JOHN HORNER AND THE COMMUNIST PARTY

John Horner and the Communist Party is a biography of a leading trade unionist and activist who became disillusioned with the Communist Party.

Known for creating the modern Fire Brigades Union during the Second World War, John Horner (1911–1997) resigned from the Communist Party in 1956. Formerly one of the Party's leading members, he afterwards refused to speak or write about his communist past. Horner's silence left him forgotten, but Horner's daughter, Rosalind Eyben, has remedied this through her engrossing account of how and why John Horner and Pat, his wife, became communist, and the events that led them to resign from the Party. She pieces the story together from a wide range of sources, including Horner's own lively unpublished memoir of his early years. The narrative occasionally diverges from the historian's voice to deliver personal reflections on the author's communist childhood and on what her father told her shortly before his death about his shame and guilt for having so long denied uncomfortable truths about the Party and the Stalinist terror.

This book is for anyone concerned with the problem of political allegiance, personal morality and associated states of denial that were to haunt Horner in later life. It will also be of interest to scholars and students researching communism and the Communist Party.

Rosalind Eyben is a historian, social anthropologist, and Emeritus Professorial Fellow at the Institute of Development Studies, University of Sussex, UK. Following a career in international development policy and practice that included working in many parts of Africa and later in India and Latin America, she became Chief Social Development Advisor at the UK Government's Department for International Development, a role that she left to research and teach about power and relations in the international aid system. Among her previous books are *International Aid and the Making of a Better World* (2014) and, with Laura Turquet, *Feminists in Development Organizations: Change from the Margins* (2013).

Routledge Studies in Radical History and Politics
Series editors: Thomas Linehan, *Independent Scholar,*
formerly Brunel University, UK, and John Roberts,
Brunel University, UK

The series *Routledge Studies in Radical History and Politics* has two areas of interest. Firstly, this series aims to publish books which focus on the history of movements of the radical left. 'Movement of the radical left' is here interpreted in its broadest sense as encompassing those past movements for radical change which operated in the mainstream political arena as with political parties, and past movements for change which operated more outside the mainstream as with millenarian movements, anarchist groups, utopian socialist communities, and trade unions. Secondly, this series aims to publish books which focus on more contemporary expressions of radical left-wing politics. Recent years have been witness to the emergence of a multitude of new radical movements adept at getting their voices in the public sphere. From those participating in the Arab Spring, the Occupy movement, community unionism, social media forums, independent media outlets, local voluntary organisations campaigning for progressive change, and so on, it seems to be the case that innovative networks of radicalism are being constructed in civil society that operate in different public forms.

The series very much welcomes titles with a British focus, but is not limited to any particular national context or region. The series will encourage scholars who contribute to this series to draw on perspectives and insights from other disciplines.

For more information about this series, please visit: www.routledge.com/ Routledge-Studies-in-Radical-History-and-Politics/book-series/RSRHP

John Horner and the Communist Party
Uncomfortable Encounters with Truth
Rosalind Eyben

JOHN HORNER AND THE COMMUNIST PARTY

Uncomfortable Encounters with Truth

Rosalind Eyben
Foreword by Kevin Morgan

Routledge
Taylor & Francis Group

LONDON AND NEW YORK

Designed cover image: Photo of John Horner. Family photo in author's possession.

First published 2024
by Routledge
4 Park Square, Milton Park, Abingdon, Oxon OX14 4RN

and by Routledge
605 Third Avenue, New York, NY 10158

Routledge is an imprint of the Taylor & Francis Group, an informa business

British Library Cataloguing-in-Publication Data
A catalogue record for this book is available from the British Library

Library of Congress Cataloging-in-Publication Data
Names: Eyben, Rosalind, author.
Title: John Horner and the Communist Party : uncomfortable encounters with truth / Rosalind Eyben ; foreword by Kevin Morgan.
Description: Abingdon, Oxon ; New York, NY : Routledge, 2024. |
Series: Routledge studies in radical history and politics |
Includes bibliographical references and index.
Identifiers: LCCN 2023051187 (print) | LCCN 2023051188 (ebook) |
ISBN 9781032671345 (hardback) | ISBN 9781032670775 (paperback) |
ISBN 9781032671352 (ebook)
Subjects: LCSH: Horner, John, 1911–1997. | Communist Party of Great Britain. |
Labor leaders–Great Britan–Biography. | Communists–Great Britain–Biography. |
Communism–Moral and ethical aspects.
Classification: LCC HD8393.H58 E94 2024 (print) |
LCC HD8393.H58 (ebook) | DDC 335.43092 [B]–dc23/eng/20231103
LC record available at https://lccn.loc.gov/2023051187
LC ebook record available at https://lccn.loc.gov/2023051188

ISBN: 978-1-032-67134-5 (hbk)
ISBN: 978-1-032-67077-5 (pbk)
ISBN: 978-1-032-67135-2 (ebk)

DOI: 10.4324/9781032671352

Typeset in Sabon
by Newgen Publishing UK

CONTENTS

List of Figures   vii
Foreword by Kevin Morgan   ix
Acknowledgements   xii
List of Abbreviations   xiv

Prologue   1

1   'Walthamstow Wide Awake!'   8

2   A Sense of Class   15

3   At Sea   27

4   The Lady of Shalott   37

5   No More War   51

6   'The Coming Struggle for Power'   59

7   'Marx for You and God for Me'   65

8   Hampstead   79

9   'Pale Pink' and 'Deeper Red'   92

10 Close to Death, August–September 1939   104

11 'Imagination and Decision' 1939–40   111

12 'Bombed But Far From Beaten'   120

13 'Known to Keep Strange Company' 1941–43   128

14 The Campaign for a Second Front   136

15 'Go to it, Housewives!'   146

16 'Dare to Make it Known'   157

17 'Sliding into the Deep Freeze'   168

18 'The World Shall Yet Live in Peace'   179

19 The Children's Perspective   195

20 'Both Betrayed and Betrayer'   202

21 Exit   214

Epilogue: Uncomfortable Encounters with Truth   231

Bibliography and Sources   237
Index   243

FIGURES

1.1 William Morris by Frederick Hollyer, 1887   10
2.1 Fred Parsons, linocut by Frank Hall, 1936   23
2.2 John Horner when a school boy   24
3.1 John, aged seventeen, in his brass-bounder's uniform   30
3.2 Labour's Struggles in Latin America, front cover   33
4.1 John rambling in Epping Forest   38
4.2 Pat aged 21   39
4.3 Pat and her brothers, 1921   43
5.1 A Friends Hall ramble with Violet, far left, front row, 1930   52
6.1 John with shipmates on the SS *Hardwicke Grange*, 1934   60
7.1 Pat walking in the Lake District   76
8.1 West Hampstead Fire Station today   81
8.2 Flyer for Hampstead's Spain Week, 1938   87
10.1 The Horners at the Surrey cottage, late 1939   109
12.1 Pat with Carol in Oxford, 1940   122
12.2 Firemen at work in bomb damaged street in London, after
     Saturday night raid, circa 1941   125
13.1 'Fire Station Discussion Group' by Reginald Mills   132
14.1 Second Front Rally, 26 July 1942   140
15.1 Violet with Reg Latham   147
15.2 The Horner Family, December 1942   151
15.3 A summer day in Epping Forest, 1943   155
16.1 Taking advice from FBU President, John Burns   160
16.2 'Hands Off Greece' Rally (announcement in *Daily Mirror*,
     16 December 1944)   161

17.1 The FBU entertains the Mayor and Mayoress of Whitley
      Bay. FBU Conference, June 1949   173
18.1 The Horners in their garden in Chingford, July 1949   179
18.2 Meeting of the Communist Party's Executive
      Committee, 4 March 1950   182
18.3 Chingford Unity Theatre Supports the Peace Petition, 1950   184
18.4 John Horner with his Leica in Moscow, 1954   188
19.1 Carol's Soviet braids   196
20.1 John's mother   208
21.1 John Horner with author on holiday, August 1957   221
21.2 John Horner with Canon Collins and Jacquetta Hawkes at
      head of CND March from Wethersfield, Easter 1961   226
21.3 Pat and John in Brighton for Labour Party Conference, 1962   227

FOREWORD

There are many accounts of the thousands who broke with the British Communist Party in the crisis year of 1956–7. Just as with the Spanish Civil War, which had drawn many of them in, they tend to be the accounts of writers, journalists, historians, cultural workers – in a word, of intellectuals. John Horner was of the same generation as the student communists of the 1930s who crowd the foreground of this picture. Leaving school at fifteen, he was a merchant seaman, then a London fireman, who for more than a decade had combined membership of the CP executive with the leadership of his union, the Fire Brigades Union. This was one of the CP's cold war success stories; on resigning from the party in November 1956 Horner made national headlines. How easy it is, even so, for these trade unionists to slip into the background or a footnote. When I mentioned Horner's name to one of the best-informed historians of 1956, it only faintly rang a very muffled bell.

As Horner's daughter and herself a distinguished academic, Rosalind Eyben has here sought to put that right while also giving us clues as to the reasons for this neglect. The most important of these clues lies in Horner himself. Like so many communists of his generation, he had a great love of words. He had wanted to be a journalist, had sailed through choppy political waters through his gift of the gab, had written much of his union's monthly journal and towards the end of his life turned his hand to autobiography. He was eminently fitted for the task and the account that follows of his earlier years is enormously enlivened by it.

There was, however, no working over the traces of his communist years. Rosalind has stepped in to make up the deficit, both by her own researches and by the imagined colloquy-cum-interrogation with which she ends her book. But Horner's was like so many autobiographies of communists or former communists in either tailing off or dissolving into generalities the closer they get to the party itself. In his case, there was just a perfunctory final chapter. As a visiting oral historian put it, he was very good at evading questions.

But why this reluctance when others could be so combative? In a passage that he removed from the final version of his memoirs Horner referred to Stalinism's defining conundrum of feeling at once betrayer and betrayed. The defectors of 1956 did not always struggle for the words to describe their feelings of betrayal. Nevertheless, those who spoke out most sometimes seemed a good deal more comfortable talking about others' responsibilities than about their own. Was it a trade unionist's instinct of collective responsibility that drew Horner back from simply displacing onto others any feelings of guilt? Resigning from the CP as Soviet tanks rolled into Hungary, he wrote of feeling personally responsible for propagating and advancing the policies which had culminated in these events. He remained in public life, at the head of his union and then for six years as a Labour MP. But for as long as the USSR itself existed, it seems that he had little more to say about what this responsibility had involved.

When he broached the subject in his final years, it was in relation to the 1930s' Moscow show trials. Here this becomes the centrepiece and moment of reckoning with which Rosalind concludes her account. Had other records been available to her, like what one imagines were Horner's abundant state surveillance files, one wonders whether episodes like his post-war trips to people's Hungary might have weighed more heavily in his own personal reckoning. Hungary had had its own treason trials, with victims of his own generation like László Rajk, under a regime whose gifts and hospitality Horner had enjoyed while bearing public witness to its accomplishments. This was what he mentioned in his resignation letter; despite the shock of the earlier Khrushchev revelations, unforgettably recalled here by his daughter, it was only at this point that he like many others finally exited the party.

There is much more than this in this enthralling personal history that is both more and less than a conventional biography. Rosalind writes as a feminist; and where 'party wives' are so often pushed to the margins of these activist histories, here her mother Pat has her full place in the story. One glimpses her at home, fretting with the children while her husband is away junketing with Barbara Castle in People's China. But in the crisis year of 1956 it is Pat who emerges as the stronger of the two, and who makes practical amends by helping settle in Hungarian refugees.

Rosalind and her sister Carol also feature as participants as well as observers. There are no friendly recollections of the Party here and Rosalind describes her euphoria at the moment of her parents breaking free from it. Carol, who was older, felt excluded and ignored, with a negativity about the whole experience that spills over into the narrative. Greasy, lecherous, fat and smelly: I felt uncomfortable with Carol's evocation of the communist visitors to the family home and wondered if these also had their personal histories and if the fat and smelly weren't found on both sides of the cold war. But even the bitterness of this children's perspective has an authenticity that adds a further dimension to what by this stage has become a family portrait.

The reader of this book is left with powerful images to reflect on. The one that has most stuck with me is the burning of John's 'communist' books in 1991. It reads like the sequel to his breakdown in 1956 – but why at this distance in time? Why the ritualising process of destruction? And according to what principles of selection, that could burn a Strachey on the rebound from Mosley towards Marxism and yet spare E.P. Thompson's *William Morris*, which is vitiated by encomiums to Stalinism for which by this time there were no extenuating circumstances?

Can one just burn some of the books, or tear out certain pages – as sometimes communists used to? In this vividly personal narrative, exploring the truths of John Horner's exemplary trade union leadership and complicity in Stalinism is a task that has required both intimate knowledge and critical distance. We can be grateful that Rosalind Eyben has had the skill to carry it out with such conviction.

Kevin Morgan
Emeritus Professor of Politics
University of Manchester

ACKNOWLEDGEMENTS

For their assistance with tracking down primary sources and materials, I am very grateful to Waltham Forest and Camden Local Records Offices, Hull History Centre, the Modern Records Centre (Warwick), Friends House Library, the British Library, London Metropolitan Archives, the Marx Memorial Library, the People's History Museum, Bishopsgate Institute and the Library of the University of Sussex. Thanks also to the archivists at Blind Veterans UK, the Fire Brigades Union and Peace Pledge Union, and to the local history societies in Aston and Chingford. Sally Coles, Susannah Stapleton and Guy Van Enst kindly assisted with the Horners' family life. I appreciate the feedback from those who came to my talks to Camden Local History Society and to the Friends of Belsize Library. Also to Matt Wrack, General Secretary of the Fire Brigades Union for his encouragement, to Rob, the firefighter who showed me around West Hampstead Fire Station and to former London firefighter David Pike and his website 'Beyond the Flames'.

Kevin Morgan's advice and interest was most helpful and I was delighted when he accepted my invitation to write the book's foreword. Richard Temple generously sent me the material he had collected for his entry about John Horner in the *Dictionary of Labour Biography* and helped me in what ultimately proved a failed attempt to locate a packet of papers sent by Horner to John Saville. Geoff Andrews, Keith Flett, Mark Freeman, Christian Hjøgsberg, James Oliver, Ruth Pearson, David Rock, Tom Sawyer, Richard Saville, Maxine Stirling and Andrew Thorpe kindly assisted me with research queries. My thanks also to Tom Linehan and John Roberts for including my book in their Radical History and Politics series and to the Routledge editorial team, Craig Fowlie, Elizabeth Hart and Sandra Creaser for guiding and supporting me through the publication process.

Stuart Mitchell from the Open University taught me about the excitement and pitfalls of the archives and how to always provide a date when writing history. At New Writing South, I benefited from comments from classmates and from our devoted tutors, Holly Dawson and Hannah Vincent. For subsequent feedback, I am grateful to an anonymous reviewer from the Faber Academy, to Wendy Moore (Royal Literary Foundation) and to Clare Christian, while Margaretta Jolly welcomed me as an associate at Sussex University's Centre for Life History and Life Writing. Finally, my loving thanks to Jane Buckley-Sander, Andrea Cornwall, Karin Eyben, Pat Holden, Margaret Kenna, Joanne Sandler, Hilary Standing and Fiona Wilson for their interest and encouragement, and, most of all, to Itil Asmon for his support and assistance, as always.

ABBREVIATIONS

AFS   Auxiliary Fire Service
ARP   Air Raid Protection
BNA   British Newspaper Archives
CND   Campaign for Nuclear Disarmament
DW   Daily Worker
EC   Executive Council (Fire Brigades Union) / Executive Committee (Communist Party)
FBU   Fire Brigades Union
HHC   Hull History Centre
IRD   International Research Department (a secret government unit for anti- communist propaganda).
LCC   London County Council
LFB   London Fire Brigade
LHA   Labour History Archives, People's History Museum.
LMA   London Metropolitan Archives
MCF   Movement for Colonial Freedom
MML   Marx Memorial Library, London
MRC   Modern Records Centre, Warwick University
NA   National Archives at Kew
PPU   Peace Pledge Union
TUC   Trades Union Congress
USSR   Union of Soviet Socialist Republics
WFLRO   Waltham Forest Local Records Office, Vestry House, Walthamstow

PROLOGUE

In an uncharacteristic fit of generosity towards a man he disliked, the Labour politician Herbert Morrison reportedly said about my father, John Horner, 'The sad thing is people never join the Communist Party for bad reasons'.[1] So what were the good reasons? My father had grown up in working-class Walthamstow under the lasting influence of the town's most famous citizen, nineteenth-century craftsman, poet and socialist, William Morris. In 1933, when in his early twenties, he met my mother Pat at Walthamstow's Quaker-run adult evening school where they joined the No More War Movement. Within a year or so my parents came to believe in the Soviet Union as the hope of the world, a country run by and for the workers where everyone had a good job and a decent home, with equality of the sexes and universal enjoyment of good health care, education and the arts. If there, why not in Britain – and indeed in the whole world? Abolish capitalism, communists argued, and there would be no more imperialist wars, no more colonial oppression, no more exploitation of man by man: a better world for everyone, everywhere.

My father had joined the fire service when unemployed in the Great Depression and five years later was unexpectedly elected general secretary of the Fire Brigades Union. It was a few weeks before the Second World War. He was twenty-seven years old without leadership experience. Yet, 'That bloke could sell sand to Egyptians, stairs to people living in bungalows', a fireman had grumbled admiringly on hearing him speak at a union meeting. He was a friendly, approachable man and people enjoyed listening to him but my father didn't always let the truth spoil a good story – a weakness with consequences when he was to tell himself (and others) about the Soviet Union.

Under his bold and imaginative leadership, the tiny firemen's union of three thousand members was to expand in 1940–41 to over seventy thousand, its

DOI: 10.4324/9781032671352-1

new members recruited from the wartime Auxiliary Fire Service. He had the capability and authority to lead one of Britain's great industrial trade unions with their hundreds of thousands members but, when the war ended, and the auxiliaries returned to their peacetime occupations, he remained in charge of a union of less than twenty thousand. In a film made to celebrate the Fire Brigades Union centenary in 2019, a fireman too young to have ever known him speaks of him as myth – 'He was a very tall man, a very, very strong man ... I would not like to have been the Home Secretary on the other side of the table because John would have won the discussion'. He campaigned for better pay, bigger pensions and greater safety for his members and for the public they served. His was a major contribution to shaping the British fire service in the second half of the last century. He successfully pressured the government to improve fire prevention measures and when he died in 1997, his obituary in the *Times* described him as a 'relentless opponent of cost-cutting and carelessness' that saved innumerable lives.[2] There would have been no Grenfell Tower on his watch.

If my father had not stuck with his union, he might have made another career as a Member of Parliament in the election that brought Labour into power in 1945. Instead, he officially joined the Communist Party, to which he had been close for about ten years.

His obituarists reflected on what John Horner could have achieved had he chosen differently: his breadth of intellect, strategic vision and charismatic leadership might have made him a senior minister in the post-war Labour government. And, when eventually he was to enter parliament in 1964, Tam Dalyell regretted that Harold Wilson lacked the boldness to bring John into the new Labour government – 'Had he been there, I believe the relationship between party and parliamentary party would have been such that victory in 1970 would have been possible'.[3] Another obituarist speculated that, had my father had the opportunity to attend university, he might have had an entirely different career as a historian.[4] But that's unlikely: he had wanted not to just study the world but change it for the better and believed he could best help do this by becoming a communist.

At an early age, he had started buying books with pennies earnt from lighting his Jewish neighbour's Sabbath fire and from chopping firewood for the local greengrocer. His library grew to encompass science, art, philosophy, and poetry and he was intrigued by the stories of people adventuring into other places and cultures. But history was his passion. Among the books acquired in his teens are the first two volumes of Harmsworth's *Universal History*, published as a monthly magazine in the year of the General Strike. Harmsworth's volumes took what was then the standard 'liberal' approach to history as Progress, a narrative that had survived unscathed from the First World War that might have made one think that history had shifted into reverse. Then came the Great Depression. No sign of progress there. But still busy reading, my father had by then discovered a country in the here-and-now, that had shaken the world in a brief ten days and thereafter was progressing in regular, well-planned intervals. The first Five Year Plan, said Stalin, had created the economic base for a classless society.[5] The Soviet Union was steadily moving towards the end of history, when time stops, described by William Morris as 'the Change beyond the Change'. In Marxist thinking, class struggle and history are coterminous. With the Industrial Revolution, the progressive force of society had become the working class, meaning people like my father, the son and grandson of building labourers. He believed he was on the side of history in the ultimate class struggle which the workers would win, as they had already in the Soviet Union. Very energizing.

My father liked writing almost as much as he enjoyed reading. His boyhood ambition had been journalism and while general secretary of the Fire Brigades Union he edited and wrote much of the Union's newspaper; he also painted in oils and water-colours, was an aficionado of chamber music, became a serious photographer (after his Soviet counterparts gave him a Leica camera) and learnt to sculpt – a family friend remembers him making an excellent bust of Lenin. All this with Pat, my mother, his constant companion and support. Her death in 1994 appears to have liberated him to talk more freely about his communist past. Some months before he himself died, he made to me what he called 'a confession' about the events that led to his breaking with the Communist Party when in his mid-forties. On another occasion around the same time, he puzzled about having hidden from himself the truth about the Communist Party and the Soviet Union that he had not wanted to acknowledge. Because I was more concerned about his evident distress when telling me about his failure to face up to the truth, I remember only some of what he recounted. He had made however a similar, separate confession to my sister Carol. Before she herself died soon afterwards she wrote in a fragment of memoir about how the Communist Party had pressurized our father 'to lie, manipulate and even help cover up a murder'.

'Blood bath at Kuropaty', *Moscow News*, November 1988. The Soviet Union's long-established English-language journal for Communist sympathizers in the West had done a volte-face; this was now the era of 'glasnost' – openness. A shocking secret is revealed. Except, explains the article's author, Zenon Poznyak, no secret to the villagers living near the forest of Kuropaty. They had known what was happening but had been terrorized into silence. They were to tell Poznyak how 'around the clock and at all seasons, came the sound of shots, shouts, cries, appeals, the howling of dogs and the purring of automobiles'. The shooting at Kuropaty had begun in 1937 and stopped only with the German invasion in June 1941.

The Soviet Union's secret police, the NKVD, had turned a forest near Minsk into a covert killing ground. The victims were brought there in vans 'soon after dinner'; the shooting started under cover of darkness and continued through the night. The dead were buried in a deep pit, each layer of corpses lightly covered with sand until the pit was full. Then another pit was dug. Each held about two hundred victims. Poznyak and his colleagues estimated that at least one hundred thousand men and women were thus buried in the forest of Kuropaty – one of five concealed mass murder sites in Byelorussia. The women's rubber shoes found in the pits at Kuropaty reminded Poznyak of those his mother wore when he was a child.

> When you pull out from, under skulls with bullet holes, long strands of women's hair, like the hair you used to see in the morning on a woman — when you see all this, and experience the smell of decay in the blossoming forest full of singing of birds …

I discovered this clipping about Kuropaty within my father's copy of Sidney and Beatrice Webbs' *Soviet Communism, a New Civilisation* (the second, 1937 edition without the question mark in the title). It is one of several cuttings dating between 1976 and 1995 secreted among its pages, my father's acknowledgement of the truth about the Soviet Union that as a young man he had chosen to ignore. The Webbs had been Britain' s leading social scientists for over forty years when they published *Soviet Communism*. Capitalism has been abolished in this new civilization. Planned production has eradicated its booms and busts and swept away the consequent evils of mass unemployment. Soviet workers share the products of their labour 'without tribute to a hereditary parasitic class'. Human wellbeing has replaced the profit motive as a judgement of value. Bound in dark, brown thick board, the title illuminated in gold against a deep orange background, everything signals authority. It was not a cheap purchase – barely affordable on a fireman's pay without his Left Book Club discount. A tombstone of a book, weighing in at one and a half kilos. If the Webbs duped themselves, little surprise that my father did also.

The clippings inserted into *Soviet Communism* track a journey out of delusion that he ignores in his memoir written at the same time and completed in 1989, the year the Berlin Wall came down. The memoir is a highly readable account of a life of which he felt justifiably proud: a working-class boy winning a rare scholarship to grammar school, his adolescent conversion to socialism during the General Strike, his Merchant Navy apprenticeship and subsequent unemployment, joining the London Fire Brigade and after five years, becoming general secretary of the Fire Brigades Union just before the start of the Second World War. The main narrative stops in 1943 when he was thirty-one years old. He has told us nothing about what he did in the Communist Party, other than the half-truth of becoming a member in 1945 and the memoir is striking for the absence of named communists.

The exception, a humorous account of an urgent consultation with the Party's general secretary, Harry Pollitt, in the toilets at the Trades Union Congress in 1943, one that left my father no clearer about what he should do. The memoir's final, dreary chapter summarizes the remainder of his trade union and political life up until 1970, including a few sentences about his resignation from the Communist Party in 1956 and his later brief career as Labour Member of Parliament.

The left-wing publishers Lawrence and Wishart rejected the memoir, having already contracted to publish an official history of the Fire Brigades Union, *Forged in Fire*.[6] The book's supervising editor, the labour historian, John Saville then persuaded my father to revise that part of his memoir covering his fire service years to convert it into a chapter in the FBU history.[7] The principal editor, Victor Bailey, meanwhile worried that such a history could not ignore the Communist Party's very considerable influence upon the union from 1940 to 1956 when my father resigned from the Party, followed by the rest of the FBU leadership. Someone 'should confront this difficult theme', Bailey wrote to John Saville, 'We simply cannot ignore it. It was an influential episode in the Union's history, but one impossible for a non-participant to deal with'.[8] Pressure was put on my reluctant father. Eventually, he sent Saville a few pages with a covering letter, 'I made numerous starts and scrapped each one in turn ... I found myself becoming immersed in a wallow of apologia'. His first draft had been too 'subjective', better fitted to his memoir but 'no thank you'.[9] The closest he got was in a chapter he chose not to include in the final version of his unpublished memoir.[10] Thus, he left no account of his life as a leading British communist during the first decade of the Cold War. Notwithstanding, his unpublished memoir provides the context of why and how he became a communist, a central theme of this book. And as for the dramatic manner of his leaving the Party, I was old enough to be a witness.

Books about British communists tend to be political biographies of interest to specialists or, if written for a wider readership, are either popular family memoirs or biographies of middle-class, well-known intellectuals whose diaries and letters provide the sources rarely available for lives of working-class activists such as my father. That lack of sources helps explain why relatively little has been published about the past lives and times of trade union leaders, leading to the false assumption that their lives must have been 'colourless, dry and dull'.[11] My father's life was anything but dull yet his lively memoir left much untold, and by the time I thought of writing the present book, it was too late to speak with his contemporaries. He had been interviewed at length by Louise Brodie for the Labour Oral History Project but its tapes contain little more than a shorter version of his memoir, already completed.[12] It was public knowledge that John Horner had joined the Communist Party in 1945, had led a Communist-run trade union and served ten years on the Party's National Executive, yet almost forty years since leaving the Party he still hates being asked about it. 'You're very good at evading questions', sighs Brodie. Listening to the tapes in a cubicle in the British Library, I am reminded how he avoided questions with an embarrassed laugh, followed up with an amusing anecdote, leaving his interlocutor puzzled as to any link between her question and his response. My mother's presence during that interview allows him to deploy a further diversion. It is just a couple of months before her death, her health already poor. When Brodie asks him an unwanted question, he responds with one to my mother, 'How are you mate?' 'Mate' being a term of endearment reserved solely for her. She is the guardian of his secrets; her presence a reminder of what not to divulge.

Other than his memoir and associated photographs, the principal primary sources are material given by my sister to the Fire Brigades Union after John Horner's death (later deposited by the FBU at the Modern Records Centre at Warwick), the digitized *Firefighter* (FBU journal) and British Library newspapers. In 1981, a fire in my parents' bedroom unhappily destroyed the letters he sent my mother during the Second World War. At times, I have had to resort to supposition and conjuncture informed by secondary sources. Regrettably, the secret intelligence services were not persuaded to release my father's files, perhaps because they had continued watching him after he became an MP in 1964 when I inadvertently witnessed them bugging the phone while staying at my parents' Westminster flat during the parliamentary recess.

As for my mother, she never wrote a memoir, nor indeed scarcely anything else. Not that she lacked the skill: a pastiche letter from Jane Austen's Mr Collins won her the weekend competition in the *New Statesman*. Yet, it simply did not appear to have occurred to her – or to my father for that matter – that she should write about her own life. As he described it, hers was so much part of his: 'The shared political action and direct involvement in the crises and excitement of her husband's work'. That he left a memoir and she did not, is mirrored in the public record: *his* political and professional life can be tracked through newspaper and other records whereas *she* is almost invisible, despite grassroots activism. Theirs had been a fifty-year habit for her to type his manuscripts, making editorial corrections and improvements as she did so. But she was much more involved than that. According to his memoir, 'She watched much of her life become submerged in the affairs of the Fire Brigades Union until at times, it was impossible to disentangle our lives together from the vicissitudes of that organisation'. That he was the public man and she the supportive woman, was then the norm of gender relations. A book about my father must include the story of my housewife mother.

It never comes easy to recognize an uncomfortable truth. By admitting it, we risk our comrades' criticism for our providing ammunition to opponents. It means we have to be brave in supporting each other so as to open our collective eyes to what might be happening in a movement we believe to be just. Only then, will we have a cause worth struggling for. I am consoled by the psychologist John Steiner, 'The fact that we do sometimes face the truth, however imperfectly, is a considerable achievement'.[13] This my father did.

Notes

1 John Horner, 'The Bells Go Down', unpublished, typescript memoir. Hereafter, all unattributed quotes are from the final version, in my possession. I have deposited another copy with Waltham Forest Local Records Office (WFLRO).
2 *Times*, 14 February 1997.
3 Tam Dalyell, *Independent*,18 February 1997.
4 Sally Holloway, *Independent*, 18 February 1997.
5 *Daily Worker*, 14 January 1933.
6 John Horner, 'Recollections of a General Secretary', in ed. Victor Bailey, *Forged in Fire*, London, 1991, 279–359.
7 'Recollections of a General Secretary'.
8 Hull History Centre (HHC), John Saville archives, UDJS/1/28, 'Forged in Fire', 1986–1992, Letter from Victor Bailey to John Saville, 18 November, 1990.
9 HHC, UDJS/1/28, Letter from John Horner to John Saville, n.d. acknowledged by Saville on 10 February 1991.
10 This final chapter is in a version of the memoir among the Fire Brigade Union records at the Modern Records Centre in Warwick. It must have been in the packet of papers sent by sister, Carol Horner, to the FBU after John Horner's death.
11 Kevin Morgan, ' "Colourless, Dry and Dull". Why British Trade Unionists lack biographers and what (if anything) should be done about it', *Moving the Social*, 2014, 51, 213–334.
12 John Horner, interviewed by Louise Brodie, 20 July and 16 August 1994, British Library sounds collection.
13 Cited in Catherine Hall and Daniel Pick, 'Thinking About Denial', *History Workshop Journal*, 84, 2017, 1–23 (14).

1

'WALTHAMSTOW WIDE AWAKE!'

Bonfires blazed all over London the night John Horner was born. Except they didn't. On writing his memoir's first sentence, he must have forgotten how Guy Fawkes parties were postponed to the Monday when November the Fifth fell on a Sunday. Or did he choose not to let this inconvenient fact spoil a good opening? His memoir is probably right however about the paucity of fireworks in Walthamstow's Boston Road, the street where he was born. Housewives were struggling with rising prices, while their husbands' wages stagnated and employers grew rich. After a long, hot summer of nationwide, working-class unrest, fresh strikes were predicted. Nineteen hundred and eleven was the best and worst of times to be born a future trade union leader. He arrived in the midst of a great storm that blew across the British Isles. Heavy seas broke the hatches of a Clyde tramp steamer and only with pumps at full pressure, did she eventually reach the safety of Belfast Lough; another vessel sank off Bolt Head with all but three of its crew lost. Luckily, Frederick John was born with a caul to protect him from drowning, were he to become a sailor. The caul's prophylactic powers were fully tested early on, he writes, when strapped into his pushchair, he pitched head first into a flooded gravel pit, to be saved by some boys swimming nearby.

He was born on a Sunday, his father's weekly day of rest from the hard labour of digging foundations for the City of London's new buildings. A faded studio photograph from Charlie Horner's wedding day in 1900 shows a handsome, well-built man, just under six foot, muscular, with large square hands and feet, and an outsized, round head. If not for the gale, Charlie would have been in their small back garden, his big, calloused hands given something useful to do. But forced indoors, I imagine him sitting beside the coke range, ready at the midwife's call to carry upstairs the simmering

DOI: 10.4324/9781032671352-2

kettle. He smokes his pipe and struggles to read the scandal in the *News of the World*, missing the help of his literate wife, otherwise occupied. The two oldest children make a racket in the passage, the weather having kept them from their street games, but his namesake, two-year-old Boy Charlie, snuggles himself comfortably into his father's lap. Together, they look at the paper's pictures.

There had been a little girl born two years before Boy Charlie. She had lived for just eight months. According to the death certificate, Gladys died of 'broncho-pneumonia meningitis'. Fewer babies died in the suburbs than in the congested housing and dirtier air of inner London and yet from every thousand babies born in Walthamstow, one hundred and thirty died before the age of one.[1] Infantile diarrhoea was the commonest cause of death. With the summer of 1911 the hottest on record, John's mother, Emily, was plagued by the flies from the coalman's stables across the street and at night she could not sleep from the sound of the coalman's dray horses who, irritated by the heat, stamped their great hooves on the stable floor. John was thus fortunate to be born after the weather had cooled down and the flies gone.

He was proud to share his birthplace with William Morris, craftsman, poet and socialist and hung a photograph of him above the table he used to write his memoir (Figure 1.1). Morris was born in 1834 when Walthamstow was still a village. It became a working-class suburb in the 1870s, with 'rows of flimsily built two-storied houses, in all their hideousness of yellow brick and blue slate, stretching in a squalid sheet over the Lea valley'.[2]

Yet, for all its hideousness, Walthamstow compared favourably with the tenements and crowded dark courtyards of the slums further into London whence many Walthamstow residents had escaped. When he was a young fireman stationed in Southwark, John came to appreciate the difference:

> In Walthamstow, we had been poor, but my father had his backyard chicken run and my mother her tiny much-loved flower garden … Here [in Southwark] I saw scores of families packed together in hutches seeking to make homes bereft of basic human decencies.

Overall, Walthamstow was not a bad place with its cheap rents, good transport connections, mains sewage, clean air and the nearby open spaces of Epping Forest and the Lea Valley marshes. When John's parents moved there in 1900, Walthamstow was considered 'sober, quiet, restrained in outward appearance, in a word respectable';[3] a description equally applicable to Emily and Charlie Horner.

They had met in Camberwell in south London, Emily's birthplace where, as she told her granddaughter, from the age of eleven she had scrubbed other people's door steps while Charlie, an orphan teenager from the rural Essex, laboured on building sites. Emily had had a London board school education,

FIGURE 1.1   William Morris by Frederick Hollyer, 1887 (Wiki Commons).

perhaps explaining why she rather than Charlie did most of the talking, thinking and planning. It may have been Emily's idea that they settle north of the river in Walthamstow. They could rent roomier accommodation than in Camberwell and Charlie could take advantage of the cheap, early morning workmen's trains to reach the city's building sites. The front entrance at 66 Boston Road led directly from the street into a passage running through to the back door and to a small garden where Charlie kept his chickens – 'Rhode Island Reds, good layers and he made a shilling or two selling eggs to neighbours', remembered John. To the right of the passage, a rarely used front parlour; and further along, the back room, the kitchen with a lean-to scullery and water tap. The toilet was another lean-to, accessed from the garden. The kitchen was the family living space where they took their weekly bath and ate their meals. Unlike Mrs Perks next door, 'whose inadequate domestic arrangements were a frequent matter for comment', John's mother insisted they sat down at the table to eat, however meagre the meal, as would have been the case when bad weather meant no work or when the Labourers' Union had voted to strike.

Walthamstow's rapid transformation into a working-class suburb had coincided with the extension of the franchise for local elections. Many men – and some women – voted for the first time, and a 'Progressive' coalition of Radicals and Liberals took charge of Walthamstow's new Urban District Council to improve public services.[4] Public 'slipper' baths were opened for people without indoor plumbing; a magnificent, well-stocked library soon followed; and Morris' childhood home in Lloyd Park was converted into a children's clinic, its grounds opened to the public. Yet Walthamstow's socialists wanted more radical change than this. When just before the Great War, working-class voters began to move further leftwards, the socialist *Daily Herald*'s headline 'Walthamstow Wide Awake', announced the ascendancy of the town's 'Rebel Reds'.[5] Of Labour's four candidates, two were skilled building workers. They and their comrades had recently devoted Sunday mornings to erecting on vacant railway land a centre for working-class education. John remembered the William Morris Hall as the base for the Unitarian minister Reg Sorensen, 'fighter for India's independence and Gandhi's friend'. The Hall's regular events included a socialist Sunday School, the Friday evening Whist Drive – 'all profits to the Socialist and Labour Movement' – and the Sunday Evening Lectures. In February 1926, when John was fourteen, these last included 'a lantern lecture' on the International Labour Organisation; Man's relations to the Planets; an Independent Labour Party speaker's views on the Power of the Press; and a play about the Tolpuddle Martyrs presented by the Reverend Sorensen.[6] A socialist education on John's doorstep.

The same year they built William Morris Hall, Walthamstow's building workers had hosted a London-wide meeting of like-minded comrades, the first step to a grassroots inter-union alliance in the construction sector. The alliance bore bitter fruit in the new year of 1914: building workers constructing the Pearl Assurance Building in High Holborn struck in support of the carpenters whose wages were undercut when contractors hired non-union workers on lower pay. Galvanized by this grassroots militancy, the official leadership of London's nineteen building unions collaborated for the very first time to bring their members out on strike. The employers responded with a London-wide lock-out: building workers were refused jobs – blacklisted – unless they consented in writing to the employers' right to hire non-union men on lower pay.[7]

John's father did not work for eight months. Whereas the unions of the better-paid painters, bricklayers, plasterers, plumbers and other skilled workers had financial reserves for strike pay, labourers' unions soon ran out of money. The *Daily Herald* urged its readers to support their starving families; the Southend branch of the Gas Workers Union raised £2 and 17 shillings (less than three weeks' wages) for the Walthamstow Lock-out Centre where John's mother, Emily, would have gone for help.[8] Money was raised from across the country. Here was trade union solidarity in action. A *Herald* reporter went along to a centre in Battersea to see for himself. He hardly knew which was most moving, the handing over of food supplies for four hundred of the fighting families or fitting boots for some of the wives and children:

> One pretty girl about fourteen years of age was leaving the counter with her arms full of bread and groceries, when the kindly eye of a taximan's wife spotted the girl's feet. 'Just look at the poor dear's boots, Mr. Jenkins', she whispered. Bob looked and the Herald man looked. My God, the 'boots' were too awful for words. The remains of the heels were sticking out at the sides, and the child was shuffling along on the uppers. 'Send her inside', said Bob, quietly, 'and try and fix her up'. The child could hardly believe it was possible, later she came tripping out smiling and happy .... 'I'm sorry, mate', said Bob to a labourer who had come to get his wife a pair. 'The missus will have to come again on Monday'.[9]

They were rescued by the First World War. Britain's trade union leaders called an industrial truce and Charlie Horner returned to work on ex-ante terms – except that now he had rent arrears and ill-nourished, poorly-shod children. When he learnt that Cubitts was hiring building workers for a government overseas contract, Emily would have urged him to sign up. Men in her family had a tradition of travelling afar, her brother was a hussar in the South African war, another in the Royal Navy, while an uncle in the Royal Engineers had helped suppress the Indian Mutiny. There were no such imperial adventurers among the Horners. Until Charlie and his siblings had left for London, they had been stay-at-homes, perhaps since the fifth century when their ancestors had taken ship across the North Sea to the Essex coast, and fearing to venture further, had settled along its mudflats and estuaries. Charlie's decision was thus exceptionally bold, writes John, 'lured on by the chance of a long period of regular pay'. It was very hush-hush. The pay was more than double what Charlie would have earnt in London for an equivalent ten-hour day; he and four others from Walthamstow were among the two hundred London building workers who signed up.

Only after boarding ship did Charlie learn he was to travel eight thousand miles to build an Admiralty wireless station in the Falkland Islands. When Charlie returned home fifteen months later, John remembered the smell of onions filling the kitchen when his father threw back the lid of his sea chest.

> Packed among the clothes were skins of Antarctic sea birds, of penguins, of a baby seal, all of them rubbed with alum to preserve them .... My father,

I believe, had some idea that the skins might be used to make hats for my mother. There were postcards of sea elephants, of penguin rookeries, of whaling stations and of the tiny Cathedral in Port Stanley.

His father's adventure across the Southern Ocean introduced John to seafaring and after his father left them again to build military installations in France, his mother transformed these postcards into a favourite bedtime story for her little son.

There was another story from this Falklands adventure that John never heard. The Admiralty and their contractors, Cubitts, must have ignored how the London building workers recruited for the Falklands had learnt solidarity during the preceding eight-month lock-out. The official records show the outward journey to have been appalling: a dirty, leaking ship with food the workers swore no decent Englishman would eat. Many fell sick. Yet, when they formed a joint action committee to protest in writing about the conditions, John's father's name was not among those who signed. After all, he didn't know how to write; he was just an unskilled labourer, not a carpenter, plumber or plasterer. Nor was he one to make a fuss. John remembered that when unpleasantly surprised, at the most Charlie might have allowed himself was a 'Jesus wept'.

On arrival in Port Stanley, the building workers were horrified to learn the Admiralty planned for them to live on board ship during their entire assignment. Promptly declaring a 'general strike' until billeted in the town, they refused to discharge the materials and equipment needed to start work. The Governor of the Falkland Islands read out to them a telegram from the Admiralty, 'The Empire being at war and the work on which you are employed being war works, the Admiralty will not tolerate for a moment further strikes or slackness'. Yet these embittered and strike-toughened building workers knew they had the upper hand. With an acute labour shortage in the Falklands and the wireless station urgently needed, the Admiralty was forced to surrender: the workers were accommodated on shore, their additional living costs, paid by the government.[10] Here is a fragment of Londoners' working-class history, hidden in the National Archives, that John Horner would have loved to have known.

With no trace of this story in the contemporary press, the incident must have been censored and the workers instructed to stay quiet if they wanted future employment. Perhaps also, it was something John's father preferred not to talk about. Charlie paid his Labourers Union dues on time and went on strike when told to. But it was wide awake Walthamstow, not his parents, that was to make John a socialist. According to his memoir, William Morris' socialist teachings were read and followed in Walthamstow by two generations of young working men and women and 'When Harold Wilson formed his first government no less than four of his ministers had their origins and had served their apprenticeship in Walthamstow's mean streets'.

Notes

1 Walthamstow Medical Officer for Health Report, 1910, Wellcome Collection On-line.
2 John is quoting from Richard Tames, *William Morris. An Illustrated Life 1834–1896*, Aylesbury, 1972, 5.
3 W.R. Powell, *The Victorian County History of Essex*, V. London, 1966, 58.
4 Tim Cooper, 'Politics and Place in Suburban Walthamstow', PhD thesis, University of Cambridge, 2005.
5 *Daily Herald*, 24 March 1914.
6 *Walthamstow Observer*, February 1926.
7 See Peter Latham, 'Rank and File Movements In Building 1910–1920', *History Group of the Communist Party*, Pamphlet no 69, n.d.
8 *Daily Herald*, 20 June 1914.
9 *Daily Herald*, 8 June 1914.
10 This account constructed from National Archives MT 10/1825/39; CO 1071/126; CO 339/8; MT 23/407.

2

A SENSE OF CLASS

The first glimpse of John is in 1919, at a street party organized for Boston Road's children to celebrate the return of peace. He is sitting in the middle of the second row in a group photograph, poorly reproduced in a contemporary's memoir of a Walthamstow childhood.[1] John's body is tilted at a slight angle, perhaps to avoid his face being hidden from the camera by the big girl in front of him but more likely to get a better view of what's going on. It may have been the first time he had seen a camera and was curious. John's curiosity soon took him beyond Walthamstow's confines to explore central London with the boy from next door, Doughy, so called because he always had with him a hunk of bread (Doughy's mother, Mrs Perks, was not too bothered with sit-down meals).

Money for tram fares was earnt by chopping and bundling firewood for the local greengrocer. One penny took them to the British Museum's Egyptian mummies where they indulged in 'horrid imaginings of what lay underneath the bandaged wrappings', or to the National Gallery where they ogled and giggled over the naked ladies. The journey was part of the fun.

Perched up on the wooden slatted seats in the brass-railed open platform at the front of the upper deck of the swaying tram, with the sliding glass door behind you shutting off the rest of the deck, you could pretend you were on a ship's bridge.

From the terminus at Liverpool Street,

we would cut down Houndsditch, along the Minories, to roam at liberty through the Tower of London .... We would study the crowded shipping

DOI: 10.4324/9781032671352-3

in the Pool, and when the tide was low, comb the tiny beach below Traitors Gate.

John also adventured by himself when visiting relatives in the Essex countryside. The charity for blind servicemen, St Dunstans, had settled his mother's brother on a smallholding at Tiptree, Uncle Arthur had lost his eyesight during the war while serving in the Royal Navy.[2] He was a jovial, approachable man and a deep, mutual attachment developed between uncle and nephew, with a visit to Tiptree the annual high point of John's school holidays. North Essex was still intensely rural with a pleasing mixture of lowland heath, woods and farmland through which John happily rambled, while slightly more distant lay the wide skies and marshes of the Blackwater Estuary. His first acquaintance with and lasting love for the English countryside originated from staying at 'my uncle's farm in Tiptree'.

The year that Uncle Arthur moved with his elderly mother to Tiptree, the Board of Education inspected Gamuel Road elementary school and reported positively on the keen spirit among the pupils and the 'earnest and stimulating work' of the headmaster and staff. The inspector was particularly pleased about the recent improvement in the range and quantity of reading material but urged the teachers to pay more attention to correcting their pupil's 'native weakness in English' that handicapped their learning and oral expression.[3] The well-meaning inspector had a point: speaking cockney was a serious impediment for any boy or girl hoping to improve their chances in life. Yet, perhaps it was just because his 'native weakness' had not been corrected that John remembered Gamuel Road as a friendly place. Grammar school was to be very different.

Of the fifteen hundred eleven-year-old boys living in Walthamstow in September 1923, only sixty-five started at Sir George Monoux, the local grammar school. From among these, seventeen had passed the local authority examination for a scholarship that paid the Monoux fees.[4] Boston Road was proud that one of their own had made it to grammar school, a rare achievement for a lad from south Walthamstow. But Doughy Perks felt sorry for John having to join 'that toffee-nosed lot' at the Monoux. Anyone higher up the class ladder than a labourer's son must have seemed snobbish to Doughy, unaware of the gradations of class superiority that John was to experience at the grammar school. The fathers of the Monoux's fee-paying pupils were local businessmen, doctors, dentists, minor civil servants and secondary school teachers. These differentiated them from the scholarship boys' fathers recorded by the school as clerks or skilled workers. Among that year's entrants, only John and one other boy were sons of unskilled labourers.[5] Even before they heard him speak cockney, the difference between John and his classmates would have been obvious. His poverty excused him from games for lack of kit: 'Cricket meant white flannels and cricket boots to be bought at a price far beyond my mother's purse and to this day I do not know the fielding positions on a cricket field'. Nor could his mother afford the school uniform of 'grey flannel slacks and the beribboned blazer' but she did buy him the striped red and blue tie and dark blue long socks with red tops. These John proudly wore wherever he went, along with his school cap emblazoned with 'its glorious badge of the Monoux arms worked in silk'.

Then, 'some busybody' reported to the school that John had been seen wearing his Monoux cap while on his Saturday job, sitting alongside the dairy man on his milk cart, and the headmaster conveyed the message to John that milk rounds and Monoux school caps did not go together. More distressing than the warning for John had been his surrender. He stopped wearing the cap on the milk round.

At the first challenge, I had given way to an unfair, snobbish dictat. The headmaster's ban implied that there was something shameful in working on a milk round, but the real shame I felt came from my own collapse in the face of authority.

With no one with whom he could share his misery, he took to wandering by himself over the Lea Valley marshes. When the wind was easterly, he could smell the soap factory at Stratford.

But the marshes had great skies and it seems to me now that larks were always singing and overall there was a melancholy solitude which matched the moods of a lonely boy. I first saw a dead body when I watched them drag the body of a woman from the river.

Towards the end of the summer holidays after John's first year at grammar school, his brother, Boy Charlie, was killed in a traffic accident. Charlie had been 'a quiet, serious boy' who had successfully escaped the family tradition of digging holes. When eleven, he had won a scholarship to Walthamstow's new, technical Central School in Queens Road and now aged fifteen was ready to start his first job as a skilled factory worker. With the light fading on an August evening in 1924, Charlie took his sister Winnie's bicycle for a spin and was knocked down by a motor car. He died in hospital a few days later. 'On the first day of term', John writes, 'I took a note to the grammar school, asking to be excused lessons until after the funeral'. There is very little more to learn about poor Charlie's death. The *Walthamstow Guardian* did not report the accident and published just a brief item about the inquest: Charlie had died from 'shock, fractured ribs and other injuries'.[6] Before dying, the lad had told his father how the last thing he remembered was signalling his intention to turn left. The driver who had killed him stated that Charlie had signalled too late to be avoided and contested a bystander's statement that his car was going at well over 20 mph (the legal speed limit). Shockingly, there appears to have been no police report. Verdict: accidental death.

The short shrift given to Charlie's death reveals the indifference of the paper's middle-class readers to the fate of working-class children. Surely, the boy's tragic death merited more than one brief paragraph? What could have been more important in that week's local news that so little space was given to poor Charlie? On the same page as the inquest is a report, twice the length, about a railway guard who had been brought before the magistrates for stealing from a passenger's portmanteau. He had taken a book, a cake of soap and a small quantity of envelopes Evidently the bourgeois readership of the *Walthamstow Guardian* was interested a good deal more in the theft from a passenger – who might have been any one of them – than in the killing of a working-class boy. Equally shocking is the driver's impunity. Although a speed limit existed for built-up areas and despite a witness reporting that Charlie's killer was going too fast, no action was taken against the driver. Cyclists' deaths from encounters with motor cars were horribly frequent in the 1920s – hardly newsworthy – and the coroner's verdict of 'accidental death' was standard practice in such cases, with the driver rarely found culpable.[7]

'Emotions were not displayed in our family and my father was as quiet and undemonstrative as ever', John writes.

> For weeks after Charlie died, on Saturday afternoons and Sunday mornings, he would hide away down the garden cleaning the chicken houses, scrubbing their nesting boxes, turning over their runs, whitewashing and disinfecting. For hours he would not come out from behind that wire netting. And my mother knew. and I knew, that alone with his chickens he wept unceasingly.

Every Sunday, John accompanied his father to the grave in Queens Road Cemetery, across the street from the Central School that Charlie had so recently left. When John came away from Sunday School, he would see his father waiting at the street corner 'dressed in his black mourning, black trilby hat and with an ill-fitting collar and black tie in place of his customary cap and white choker'. Standing together at the grave, no word would pass between them. John writes how afterwards he was to remember with shame those visits to the cemetery: when he saw his father's lower lip tremble, he would impatiently turn his face away.

Still feeling guilty in old age for having thus dissociated himself from his grieving parents, John writes, 'Now there remains the remorse that when he knew that in their misery he should have been closest to his parents, their remaining son – their baby – was at his most distant'. Strangely, he misremembers the year of Charlie's death, believing himself to have been eleven when Charlie died and thus resenting that his brother 'had gone and got himself killed just when I was going to my grammar school and so had spoilt everything for me'. Yet, Charlie died in August 1924 when John was twelve and at the end of his first year at the Monoux School. Did this misremembrance allow John to indulge in greater feelings of guilt? 'Yet I knew then that was all that my parents had. That knowledge was a heavy burden for a boy lonely in his new school'. Altogether, it would have been a miserable autumn for the grieving family. Boy Charlie's death afflicted a family already stressed by a building strike that had begun in July. The second strike in less than two years lasted seven weeks. Once again, Emily must have struggled to put food on the table and buy the clothes and boots needed for a growing boy at grammar school.

Life only improved the following summer when Charlie Horner secured longer-term work, digging the foundations for the new Lloyds Insurance Building in Leadenhall Street. He enjoyed bringing home interesting finds from his labours: when working on the reconstruction of the Bank of England he had found a wild boar tusk that he placed on the mantelpiece next to his Falklands sealion tooth and a fragment from a Zeppelin brought down from above Walthamstow in 1915. Charlie was to strike really lucky in Leadenhall Street.

As the steam diggers and their attendant navvies opened the immense crater, they penetrated stratum after stratum of London's history ... In the corner of the excavation where my father was working, he and his mates came across what must have been a rubbish heap of Roman London. Night after night he would open the saddle bag of his bike, take out the red spotted handkerchief which had held his dinner on its two enamel plates and unroll the rag which held the treasures he had brought home for me. Bronze pins, styli, brooches, beads, sandals, tiny coins and shards of decorated red Samian ware from Gaul.

As they sat together at the kitchen table examining that day's discovery, his father used the finds to bring John closer to him. Charlie's silences, his heavy brows and strong jaw made him look stern, but the boy now began to understand that 'in reality he was only shy'. John had also, at last, started to enjoy his new school. Most of the masters were approachable, and if he showed interest, generous with their time. English became his favourite subject. His teacher, marvellously named Percy Bysshe Whitt, 'kind, humorous and ever patient', introduced the class to William Morris with 'Sigurd the Volsung' that John learnt by heart and later lectured on. Percy Bysshe started him 'on an exploration of English literature that would last a life time', aided by the nearby public library and a second-hand book seller who positioned his weekly barrow in the High Street close to the school gates. Among the books on John's shelves when he died, were some from that barrow's penny and tuppenny boxes, along with Robert Louis Stevenson's *Virginibus Puerisque*, never returned to the school library.

From the school inspectors' report, it seems biology was not on the curriculum, possibly making John more susceptible to the Christian fundamentalism of his mother's younger sister. Aunt Mill encouraged him to attend a Baptist chapel whose minister preached how God created the world and all living creatures in just one week. It was a divisive theology: you believed this or you were out, no vacillation nor doubts allowed. The congregation sang a hymn with a cheerful lilt that was to become an ironic favourite of John's –

> One door and only one
> And yet its sides are two.
> I'm on the inside
> Which side are you?

He worried about the fate of his soul. The books from Walthamstow's central library led him to question God's creation of the world. Yet Aunt Mill's Baptists forbade uncertainty; to a doleful tune, the chapel's congregation lamented the fate of doubters-

> 'Almost persuaded' doom comes at last;
> 'Almost' cannot avail;
> 'Almost' is but to fail!

John's detailed account of his adolescent religious fervour and of his subsequent doubts arguably serves as a surrogate for what he was to find so difficult to write about: that moment in the early 1950s when he began questioning communism. He told his daughters that his teenage devotions had ended on a summer evening after he glimpsed the Baptist minister hiding behind the chapel wall, kissing a woman who was not his wife. Chuckling at the impious analogy, John likened himself to the pilgrim whose burden rolled off his back at the sight of the City on the Hill. The minister was a hypocrite; Aunt Mill's religion a fake; it was all rubbish; there was no Hell. Thus, John lost his faith and gave himself permission to believe in evolution. This much he told us. His memoir takes a rather different slant on his rejection of religion that he associates with the General Strike, his political awakening, and a new friendship.

The General Strike of May 1926 had obliged Charlie Horner to once again put down his shovel and pick. This time in solidarity with one and a half million miners, locked out after refusing to work longer hours for lower wages. Walthamstow was 'as solid as a rock', the local organizers reported to strike headquarters, and the Labour-controlled council was so enthusiastic in its support that it voted to disconnect the municipally controlled electricity supply to local factories.[8] But the government had long been preparing for such a contingency; middle-class volunteers broke the strike by driving buses, trucks and trains; and according to a northern provincial newspaper report (the national press was on strike), workers in Walthamstow had overturned a volunteer-driven bus.[9] Although alarmist talk and fake news from the government, particularly from Winston Churchill's daily official bulletin, stirred up middle-class fears of a communist revolution, the closest this came in Walthamstow was when two thousand strikers attempted to storm the local army recruiting centre.[10]

One week into the strike and the unions stayed solid; on the Sunday, 'two eloquent miners from Yorkshire' addressed a meeting in Walthamstow of ten thousand strikers and sympathisers'.[11] On the Monday, Walthamstow Trades Council informed the central organizing committee, 'the position here is excellent'; yet, the very next day it was querying the absence of strike pay, causing 'grave unrest' among the strikers. On the Wednesday (12 May), the Trades Council issued a bulletin with a stop press – 'THERE IS NO TRUTH TO THE RUMOUR THAT THE STRIKE IS OVER'. But it was. Margaret Cole, the social historian was to write,

> The Government had made up its mind that "direct action" must be scotched once and for all, and, that being so, the Unions had no choice between surrendering and going on to civil war and revolution, which was the last thing they had envisaged or desired.[12]

Their unions instructed the strikers to return to work, the miners abandoned to their fate.

Later that summer, the middle-class, sixth-form editors of the annual Monoux school magazine made the General Strike a subject for mild irony, ignoring their schoolmates who must have gone hungry when their fathers' strike money had failed to arrive.

> Without wishing to associate this editorial with any definite political opinions, we must nevertheless confess that from our point of view it was a complete failure. Only one cricket fixture had to be cancelled, and School routine continued just as usual. In fact, the only indications of anything out of the ordinary were, firstly, that motor cars made their entrance with great éclat into the playground and were given a delirious welcome; and, secondly, that little boys from South Chingford, who arrived after the second bell, could no longer offer the excuse that they travelled by tram.[13]

The General Strike had been an amusing incident, with the minor inconvenience of a cricket fixture cancelled – a game that John had never learnt to play because his parents could not afford the kit. The appearance of the motor car owners, the fathers of the school's wealthier pupils, must have further reinforced John's consciousness of his class difference.

'It was inevitable', writes John, 'that those few scholarship boys whose fathers were on strike should find themselves defending the miners and the strike against the attacks and jeers of the sons of shopkeepers, doctors and solicitors'. The leader of the strikers' sons was a tall red-haired boy whose mother John remembered as a well-known outspoken Labour councillor in Walthamstow. 'My mind was a ragbag of confused ideas about the school and its class differences, the politics of snobbery and the consequences of the debacle of the General Strike. My new friend was a useful guide through these thickets'. From politics to religion was an easy transition. When John told his new friend of his doubts about the Bible story of the Creation, he was reassured that if that was all that worried him, he should skip Sunday school and come with him to Friends Hall, a Quaker-run education centre in Greenleaf Road. There, his friend introduced him to Fred Parsons, who transformed John's despondent adolescence into joyous discovery.

Fred was the antithesis of Aunt Mill's fundamentalist, puritanical gloom. One of Fred's students remembered how a room glowed when Fred was present: 'It was a glow of youth, of exuberance, of health, of combat even'. 'He never seemed old, even at 70, and young people delighted in his company. They argued with him, for they often disagreed with his views … but they really and truly loved him. He was a fire you could warm your heart by'.[14] John placed on the wall above his writing table Fred's picture, next to William Morris.

Fred had retired early from the civil service and, when the teenage John first met him, had been running Sunday afternoon classes at Friends Hall for about four years. Fred's class was definitely not a Sunday school but rather for young people to learn about and discuss whatever they wished. Another fellow student remembered that everything that mattered was talked about at Fred's class – 'from Job to Communism'.[15] For the summer of 1926 the topic was human evolution, 'The Rise of Man'. Fred concluded the last session by declaiming from Shelley's *Prometheus Unbound* –

The loathsome mask has fallen, the man remains
Sceptreless, free, uncircumscribed, but man
Equal, unclassed, tribeless, and nationless,
Exempt from awe, worship, degree, the king
Over himself; just, gentle, wise …

Fred freed John from 'the hobgoblins and worries about religion'. And his class mates were such fun, 'Were these Quakers? And Fred Parsons? White-haired

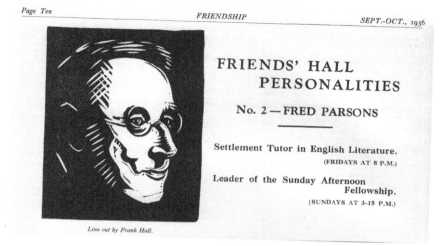

FRIENDS' HALL
PERSONALITIES

No. 2 — FRED PARSONS

Settlement Tutor in English Literature.
(FRIDAYS AT 8 P.M.)

Leader of the Sunday Afternoon
Fellowship.
(SUNDAYS AT 3-15 P.M.)

Lino cut by Frank Hall.

FIGURE 2.1   Fred Parsons, linocut by Frank Hall, 1936.[20]

Fred, whose blue eyes were the merriest of all, was he a Quaker?' Sometimes. Fred converted his Sunday class into a full day's ramble, introducing John to nearby Epping Forest. He didn't need to travel to Tiptree for a country walk. During those rambles and over tea and toast at Fred's East End home, John learnt to discuss ideas and to understand there were different ways to think about the world. 'We spent the next three hours listening to jolly records and readings', wrote another student about an evening at Fred's. Records varied from 'Dance Little Lady' to the 'Flying Dutchman Overture' and the readings from 'Little Tommy Tucker' to Wordsworth Sonnets and Shakespeare …. A cheerful memory of Fred's flat, soft light, warm fire, comfortable chairs, pleasant music and poetry.[16]

   On one such an evening, John met his first communist. Fred's daughter, Iris had been volunteering in a Quaker scheme offering material help and adult education for distressed South Wales miners and their families.[17] She had returned home with a young communist, an out-of-work miner.

   Of Welsh miners, I had seen plenty. Out of work and singing in the gutter for pennies – but now I was actually talking to one, and he a communist. In the intervals between the music he had much to say to me. I was in turn much taken by Comrade Bryn.

Fred may have been less enthusiastic. He distrusted centralized organizations that demanded orthodoxy. 'Man's own private experiences, his idea of life, his sense of values, puts in its claims. Is a man to prostitute his God to such force of the political arm?' he later asked.[18] His suspicion of organizations had led Fred to work locally and independently for the good of society.

He and his wife Muriel – a social worker – had moved to one of the most deprived districts of London's Dockland to live upstairs above a disused pub in Shadwell they had converted into a hostel for ex-prisoners. Any help with the hostel was welcomed. 'A kind of extra-mural class with the jailbirds', John remembered. Fred gently showed the young people from Friends Hall how to make a better world through hands-on, loving support. But communists, like his daughter Iris and her boyfriend Bryn, would have believed Fred and Muriel's social work only delayed the inevitable revolution that would usher in the new era of peace and plenty for all.

FIGURE 2.2 John Horner when a school boy (family album).

The first photo I have of John was probably taken at his uncle's farm in Tiptree. A sturdy, cheerful teenage boy is outdoors with a dog and is wearing Monoux School's striped tie and knee-high socks. It may have been the summer holidays following the General Strike and he was not looking forward to September and the new school year. That July he had made the mistake of attracting the headmaster's attention, with life-changing consequences.

At the end of his third year at Monoux School, John had won a prize in English literature – and then failed to show up at the prize-giving ceremony. Even before his bruising from the school's attitude towards the General Strike, he had decided that anything involving 'nice boys with nice sisters and posh parents were not for me'. His no-show before the assemblage of Walthamstow dignitaries had however embarrassed Mr Midgely, the school's recently appointed headmaster. Summoned next morning to the headmaster's study, John refused to explain his absence. 'I could hardly stay away on principle and then cook up some excuse … Yet I dearly wanted the prize which he was now threatening to withhold for my dumb insolence'. A puzzled Mr Midgely then changed his tune. He asked John to sit down, enquired about his parents, his interests, and what he wanted to do when he left school – and then gave him his prize: the *Oxford Book of English Verse*, its navy-blue front cover emblazoned with the arms and motto of the school – 'Virtute et Probitate' ('Virtue and Integrity').

Afterwards there was a letter for him to take home to his mother, requesting she visit the headmaster. Mr Midgely suggested to Emily an experiment. Her son was doing well enough at school to leap-frog a year of study: by going straight from the third to the fifth form he could take his School Certificate exam a year earlier than normal. It would save her almost a year of his keep. Although she left the decision to John, he felt he had no choice. He lost all pleasure in his education. His last year at school was 'a long, dreary swot'. Up until then, he had enjoyed taking exams, liked to do well in his favourite subjects, proud of taking his school report home to his mother. Sadly, the report for 1927 shows him far from top of the class, even in his strongest subjects, English and history. He envied his erstwhile class mate David Thomson, another scholarship boy and, like John, good at history. No one had suggested Thomson should jump a year. John afterwards learnt that Thomson had stayed on into the sixth form, had won a scholarship to Cambridge to become a distinguished historian and eventually became Master of Sidney Sussex College.[19] Thomson represented for John the education he himself might have enjoyed, if only Mr Midgely had not interfered. 'Whenever my eye hits upon [Thomson's] magisterial volumes on nineteenth century France upon my shelves, the old grudge still grumbles up inside me'.

Did class influence these different outcomes for John and David? Ancestry's records show David's mother a couple of steps up from Emily: she had been an office clerk before marrying a skilled worker, a printer killed in the Great War. The widowed Mrs Thomson may have struggled as much as John's mother to keep her clever son at school yet with ambitions for David's education beyond Emily's imagination. To leap from hard, manual unskilled labour to an office job in one generation was already a bold maternal aspiration; Mr Midgely may have also considered it sufficiently ambitious for a boy located on the bottom rung of the class ladder. He concluded that leapfrogging a year had been a success, writing in John's final report that he was 'a boy of intelligence and common sense [who] had fully justified the double promotion … by his steady industry and perseverance'; while his form master, Percy Bysshe Whitt, observed that John's diligence had been 'praiseworthy and ought to ensure success'. Yet John was sadly disappointed: he had passed his School Certificate examination 'with barely more than average marks'.

Notes

1 Harold Walker, *Mainly Memories 1906–1930*, Waltham Abbey, 1986, 21.
2 From the file on Arthur Trigg, Blind Veterans UK (previously St Dunstans).
3 Inspection report NA/ ED 21/28560.
4 This number derived from the Ministry of Health report for 1910 (1911 unavailable), Wellcome Collection.
5 Monoux School records, Waltham Forest Local Records Office (WFLRO).
6 Inquest report, *Walthamstow Guardian*, 12 September 1924.
7 Peter Cox, ' "A denial of our boasted civilisation" Cyclists' views on conflicts over road use in Britain, 1926–1935', *Transfers*, 2012, 2, 3, 4–30.
8 TUC Library collection.
9 *Sunderland Daily Echo*, 6 May 1926.
10 UPI, 8 May 1926.
11 *Fraserburgh Herald*, 11 May 1926.
12 Margaret Cole, *Growing Up into Revolution*, London, 1949, 123.
13 *Monrovian*, 1926.
14 'Fred Parsons, An Appreciation', Ed. Will Hall, 1947 (pamphlet).
15 Hall, 1947, 3.
16 Maud Bird, Association of Students and Friends (ASF) Logbook, 1930, Friends House Library, Box 714/9, copy number 64655.
17 Maes y Haf papers, Friends House Library.
18 Fred Parsons, *Friendship*, April 1933.
19 Derek Beales, 'David Thomson (1912–1970)', Oxford Dictionary of National Biography, https://doi.org/10.1093/ref:odnb/38060; published online: 2004; *Monrovian*, 1931.
20 *Friendship*, September–October 1936.

3

AT SEA

The headmaster sent John to be interviewed by a panel of gentlemen 'able to recommend grammar school boys to certain employers of repute'. On hearing that John wanted to be a journalist, they doubted this would suit, it being a most uncertain profession. They had another suggestion: because he had achieved good marks for Spanish in the School Certificate exam, he was offered a position as trainee buyer in the London office of Harrods' South American subsidiary. Its department store in Buenos Aires catered especially for high-class trade and business was booming. He would work in the department of 'Cotones y Camiseria' (Cottons and Shirts) whose buyers, writes John, 'roamed through Europe searching out the finest fabrics for Argentina's pampered elite'. It was a plum job. 'The headmaster congratulated me (and I think himself). My parents were overwhelmed. In the face of their pleasure I put up no more than token resistance'.

It is hard to conceive a more inappropriate career. At sixteen, already a confirmed socialist, John was catapulted into servicing the luxurious world of upper-class consumption. Harrods' London store was then at the height of its grandeur. The 840 pages of its 1928 catalogue itemize all and more that a wealthy family might desire. To familiarize John with the selling end of the business, he was assigned for his first fortnight to shadow Knightsbridge's snobbish, frock-coated floor walkers who assisted customers with their shopping. This induction confirmed John's doubts; he hated the customers' arrogance, typified by Oscar Wilde's Lady Bracknell, whose loud, clipped upper-class, 'la di dah' voice, as performed by Edith Evans, he enjoyed imitating when reminiscing about Harrods.

Then from the store in Brompton Road to the buyers' department of Harrods (Buenos Aires) in Moorgate; there he had little to do other than filing

DOI: 10.4324/9781032671352-4

or practising his Spanish with the occasional South American visitor. Idle and unhappy, he persevered because of his mother. Her pride found expression in a dozen different ways. If he were going out in the evening to the theatre, 'the carefully laundered shirt would be laid out with cufflinks inserted'. If running late in the morning, and risking to miss his train to Liverpool Street, she would polish his shoes for him because, as she loved to tell the neighbours, 'My son goes to business in the City'. And the job became more interesting after his probationary period, with trips to Lancashire manufacturers, while the buyers were pleasant, friendly men who put up with John's long lectures on the evils of capitalism. And yet, 'The ostentatious opulence, the display of wealth and luxury which I had witnessed at Harrods constantly raised doubts, doubts to which I began to feel there could be but one answer'. Furthermore, he was not kept busy enough – to the extent that he literally started climbing the wall. One afternoon, the managing director opened the door of John's room to discover him practising rock climbing on the floor-to-ceiling shelving. 'Filthy from the undusted files, my hands had left a row of prints across the ceiling. The managing director cocked an eye upwards. "Are you happy with us?" he asked'. John's distaste and boredom by now very evident, Harrods did not dissuade him when he announced that buying shirts for rich men was not for him. He was going to sea.

Since his father's return from the Falklands, John had been attracted to the sea. When a small boy he had gazed at the world's shipping in the Pool of London and ridden back and forth across the Thames on the free Woolwich Ferry. An 1800 edition of *Anson's Voyage*, an early purchase from the barrow outside Monoux School, stayed a favourite as an epic story of heroic endeavour against the elements. While from overtime earnt in digging the foundations of the Lloyds building, Charlie had given his son five shillings to buy two imposing, solidly bound volumes of Frederick Whymper's *The Sea*, described in the frontispiece as a 'stirring story of adventure, peril and heroism'. And as a bookplate for his precious school prize, John had made a pen and ink drawing of a line of galleons in full sail, gliding over the billowing waves. The sea was the pull but there may also have been a push, omitted from the memoir but that he spoke of later: 66 Boston Road had become crowded. After Uncle Arthur had married in August 1928, John's grandmother moved into the third bedroom while his sister Winnie returned home with a baby and no wedding ring. Since his brother's death, John had been the sole occupant of the smallest bedroom but now a sheet was hung down from the middle of the ceiling, with Winnie and baby on the other side. He had little love for his sister, the baby cried, and the proximity and lack of privacy were intolerable.

He had the good sense not to ship as a deck hand. During his many idle moments in Harrods, he visited the friendly staff in the shipping department where to talk about ships and sailing routes was a relief from the tedium of 'Cotones y Camiserias'. Advised that with his school certificate in mathematics, he could become a Merchant Navy officer, they helped him apply for an apprenticeship with Houlders Brothers, a shipping company involved in the South American freight trade. Harrods was a regular client and the usual fees must have been waived. Apprentices were indentured for four years to learn seamanship and navigational skills; they then took a Board of Trade examination in nautical theory to acquire a second mate's certificate; further experience and more examinations allowed a competent officer to move up the career ladder to commanding a ship. How much theory could be acquired during his four years of indenture depended largely on the willingness of the ship's captain to give the apprentice time and help with his studies; there were still many ships where apprentices were used as cheap labour (as happened to John during his first two years).[1] However, his small wage would help cover the fees to study at a nautical cramming school on completing his indentures.

He drew on his parents' small savings to buy his kit, including a brass-bounder's uniform, to be worn only when reporting for duty or on ceremonial occasions. A studio photograph, surely taken at his mother's behest, reminds me of 'the slim lad with large hands', portrayed in H. M. Tomlinson's 'The Master', in *London River*, a collection of short stories about men who go to sea. John's is the 1925 edition. He wore his new uniform for the journey to Cardiff, his mother travelling with him as far as Paddington where he left her in tears. That night he embarked on the SS *Orange River*, a tramp steamer busy loading a cargo of South Wales coal. John was now in charge of his own life.

He was quickly disabused of any romantic dreams: a cold, cramped, comfortless cabin, thick in coal dust and shared with the other new apprentice; seasickness in the Bay of Biscay; the most demeaning and dirtiest task of cleaning out the bilge pump to test his endurance; filthy food – and not enough of it. John's tribulations are familiar tropes. The captain, rarely sober, only appeared for the noon sights or when entering and leaving port, while the Swedish first mate, Mr Jackinson, was a tyrant and his bosun side-kick, a bully. On the first day out, John and the other new apprentice, Bill, were summoned before the first mate. Bill was unfazed; he had already informed John that he was a deep sea fisherman's son and his older brother a deck officer on another of the company's ships. 'Mr Jackinson did not shake hands. He proceeded to examine us. "You're the fisherman", he said to my companion. "And you", he turned to me, "have you worked before?" I confessed, "Only in an office". "Then you'll be in my watch". It sounded like a threat'. They were on the point of leaving the saloon, when Mr Jackinson called John back. Had he ever imagined that by coming to sea that he had broken his mother's heart? 'Indeed, I had had such imaginings

FIGURE 3.1   John, aged seventeen, in his brass-bounder's uniform (family album).

but what could I say to this unfriendly stranger. I stood before him, dumb. "Just remember", he added, "You're not going to break mine" '.

The daily shipping news of the time shows the *Orange River* leaving Cardiff on the twenty-seventh of January 1929, passing Cape St Vincent after eleven days to head southwards across the Atlantic. That was when a pail of drinking water laced with lime juice was placed outside the steward's pantry. Without electricity there was no means of conserving fresh produce and 'Bill laughed at my queasy rejection of the ship's food, helping himself to my untouched plate'. He had often been out on his father's trawler. 'Tales of entertaining Argentinian gentlemen to the music of a string orchestra could not rival Bill's tales of fishing off the Skerries in December'. Bill had spotted John's Spanish dictionary and his Oxford Book of English Verse, with John's proud inscription 'SS Orange River' on the fly sheet. He was intrigued why John should have chosen a career at sea he so evidently disliked.

Yet, as the ship voyaged south and they left winter behind them, John recovered from the first shock, made friends with Bill and started to take an interest in the crew. Mr Jackinson had signed on Irish deckhands 'because he hated Irishmen and thus could look forward to a voyage in which he had readily available targets for his foul-mouthed abuse'. But the crew were kind to John. Seafaring was a dangerous occupation and they protected him from his inexperience. He loved their soft, melodious voices and was delighted by their seamen's bawdy.

Working with one of them as his unskilled labourer and in my tardy clumsiness delaying him finishing his work, he admonished me as eight bells struck and his watch ended and his task unfinished. 'Eight bells', he lamented 'and there you are' – he caught site of the mate making his way across the deck and added, 'Eight bells, as the Madam said, not a whore in the house washed and the street full of Spanish captains'.

Or,

When I was homesick and in the dumps, a sailor would seek to cheer me up, saying I was as miserable as 'a whore at a christening'.

Argentina suffered its first military coup in September 1930. It happened when, according to John's memoir, the *Orange River* was steaming down the coast of South America, only to learn about the coup on entering the mouth of the Plate –

The Wall Street crash and the ensuing world slump had knocked the bottom out of the world economy and put an end to a decade of progressive, liberal rule. All over the great river basin across which we were steaming, dockers, railway workers, transport workers were on strike, defending their fledgling social security schemes and their country's democracy. When we anchored in mid-stream we joined a queue of vessels waiting to move up river.

The *Orange River's* destination was Villa Constitución, a small port and railhead on the Paraná, thirty-five miles south of Rosario and, like every other port, closed by the general strike.

John writes,

> We knew that there had been outbreaks of violence in a number of provinces and gun battles had been fought around the presidential palace in Buenos Aires [and] we had been long enough up river for the politics of what was happening to filter into the focs'le.

After the captain decided that the ship's crew of Danes, Maltese, Norwegians and a Barbadian would have to use the ship's winch to discharge the cargo, a worried bosun came to tell Mr Jackinson that they too had a strike on their hands. Jackinson wasted no time arguing with the crew. The deck officers, the bosun, carpenter and donkey-man, aided by the two apprentices would have to shift the two thousand tons of cement, the crew's bonus to be shared among them. Having already made his sympathies for the Paraná River dockers known to the deckhands, John thought he could hardly join the ship's officers to break the strike. But Bill told him he was a fool, that he was jeopardizing his indentures; even the striking crew told him not to ruin his career, that they would not hold it against him. In his heart, this is what John wanted to hear and yet despised himself for it.

> And so, I helped to work that cargo – helped to break a strike – and took the money, one hundred and sixty-four dollars, more than I would receive in the whole four years of my apprenticeship. The cement was dumped on the quay, deserted but for soldiers and vigilantes. We were warned not to stray along the wharves after dark. The crew spent the whole two weeks idling around the ship.

He had written a briefer version of this incident in the introduction to his pamphlet published on the occasion of the first conference of the World Federation of Trade Unions in London in 1945. In 'Labour's Struggles in Latin America', the strike still occurs in 1930 but is described as against 'a corrupt bureaucracy', rather than in protest at the military coup. Otherwise, apart from the pamphlet's omission of his strike-breaking role, the two versions are similar. Both emphasize the courage of the crew that, despite the promise of *treble* pay, struck in support of the local dockers although the impending slump in British shipping meant that this would minimize any chance of further employment at sea. 'I have yet to witness a finer example of International Working Class solidarity', John wrote in the pamphlet's introduction, 'If this modest essay were worthy I would dedicate it to the members of that polyglot crew who believed they were helping to build a lasting brotherhood among the working people of the world'. Having asked Lombardo Toledano, the leader of the Latin American Workers' Confederation, to write a foreword, John felt he should confess

BY JOHN HORNER

FOREWORD BY LOMBARDO TOLEDANO

PRICE 6ᴰ

LABOUR'S STRUGGLE IN LATIN AMERICA

FIGURE 3.2   Labour's Struggles in Latin America, front cover.

to him how he had helped break the strike described in the pamphlet's introduction. Ironically, the *Orange River* episode was to be John's unique opportunity in his trade union career to participate in a strike – and he had helped break it. Yet, his memoir exaggerates the strike's extent and misremembers the date.

There was no general strike during the coup of 1930. The new military government had prevented all industrial action by deploying troops to the ports and through arbitrary arrests of anarchist and communist trade union leaders.[2] Only in 1932, during the final months of John's apprenticeship, did a general strike occur of the kind described in his memoir. Had he had access to the *Times* newspaper archive when writing his memoir, he would have discovered that there had been a dockers' strike the previous year, in July 1929, in the Rosario section of the Paraná River, one that had threatened to spread down river to Buenos Aires. Locally organized, anarcho-syndicalist dockers' unions in the Rosario sector were a close-knit federation and when a strike started in one port, their neighbours came out in support.[3] The *Orange River* had arrived in Villa Constitución on the 15 July 1929, the day that the *Times* reassured its readers how reports of a general strike were 'grossly exaggerated'. The strike had started at a Rosario flour mill after it hired non-unionized labour and from Rosario spread to the smaller, neighbouring ports: 'San Lorenzo, Villa Constitución, Puerto Gaboto and Grandona all are now idle *except from the work of crews who are discharging cargo*' [my emphasis]. It seems John's faulty memory had merged two voyages into one: According to shipping reports, the *Orange River* was not only in Villa Constitución in July 1929 during that upriver strike but also there again in September 1930, having arrived in Buenos Aires, once again with a cargo of steel rails and cement, five days after the military coup, when there were no strikes.

John may never have known why the Villa Constitución dockers struck in 1929 but he delighted in telling a good story and his misremembrance increases the dramatic tension through situating the strike in the context of the following year's military coup. The change of date also permits him a heightened sense of guilt – to be a blackleg at such a critical turning point in Argentina's history! Is there a resemblance here to his misremembering by a year the date of his brother's death, so that it coincides with John's starting at grammar school, thus increasing his consequent guilt for being angry with his dead brother for 'having spoilt everything'? Are these misremembrances displaced remorse? Remorse for having connived in untruths when a member of the British Communist Party, untruths that he found impossible to write about because they laid so heavily upon him.

For nearly two years he served on the *Orange River*. He writes that by the time he left he had lost his adolescent priggishness, had stopped lecturing at people and started listening to them. He was becoming the cheerful, outgoing man that I was to know: easy to chat with, someone whose company other men enjoyed because he was interested in them and their work. He was also becoming a competent sailor, able to scull the heavy jolly boat with a single oar and to take the ship's helm. His relationship with the first mate had changed. 'I had grown tall enough to look him in the eye – though I seldom did – and I had put on a deal of muscle'.

John's next ship was the *Tasmanian Transport* that left South Wales for the River Plate in early December 1930, returning in late March 1931 with wheat for Manchester's flour mills.[4] It was to be his only voyage with the ship and its captain, Charles Nugent St Clair, described in his memoir as 'friend and mentor'. The *Tasmanian Transport* afterwards lay idle at Newport where St Clair died fourteen months later.[5] The world wheat market was glutted, and in a deeply depressed global economy no one wanted South Wales steam coal. Houlders had accordingly reduced its fleet of twenty-three steam ships to its nine refrigerated vessels that carried beef from Argentina and Uruguay and fruit from Brazil.[6] John was thus transferred to the *Princesa* that made the trans-Atlantic crossing in three weeks with conditions on board more comfortable than on the old *Orange River*, by then laid up in the Blackwater Estuary for want of cargo.

When the *Princesa* arrived at London's Victoria Docks on the twenty-fourth of February 1933, he had completed his indentures. An able seaman's discharge certificate records his height as 5ft, 11, with grey eyes and dark hair, a slight scar on the upper lip.[7] He signed the certificate as 'F. John Horner' and I imagine took the tram home. Whereas seventeen-year-old Freddie could have reasonably expected to make a career with Houlders, the future was bleak for twenty-one-year-old John. His memoir tells of how when his ship was in Liverpool some months earlier, he had been approached by a man carrying a small suitcase that when opened revealed razor blades, notepaper, French letters and other small items useful for sailors in port; pasted on the inside lid, was a Board of Trade Master's Certificate, a mute appeal for business from a proud man who had once commanded a ship.

Back in Boston Road, he used his strike-breaking bonus to pay his fees for a three month course at nautical school. The three hundred and fifty pages of Nicholl's *Requirements for Second Mate, Steamships* makes for a daunting read. It includes a list of likely questions and model answers for the oral part of the second mate's examination. From his underlining of page 266, John appears to have been specially concerned with a question about the 'heaving to' of a steamer in heavy seas.

Bring her head slowly in the direction to which you find she lies easiest and makes the best weather of it. That would probably be with the sea a little on either bow. Keep the engines turning just fast enough to maintain her head in that direction.[8]

Perhaps he was reflecting on how to make the best possible weather of it when tossed about in the Slump's heavy seas.

Notes

1 Alston Kennerley, 'Aspirant navigator: training and education at sea during commercial voyages in British merchant ships c.1850 to 1950', *The Great Circle*, 30, 2, 2008, 41–76.

2 Nicolás Iñigo Carrera, 'La huelga general política de 1932: descripción de los inicios de un ciclo en la historia de la clase obrera argentina' www.pimsa.secyt. gov.ar/publicaciones/DT%2031.pdf accessed 21 February 2023.

3 Natalia Alarcon and Oscar Videla, 'Fortaleza local, solidaridad regional, Un ciclo des huelgas de las estibadores portuarios de Villa Constitución (Argentina 1928–1932)'. *Historia Regional*, 4. 6, 2022, 1–31.

4 *Liverpool Journal of Commerce*, 7 January 1930.

5 See probate notice, *Daily Telegraph*, 6 September 1932.

6 Houlder Line annual report, the *Times*, 19 January 1932.

7 Registry of Shipping and Seamen: Register of Seamen, Central Index, Alphabetical Series (CR 1) FindMyPast.co.uk. Accessed 8 May 2017.

8 F.W. Maxwell, *Nicholl's Seamanship and Viva Voce Guide*, 15th Edition, Glasgow, 1927, 266.

4

THE LADY OF SHALOTT

John never said exactly when he met Pat, only that it was on a spring Sunday during a Friends Hall ramble. Assuming their first encounter was shortly after he had finished his apprenticeship, there was just one Sunday ramble in the spring of 1933. According to Friends Hall's monthly magazine, *Friendship*, on the second of April, Harry Huckett was to lead a 'good long tramp'; participants to meet at 10 am at Chingford Station, 'Bring lunch and thermos flask', with tea at Epping Friends Meeting House.[1] With the weather predicted warm and sunny, Harry must have had a large group to lead.

Apart from Fred Parsons, whose Sunday class had delivered teenage John from Aunt Mill's hobgoblins, none of the ramblers would have remembered nor recognized him from four years earlier. He had returned a transfigured, strapping John Horner standing almost six-foot-tall. After a week spent cooped up cramming for his second mate examinations, he would have needed more than the ramble's fourteen miles to Epping and back to stretch his legs.

So, I imagine him rising before dawn to walk from Boston Road through the streets of terraced cottages to Hollow Pond, then along the narrow woodland trail that cuts through Walthamstow's urban sprawl. Past the boating pond in Highams Park and up the hill to Chingford Plains, packed on bank holidays with East Enders but quiet that Sunday morning, just a few early risers walking their dogs. John's memoir describes his favourite walk through the forest and perhaps the path taken that morning.

At Queen Elizabeth's Hunting Lodge, he turns into the forest. Pressing through the hornbeam thickets, he pauses to touch oaks already old when their fellows were felled for the ships that fought at Trafalgar. From the forest's heights, he chooses the path that passes through the great beeches

DOI: 10.4324/9781032671352-5

FIGURE 4.1　John rambling in Epping Forest (family album).

of Ambresbury Banks, an Iron Age earthworks. A brief halt to honour Boadicea. Here, she and her Icenii tribesmen made their last stand against the Romans who had pursued them northwards after the Icenii had burnt London to the ground. Then on to the forest edge at Bell Common where today the M25 runs. Here, perhaps John rested among the early spring flowers, dozing in the warm sunshine to the bees' humming. After a while, he would have heard another, different buzz. Young voices putting the world to rights, alerting him to the ramblers' arrival. It was then, he told his daughters, that a girl stepped out from among the trees. Paused, a moment. Taller than average, long legs in shorts, dark brown curls, intelligent eyes. He was immediately smitten.

　　Love at first sight. So he told his daughters who knew their romantic father liked a good story. And Pat enjoyed his account, admitted he was certainly good-looking. Taller and fairer than her, broad-shouldered, muscular. His voice a pleasant, light baritone. He had his points, she said. But, oh so very

FIGURE 4.2   Pat aged 21 (family album).

shy with girls. When the ramblers ate their sandwiches in Epping, he may have made sure to sit close by, saying little to her while cheerfully arguing with the men. On their return, back through the forest to Chingford, he would have manoeuvred himself close. Without his asking, she might have told him the names of the woodland flowers spotted alongside their path – violets, anemones, lesser celandine …. Later in their lives, after fifty years of marriage, no longer shy, he still liked asking her their names when they walked together in the woods.

It could have been after that first meeting that he leafed through his *Oxford Book of English Verse*, his much-treasured school prize that had criss-crossed the Atlantic with him and found this poem by Thomas Ashe –

> Came, on a Sabbath noon, my sweet,
> In white to find her lover;
> The grass grew proud beneath her feet,
> The green elm-leaves above her . . .

It fits closely enough to their encounter in Epping Forest and Ashe's next lines match Pat's colouring – 'O sweet brown hat, brown hair, brown eyes / Down-dropp'd brown eyes, so tender!'. These last are neatly underlined with a blue pencil.

She was the fourth child and second daughter, born in August 1912, named Edith after her mother's older sister. The energetic and enterprising Edith Elliott was probably relieved that her niece later switched to using her second name, Patricia. Mrs Elliott was by then a Conservative councillor who had broken off all connections with her communist niece. Pat's mother, Alice and her aunt, Edie, had endured a difficult start; they never knew who was their father, their illegitimacy sufficiently shameful for their maternal grandparents to hide them from the 1891 census. Edie invented a father when she registered her marriage to Henry Elliott. 'Who can blame her for this fabrication, otherwise doomed to spend her life, marked by a stigma that was not of her making?' asks Susannah Stapleton, the biographer of the woman detective, Maud West, Edie's professional alter ego. Maud claimed her origins in a middle-class family of lawyers and as 'the female Sherlock Holmes' enjoyed cross-dressing, and assuming disguises for her detective work.[2]

Pat's mother, Alice Palmer, never pretended to be anyone else. Introvert, shy and home-loving, when her turn came to marry she did not lie about her origins. Her husband Geoff was an ambitious boy apprenticed to a law-writing firm. A sailor's son from the Deptford docks, he had been assured by a friendly solicitor's clerk that a clerical career would give him the chance of becoming a gentleman. 'Put on a black coat and go into society', as the saying went. Yet by the time Violet, their first child, was born in 1906, Geoff's expectations of a life-time's secure and respectable office-employment had been dashed: the typewriter was replacing copperplate script in legal documents. Work was scarce and even an experienced law writer, made only 26s a week, the same as Charlie Horner's labourer's wage.[3] Nevertheless, Geoff seemed to be making enough money when Pat was born to rent a house with a bathroom and indoor toilet in a south London lower-middle-class suburb. It did not last. By her first birthday, they had to move somewhere cheaper. A mile north from the Horners' home in Boston Road, lay a nicer part of Walthamstow: Adjacent to Lloyd Park's ornamental lake and flower beds was a newly built area of tree-lined streets whose red-brick, self-contained maisonettes were widely advertised as somewhere to live 'In a healthy district, well and cheaply, [with] night and day train service and cheap fares'.[4]

Their new ground floor home in Fleeming Road consisted of a front parlour, two bedrooms, an indoor toilet, and a kitchen with a scullery leading out into a garden shared with the flat upstairs. Built to a high standard in pleasant surroundings, a Warner maisonette was a more agreeable than a jerry-built cottage with outside toilet in south Walthamstow's fly-invested Boston Road while the weekly rent was not dissimilar. Fleeming Road was nevertheless a step down for the Palmers: the 1911 census shows the male residents to be skilled manual workers – telephone engineer, bus driver, factory foreman, house painter, plasterer. Office workers like Pat's father, commuting to the city on the cheap workmen's early morning trains, were a rarity. The move to Walthamstow had dashed Pat's parents' lower-middle-class pretensions and seven-year-old Violet felt it keenly. Used to living in a roomy house with a bathroom, she had to accustom herself to cramped living and to bathing in a tin tub in the kitchen while next door lived a family that had moved from Bethnal Green in London's East End. 'A rather unrespectable family', remembered Violet. 'No, that is that is not true they aimed at being respectable, I'm sure. They just were very Cockney. "Arry! Yer egg is cooked", we used to hear over the garden fence'. Violet looked longingly at the 'more genteel estate', a few minutes' walk away with its 'very pleasant small houses'.[5]

In my childhood I was as sensitive to subtle class differences as was Violet at the same age. Alice Palmer was slim and well-dressed; she read novels and hung pictures on her walls: Sir Galahad and his white charger walked soulfully through a dark forest in her living room, while halfway up the staircase, Hope drooped over the last string of her lyre. John's mother's body in old age had assumed the shapeless form of a woman who had lived all her life on a high carbohydrate, low protein diet. I knew her as a garrulous old woman with ill-fitting false teeth, who read nothing other than the newspaper and whose principal topic of conversation was the doings of Mrs Perks next door. Emily Horner was respectable and practical, always wore a hat when she went out, spent her little money wisely and kept her house clean. But *her* middle-class aspirations had been for her youngest son, not herself.

During the Great War, Geoff had been in the administration of an army reception camp on Blackheath. He struggled to feed the family on a corporal's pay until a temporary commission in early 1918 placed them on a more comfortable footing. Correspondence between him and his daughter Violet reveal the family as gradually adopting elements of a middle-class lifestyle: a piano was purchased; they acquired a dog and even went away to the seaside with their Elliott cousins. Geoff had luckily avoided the slaughter on the Western Front by transferring from a line regiment to the Imperial Camel Corps where he was soon promoted to the rank of Captain serving in Egypt and Palestine. His fragment of memoir pleasurably – almost gleefully – recounts how he was looked after by two private soldiers, his batman and his groom, effectively his personal servants. He slips into the pukka sahib's manner of speaking when describing them – 'Splendid fellows, both, who conspired happily to make my life as comfortable as conditions would permit'. Geoff was a fast learner who enjoyed both the performance and the social and financial benefits that officer status gave him. With his lack of a secondary education a hurdle to receiving a commission, he invented his having attended grammar school and afterwards lied his way into the Camel Corps by falsely claiming to be an experienced horseman. Not that Pat's father thought the upper classes were any better than him. On the contrary, he considered them useless at adapting to changed circumstances. It was men like him with administrative experience whose 'exercised imaginations [were] more elastic and capable of development in hitherto unknown spheres'.[6]

After helping suppress the Egyptian National Revolution, Geoff transferred to India, just in time to catch the tail end of the Third Afghan War. Good at his logistics job, he was offered a permanent commission in the Army of the Raj. According to family history, they would have all moved to India were it not for General Dwyer ordering his troops in Amritsar to fire on an unarmed, peaceful crowd demanding Indian independence. The resultant nationwide protests and disturbances eventually decided the authorities to cancel army families travelling to India until order was restored. Geoff turned down the commission and came home to Walthamstow where he photographed his younger children outside 130 Fleeming Road: Pat is scruffier than her brothers: Ken and Eric have pulled up their socks; hers are halfway down her legs. The boys have combed their hair; Pat's is a tangle of thick dark curls, too quick and impatient to give her hair the good brushing that her mother desired.

Perhaps the children had just come home from school in nearby Winns Avenue. 'It was a splendid school', remembered Violet, 'It had the reputation of being the best in Walthamstow'. And yet, Pat hated it because her teachers tortured her. Day after day, month after month, they bound and immobilized the little girl's left hand, to force her into right-handedness. The medical historian, Howard Kushner, quotes a 1924 letter to the *British Medical Journal* justifying such cruelty, because 'otherwise the left-handed child would risk "retardation in mental development; in some cases, … actual feeble-mindedness"'.[7] Forced to use her right hand for all her lessons, Pat stayed forever cack-handed with a needle – John used to sew on his own buttons – and clumsy with a screwdriver; and she never learnt to draw, paint or play tennis. Yet, her teachers must have judged the 'treatment' a success: she had

FIGURE 4.3   Pat and her brothers, 1921 (family album).

avoided mental retardation and despite the clumsy handwriting, was top of the class in English composition and an avid reader. Books were her escape from the daily misery of school. Walthamstow's central library was just a twenty-minute walk from home and the council boasted of the children's section as 'one of the best in Great Britain [providing] profitable recreation for leisure hours and a general brightness in the lives and outlook of our young people'.[8] Pat headed towards the fiction shelves to read stories about ordinary people. Unlike John, she rarely read non-fiction.

At the end of the war, Labour had captured four seats in Walthamstow's local elections, enough to influence the council to contract its post-war house-building programme to a builders' 'guild', a kind of cooperative (the name derived from William Morris' ideals of medieval craftsmanship). In early 1921, the works manager showed a *Daily Herald* reporter around the site at Higham's Park 'It is really wonderful', said the manager, 'to see how craftsmen of all kinds and labourers, have become imbued with the idea that they are doing something worthwhile'. And the architect added, 'I have never seen a contractor able to get his men to work so well'.[9] With priority on the waiting list for ex-servicemen, Pat's family was among the first to move in. The house was plain, if not austere, without the bay window, decorative corbels and tiled path of their maisonette in tree-lined Fleeming Road. Yet it had a private back garden, an indoor toilet and bathroom with hot and cold running water and, in the kitchen, an electric cooker, a rarity in the 1920s. There were four bedrooms, a living room *and* a parlour, the latter given an oriental character by Geoff's wartime souvenirs – a leather pouffe from Cairo, a Benares brass pot serving as a plant holder, and, on the wall, a Pathan curved sword and shield, mementoes from his defence of the Empire against the Waziris.

Geoff set up his own law-writing and stationery business and despite living in a council house built by a workers' guild, was no socialist; in 1923 he stood as the Liberal-Conservative candidate for the Highams Park ward in the council elections. The two parties had formed an alliance, 'shoulder to shoulder to against a common enemy, socialism', he explained in the *Walthamstow Guardian*.[10] His was not the majority view: his neighbours voted mostly Labour (a hundred years later, they still do). By then, the post-war depression had caused Geoff's business to collapse and, with the birth of Mavis in 1924, there was a further mouth to feed. After subsequent failures, he turned for help to Edie, his sister-in-law. While the lower classes were struggling to put food on the table, posher people were merrily committing adultery and Maud West's Detective Agency employed Pat's father to spy on them.[11]

While Geoff was trying to come to terms with the collapse of his dreams, Pat was the first of his children to pass the scholarship examination, and this despite her clumsy handwriting that would have compared unfavourably with the 'beautifully formed' script of most of the girl scholarship winners.[12] In September 1924, she started at Walthamstow High School for Girls and loved everything about it – friends, lessons, teachers. Compared with the boys in the cramped, smelly and noisy Monoux School, the girls were highly privileged. The High was in a new, large, airy and purpose-built building on substantial grounds, away from the sound of traffic. With a dynamic headmistress and highly qualified staff of unmarried women graduates, the school provided a wide and liberal education; an inspection during Pat's first year reported that twenty former pupils were then studying at university, compared with just eleven from the Monoux.[13] The headmistress, locally famous for her passion for everything ancient Greek, had obtained funds for unemployed men to construct an open-air amphitheatre on the school grounds. Pat remembered attending the theatre's inaugural production of *Medea*, translated by Gilbert Murray and performed by Sybil Thorndike and her troupe. Reported in the national press as a triumph, surprisingly no one commented on the play's suitability for school girls. A mother who kills her children is scarcely a role model, yet Murray had told Thorndike how *Medea* was a play for the women's movement, and she regularly performed the title role as a woman crying out against male oppression.[14] That was how Pat described it to me.

Pat's preferred class was English literature which the School Inspectors reported as well-taught, with a wide reading of prose and verse, combined with 'careful study of selected authors'.[15] Among these, Shelley, Browning, Keats and Tennyson figured, and Pat remembered many of the lines when reading these poems to her daughter. A favourite was the 'Lady of Shalott'. Shut up in a high tower, the Lady can take no part in the world that she sees only in a mirror, and she spends her time weaving into a tapestry the images she sees therein. One day she sees in the mirror a handsome young knight, riding cheerfully along the riverbank; 'Tirra Lirra' sang Sir Lancelot. *He* is free to go where he likes and do what he wants to do. ' "*I* am half-sick of shadows", said the Lady of Shalott'. She too wants real, first-hand experience. She wants a life. Pat raises her voice; pushes a curl back from her eyes and grips her daughter's hands. Together, they utter the fatal lines –

> She left the web, she left the loom
> She made three paces through the room
> She saw the water-flower bloom,
> She saw the helmet and the plume,
> She look'd down to Camelot.

But, alas! The Lady is denied what Sir Lancelot enjoys –

> Out flew the web and floated wide;
> The mirror crack'd from side to side;
> 'The curse is come upon me,' cried
> The Lady of Shalott.

The Lady died when she left the tower for the real world but women like Sybil Thorndike and the headmistress of Walthamstow High had escaped from the tower to lead full, rewarding professional lives. Sadly, it was not to be Pat's own future. At the end of Pat's third year, on her fifteenth birthday, her parents told her she was not returning to school for the new term. Had she stayed for a further two years, she would have received her School Certificate. She was not consulted and given little warning. She remembered it as her father's decision. Her three older siblings had each left school at fifteen after studying at commercial or technical school. Thus, from her father's point of view, there would have been nothing unusual in Pat also leaving at the same age. It was expensive to keep her at grammar school: her uniform could have cost as much or more than the weekly wage of an adult male worker.[16] Her parents did not attach as much importance to her education as had John's for his. Pat never remarked that if she had been a boy, it might have been different.

'Read this, if you want to know about my childhood,' Pat said to me one day, passing me V.S. Pritchett's autobiography, *A Cab at the Door*. I immediately recognized Geoff in Pritchett's account of his father. Both were quick to take offence, yet, 'expansive with optimism, walking in and out of jobs with the bumptiousness of a god'.[17] And as with the Pritchetts, the moving van was often at the door, taking the family and its furniture 'from financial calamity in one neighbourhood to fresh hope in the next'. The Palmers' moves were not as frequent, but like the Pritchetts, 'Every time we moved house, Father had lost his job or was swinging dangerously between an old disaster and a new enterprise, that he was being pursued by people to whom he was indebted'.[18] Mrs Pritchett screamed at her husband for housekeeping money but Alice Palmer never raised her voice, quietly earning from her dressmaking and accepting gifts from her sister Edie.

After Edie had paid for Pat to do an intensive course in shorthand typing, she gave her a job at Maud West's Detective Agency in Oxford Street. Pat recalled the agency as widely advertised by a picture of the shadow of a bowler-hatted man opening a door but not mention about how Maud West courted publicity through newspaper interviews where truth blurs into fiction, nor about her globally syndicated adventure stories which and brought Maud fame as the 'female Sherlock Holmes'.[19] There was much that Alice did not know – or chose not to know – about her sister's flamboyant alter ego. Quiet, conventional, introvert Alice may have preferred to ignore Maud West's existence and think only of Edie as a successful businesswoman. The Palmer children frequently visited the Elliotts' large comfortable house in Finchley, and in the year Pat left school she may have spotted a newspaper photograph of Maud West in her office, a sensibly dressed, hardworking professional, with the caption, 'Another sphere where a woman can hold her own'.[20] It was a rare chance for a young girl to work with a woman boss as a role model and her aunt would have certainly let Pat know how lucky she was. Maud West told the newspapers that she was turning away dozens of competent applicants.[21]

Notwithstanding Maud West's accounts to the press of her exciting and varied work in the highest reaches of society, her income came from the humdrum business of divorce, fraud and blackmail. We know from the *Middlesex County Times* that Geoff handled at least one divorce case: he told the court how he had followed an adulterous wife to a Bloomsbury Hotel for a rendezvous with her lover, rode up in the lift with the couple and watched them enter a bedroom; 'In the morning he saw the gentleman leave and ascertained his identity'.[22] Yet the sleaziness of her sister's business only came home to Alice when Pat told her mother how she spent her days typing reports like this one. Alice then acted promptly, told her sister that such employment was unsuitable for a young girl and took Pat away. 'You must have something of the primitive hunter's instincts to enjoy detective work', reflected Maud West.[23] Although Pat was imaginative and intelligent, she never struck me as a hunter.

Alice now found Pat a job in a more conventional business in the City. Shorthand typing was the only option for a lower-middle-class girl whose parents wanted her to start earning relatively quickly after leaving school.[24] Six mornings a week (Saturday, a half day), Pat joined thousands of other Walthamstow commuters for the half-hour train ride to Liverpool Street Station in the heart of the City where she had a succession of routine secretarial jobs – filing, answering the phone, taking dictation and typing dreary business letters. By twenty, she would have been earning about three pounds a week, most of which she gave to her mother.[25] She kept enough for occasional trips to the theatre and weekend outings and either Alice or Violet – who in the late 1920s was ill at home – made her dresses. Pat's emotional and intellectual energies were reserved for weekends and evenings.

Shortly after the Wall Street crash in October 1929, an accountant friend of Geoff Palmer invited him to join in rescuing from bankruptcy a gramophone record company. Dominion was one of nine record companies launched the previous year when sales were booming. Should he and his friend Herbert Booty succeed in turning the company around, Pat's father would finally achieve middle-class prosperity and status. Following a decade of painful failure, he threw himself into the job, later summarized in a curriculum vitae, 'After having re-organised the office and putting credit on better basis, assumed the management of the company's factory, in Luton'.[26]

The Palmer family discovered a new world of modern entertainment. Dominion's musical director, Jay Wilbur, was a Big Band musician popular in West End clubs, and some of Britain's best jazz players recorded for Dominion. Today's vinyl collectors consider that Dominion records delivered a rather muddy sound, a problem when operating on tight margins in a highly competitive market: the Slump had started, people were losing their jobs and had stopped buying records. In the run-up to its Christmas 1929 releases, Dominion disposed of some of its old stock at cut prices. I doubt that Violet ever danced, but the younger ones, Ken with his girlfriend, Eric a rather pompous young policeman, Pat and little Mavis, might have rolled up the carpet in the parlour to foxtrot to Jay Wilbur's 'Let's do the breakaway'.[27]

Even Alice, constantly worried by Geoff's impetuousness and the fluctuations in household income, may have smiled and tapped her feet. But it was to be a gloomy New Year. Record shares had collapsed. Geoff had meanwhile set up a research and development unit that improved product quality and afterwards claimed he had been on the verge of a breakthrough in developing Britain's first long-playing record when in June 1930 the company went into liquidation. For Geoff, it had been 'Success almost achieved'.[28] Research in record production had collapsed. Wireless sets had become a popular alternative to the gramophone. Geoff switched his interest to wireless technology, assembling in his garden shed simple sets encased in wooden cabinets.

I can only guess how the Dominion fiasco influenced Pat's politics, making her receptive to communism's message. Aged seventeen, she must have observed her father at breakfast gloomily scanning the city pages of the *Telegraph*; she would have listened to him talk about the steady fall in the value of record shares; and would have heard his account of the death of his friend, Hubert Booty, unbalanced by the stress of trying to save the company. All this must have made her wonder about the topsy-turvy world of speculative finance that had sucked Geoff in and then spat him out. Her father, like Mr Micawber, was an irrepressible optimist, but she worried for her poor mother, observing Alice become increasingly weary and anxious, never telling Geoff how angry she was with the mess he was making of their lives.

After disposing of Dominion's factory plant, Geoff bought a derelict breeze slabs business, with a coffee bar as a side-line. The business soon collapsed. Mavis was still little, and the household depended on the earnings of the unmarried older children, Pat, her brother Eric and Violet, now well enough to be working again as a shorthand typist. Meanwhile Maud West continued to prosper and Edith Elliott, kept very busy with running the detective agency, may have tasked Geoff to ghostwrite a new series of Maud West stories for syndication. These were advertised as 'Amazing adventures among blackmailers, dope smugglers, vice gangs! More astounding than fiction, her own story of her remarkable and hazardous career'.[29] Geoff liked to tell a good story and was as relaxed as his sister-in-law about mixing fact and fantasy.[30]

Pat had learnt from Alice not to express openly her anger but her judgement on her father's capitalist adventures may be gauged from her eventual disposal of the Dominion records Geoff had left with her after moving from London to Birmingham in 1941 while working for the Fire Brigades Union. When in 1953 it was her turn to move house, rather than leave the boxes of records with a local comrade for the next *Daily Worker* jumble sale, she asked her daughters to help her carry them into the back garden. From the box closest to her, she grabbed a record, brusquely ripped off its paper cover, and with both hands lifted it high above her head to let it drop onto the crazy paving. With a manic laugh, she kicked aside the detritus at her feet to grab another foxtrot. 'Come on', she invited the astonished girls. 'Have a go! There's a lot to get through!' Was she quietly humming to herself 'Let's do the breakaway …' as they smashed to pieces those vestiges of capitalist folly?

At her final height of five feet, nine inches, Pat had become a tall, slim young woman, her dark brown curly hair cut short and set into waves; a photo with her cousin at a suburban club shows her poised and elegant compared with the plain and rather frumpy Evelyn Elliott. Pat was to tell her rather unsociable daughters how at their age she had enjoyed parties, going out on Saturdays, meeting boys. In 1931, she started a commonplace book for her favourite poems or interesting extracts from great literature. On its first page is a sonnet by J.C. Squire, about a break up of a friendship, possibly a rupture with a boyfriend, that she appears to have copied with some emotion, her handwriting larger and more unevenly formed than in subsequent entries. Perhaps, Alice had been hoping that this boyfriend would make her daughter happy, or if not someone similar, with a steady office job and good prospects. Instead, Pat began going to Friends Hall where in the spring of 1933, she met a young man with no prospects.

Notes

1 *Friendship*, The Journal of the Friends Hall and Walthamstow Educational Settlement, April 1933.
2 Susannah Stapleton, *The Adventures of Maud West, Lady Detective*, London, 2019.
3 Law writers pay: *Daily Telegraph*, 23 June 1908.
4 Lucy Harrison and Katherine Green, *WE, The Ex-Warner Estate in Waltham Forest*, 2nd ed., 2016, 8.
5 Violet's letter to author, 1999, author's collection.
6 Geoff Palmer, unpublished memoir, n.d. author's collection.
7 Howard Kushner, *On the Other Hand: Left Hand, Right Brain, Mental Disorder, and History*, Baltimore, 2017, 47.
8 Walthamstow Education Week, 1923, WFLRO.
9 *Daily Herald* 18 February 1921.
10 *Walthamstow Guardian*, 23 March 1923.
11 Geoff Palmer's curriculum vitae, 1945, author's collection; for his work as a detective, see *Middlesex County Times*, 26 December 1925.
12 *Chelmsford Chronicle*, 15 July 1921.
13 Walthamstow: County High School for Girls: Full Inspection 1925, NA/ ED 109/ 1485.
14 Jonathan Croall, *Sybil Thorndike: A Star Of Life*, London, 2009.
15 School inspection report, NA/ ED 109/1485.
16 Selina Todd, *Young Women, Work, and Family in England 1918–1950*, Oxford, 2005, 67.
17 V.S. Pritchett, *A Cab at the Door*, Harmondsworth, 1970, quote on back cover.

18 Pritchett, 26.

19 Stapleton.

20 *Sheffield Daily Telegraph*, 14 May 1927.

21 Stapleton, 235.

22 *Middlesex County Times*, 26 December 1925.

23 *Belfast Telegraph*, 24 November 1938.

24 Teresa Davy, 'A cissy job for men; a nice job for girls': women shorthand typists in London, 1900–39 in eds. Leonore Davidoff and Belinda Westover, *Our Work, Our Lives, Our Words: Women's History and Women's Work*, Basingstoke, 1986, 124–44.

25 Davy.

26 Geoff Palmer's curriculum vitae.

27 Jay Wilbur is doing the break away at www.youtube.com/watch?v=MaP8gjCm EMI accessed 21/2/23.

28 Curriculum vitae.

29 Advertisement in the *Gloucester Citizen*, 14 November 1931.

30 Geoff included 'ghost writing stories' in his curriculum vitae.

5

NO MORE WAR

A photograph in the Palmer family album (Figure 5.1) shows Violet to have been at Friends Hall by 1930 and an enthusiastic rambler. In an article for *Friendship* in 1932, she compared how she used to spend her leisure time with people who viewed discussion of controversial subjects as 'not quite the thing' and 'politics definitely bad form'. But at Friends Hall, she had learnt to argue in a friendly way about what mattered in life: Shakespeare and swimming; economics and Esperanto; vegetarianism and disarmament – and much else besides. Violet was delighted by these new friends who preferred tramping through the countryside to hanging around in tennis clubs. She had found, she wrote, 'a group of young people with mud on their boots, books of verse in their pockets and arguments in their eyes'.[1] She soon became pacifist. In autumn 1930, the well-known author, Mrs Henrietta Leslie spoke at Friends Hall about her new, best-selling novel, *Mrs Fischer's War*, that tells the story of an Anglo-German family torn apart by the war. Mrs Leslie then invited Friends Hall students to tea in her luxurious Chelsea flat. The *Oxford Dictionary of National Biography* describes Leslie (the pseudonym for Gladys Schütze) as 'an outspoken critic of the limitations society placed on women and a tireless worker for women's rights, for children's welfare, and for peace' and despite the grandeur of the surroundings, Violet may have felt emboldened to speak in Mrs Leslie's home when at first too shy to do so at Friends Hall where the young men would have dominated the discussion.

Arthur le Mare, the socialist Warden of Friends Hall, had transformed a Quaker Sunday school into a thriving adult education centre for Walthamstow's young office workers and shop assistants and encouraged them to participate in the running of the centre.[2] Thirty minutes strap-hanging in a densely-packed carriage from Liverpool Street to Walthamstow,

DOI: 10.4324/9781032671352-6

FIGURE 5.1   A Friends Hall ramble with Violet, far left, front row, 1930 (family album).

home to tea and a fast walk to arrive in Greenleaf Road by eight o'clock. For an annual fee of fifteen shillings (about quarter of a week's wages), each weekday evening you could go to a different class. When John first met Pat she was studying psychology and drama as well as attending Fred Parson's Friday's class on English literature that John then also joined. Fred ranged from Chaucer to contemporary authors but was best known for Shakespeare that he used to quote in the middle of ordinary conversation, a habit that John was to adopt. Shakespeare at school had been alright, yet there it had been an examination subject, whereas with Fred, John remembered it as 'a glorious romp'.

According to its art teacher, Walter Spradberry, Friends Hall was inspired by William Morris' revolt from ugliness, its curriculum designed to bring to leisure, 'that fullness of interest and perception of beauty in life that the Arts holds for those who take means to extend their consciousness and ability'.[3] Pat and John's breadth of mind and delight in arts and literature were later to surprise communists with a university education who had imagined lower-class comrades more interested in football, the dance-hall and the pub. Violet and Pat must have found Graham Greene snobbish and patronizing with his scornful allusion in *Journey without Maps* to typists as the archetypal lower-middle class, middle-brow reader. Yet, Friends Hall was no modernist project. Spradberry did not teach abstract art; Fred's gramophone recitals were a musical education in the nineteenth-century classics; and there was little enthusiasm in the literature class when someone proposed they read T.S. Eliot's 'The Waste Land'. The historian Jonathan Rose suggests that working-class adult learners were uninterested in the modernist disruption, preferring to acquire the culture that had equipped the upper classes before the First World War; The Waste Land's sense of autumnal disintegration, he writes, may have felt utterly strange to young, self-educated readers aspiring to a brighter, socialist future.[4]

Encouraging their students to think about the big issues of the day, Arthur le Mare and Fred Parsons used their network to attract well-known speakers to Friends Hall's Sunday evening 'Fellowship Meetings'. So impressed was John by Friends Hall's pulling power, that he erroneously believed Mahatma Gandhi had addressed the students in 1930 while John had been at sea. Gandhi had indeed come to Walthamstow, rambling in Epping Forest with some local Quakers among whom must have been Arthur le Mare. 'It was good to see [Gandhi] enjoying the greenness of the forest, his sandalled feet carrying him along at a pace it was quite hard to keep up with', wrote the ramble's organizer in a Quaker monthly. They had met an old man gathering blackberries who took out from a shabby attaché case some he had just picked and offered the blackberries to Gandhi 'who accepted with a friendly word of thanks'.[5]

Gandhi's non-violent direct action for Indian independence had long been supported by many at Friends Hall but not everyone there believed in the Gandhian path to world peace. Marxism was a hot topic. On returning to Friends Hall in early 1933, John was surprised to find that the Depression had transformed the place into 'a veritable hotbed of pacifists, anarchists and communists'.[6] Arthur himself had just given three lectures on Karl Marx and these were followed by 'a brilliant talk' from Douglas – 'Harry' – Parsons, Fred's eldest son and already a communist.[7] The striking diversity of views at Friends Hall decided some students to form their own Peace Group to create the space for students to consider how to secure peace and social justice. Some were like Arthur and Fred, absolute pacifists. Others argued that should the state conscript them to fight, they would take a Gandhian stance of collective non-violent resistance. A third group composed of communists and radical socialists expanded the notion of resistance to include a general strike should their capitalist governments go to war, particularly if to fight the Soviet Union; and among this last group were contingent pacifists, ready to use violence should their strike be forcibly repressed. But everyone at Friends Hall wanted to reduce arms expenditure to reduce the risk of war. Violet and Pat would have been among the Friends Hall students who had collected signatures for an international declaration to be delivered to the World Disarmament

Conference that met in Geneva in 1932. *Friendship* believed the conference could mark a turning point in the world's history, 'setting all nations on the road to peace and economic prosperity'. Yet, should it fail, 'It will simply mean that we must renew and redouble our efforts, beginning again from where we have just left off'.[8]

In the summer of 1933, hopes for world peace were still high. The Nazis had only just come to power in Germany and the threat of a second and more terrible war than the first was more theoretical than imminent reality. And the weather was lovely. The Saturday night following Pat and John's first meeting was a full moon with a Night Ramble. 'Meet at Chingford Station at midnight' instructed *Friendship*. 'Home in time for an early breakfast. Bring thermos and tuneful voices'.[9] And so into a warm and sunny May: more rambles in Epping Forest, a camping weekend at Amersham, and a performance in the forest of *Midsummer's Night Dream* by the Friends Hall drama group.

Having successfully passed six written and one oral exam, on the 24 June John collected his Merchant Navy officer's certificate.[10]

> My father was at the bottom of the backyard in his chicken run on the Saturday afternoon when I came away from the Board of Trade. In my pocket I had my second mate's certificate bound in its hard, gold-crested cover. Stooping, he left his hens to join my mother in expressions of pleasure (typically muted) at my success. Unemployment then stood around the three million mark and my parents needed no reminder that I could not have qualified at a more inopportune time.

While he had been at nautical school, Houlders had sold eleven vessels from their fleet.[11] Or as John would have put it, a further eleven masters, first mates and second mates dumped on the beach to join the hundreds of officers already unemployed. He decided to take a long walk to sort things out and to think about Pat. How could there be love on the dole, dependent on his girlfriend for his bus fare or a cup of tea?

He went down to the Lea Valley Marshes where as a boy he used to wander during the unhappy days following his brother Charlie's death. He walked northwards along the tow path of the Lea, from time to time making way for the horse-drawn barges that carried hay, brick and straw from the river's upper reaches down to East London. North of Waltham Abbey, he cut across eastward to head up to Cambridge. Here he spent a day on the banks of the Cam, pondering over his ruined future.

> I was getting to my twenty-second birthday. I stood a fraction under six feet and weighed fourteen stone. Of my demands at the table, my mother proudly, and not in complaint, said that I could eat a horse. I had worked

hard to qualify for my profession. After a couple of years sea service with Mr Jackinson I could stand up to any man. I thought a lot of myself.

Then up to Ely with a morning in the Cathedral, 'Its majesty and its silence seeming to sooth the bruising my self-esteem had suffered at the tribunal'. Sleeping in woods and barns, in the high summer weather, he wandered across the Fens to Kings Lynn, by now having tramped over ninety miles north of Walthamstow. Almost out of money, he walked a further sixty miles south-westwards to Henlow in Bedfordshire where lived his Uncle Arthur. John does not relate the advice and encouragement his uncle must have given him, only that he now had the fare home to Walthamstow.

He did not immediately abandon hope of a berth; with two friends from nautical school, he spent an hour each morning at the Board of Trade in West India Docks where a Royal Naval Yeoman of Signals kept their skills from rusting. But the Labour Exchange queues reserved for workless seamen grew ever longer and 'I might spend a whole morning waiting to sign on, then join the group in the public library for my turn to study the jobs vacant pages in the *Daily Telegraph*'. My own scan of the *Telegraph*'s classified advertisements for the last day of June 1933 shows not a single proper job with a regular salary, nothing but vacancies for travellers and salesmen working on commission. One of these reassures the jobseeker he will not be required to deal in water softeners or vacuum cleaners; another seeks salesmen for automatic cigarette machines for home use. John spotted something more promising. The advertiser was looking for 'personable young men with initiative and readiness to take risks, to work late at night, sometimes in unorthodox circumstances. Service in the Armed Forces or the Merchant Navy would be a recommendation'. He rushed to join a long queue of eager young men to discover that the job was selling silk stockings to chorus girls at the stage door. He even momentarily flirted with an application to the Palestinian or Rhodesian police force. Meanwhile, he was receiving just nine shillings and sixpence a week for 'transitional benefit' that made him partly dependent on his father's earnings for his upkeep.

The threat of long-term unemployment increased John's respect for Charlie Horner who had never had a secure job. John writes, 'Poverty, unemployment and the <u>constant</u> search for work had made work for him the basis of his own system of ethics. For him, work meant more than security. It meant self-respect'. He began also to appreciate that Charlie was not just mindlessly digging holes but had always taken an interest in the buildings on which he worked.

He used the thin cardboard covers of his Rizla cigarette papers as a notebook in which he kept check of his current overtime earnings. On one such Rizla packet he had pencilled the dimensions of the Statue of Justice when he had worked on the last stages of the building of the Old Bailey.

He eventually accepted his father's offer to help find him work as a navvy and was taken underground at Chancery Lane tube station where the foreman showed him the men tunnelling an extension and offered him a job. But after four years on the wide ocean, John found insupportable 'the hot compressed air in those confined spaces, the noise of the pneumatic drills, and the thunder of the compressors'. He continued his search.

In the end, it was not too difficult. They were recruiting for the London Fire Brigade and John's naval background would be an advantage. John applied and, after some tests and an interview, was accepted. 'We took you from a queue of two hundred', he was later told by Sir Aylmer Firebrace, the former Royal Navy commander in charge of the London Fire Brigade. A fireman's job was a steady one with a reasonable starting wage and good prospects. Charlie was greatly pleased: his son would be getting a policeman's pay with a uniform and two pairs of new boots. So different from a navvy who had to work in his own clothes, with just an ancient pair of boots that as a child John used to clean weekly to remove the mud and clay.[12] The London Fire Brigade had told him to report for training on 21 December. What to do meanwhile? Houlders offered him a voyage before the mast as watch-keeper – four hours on, four hours off with Able Seaman's pay. The *Hardwicke Grange* left Tyneside on 4 August to pick up cargo in Newport and Liverpool before heading out for Buenos Aires. John writes that the grub was horrid and the bosun disagreeable but after the stress of unemployment and with the prospect of future steady work, he felt greatly relieved. 'Compared with the Chancery Lane tunnels', the *Hardwicke Grange* 'was paradise'. And during the warm night watches, he looked at the stars and thought of his girl.

When the No More War Movement opened a Walthamstow branch in January 1934, Pat responded to its call to action: 'What can we *do* so it may not be said of us by generations to follow that we failed them in this great day ... We are forced back to the startling truth that the destiny of the human race lies in our hands'.[13] The Movement's relatively small membership with a largely Quaker leadership, was inspired by socialist war-time conscientious objectors like Arthur le Mare, who saw capitalism as the root cause of war.[14] Pat's pacifism however was, above all, a visceral rejection of the evil stupidity of war. Her commonplace book mostly contains extracts about love and nature, but she also included lines from 'The Dilemma' by a favourite poet, J.C. Squire, about how during the Great War both the Germans and the English believed God was on their side.[15]

She was profoundly affected by Vera Brittain's *Testament of Youth* that recounts Brittain's experience of the Great War and the death of those she most loved. Brittain articulated Pat's own fears.

Oh life, if I do finally decide to marry G and have a family – and I'm not absolutely certain yet that I want to do either please grant that I have only daughters; I'm afraid, in the world as it is, to have a son. Our generation is condemned, condemned and the League and all that it stands for, is only a brittle toy in the hands of ruthless primeval forces!

But then Brittain reflects. The last war had killed her brother, friend and fiancé, all of them soldiers. The next would be more terrible and total. Mass aerial bombing would slaughter man, woman and child and would annihilate impartially her sons and daughters alike.[16]

Friends Hall students began to worry that the biggest threat to world peace might be the rise of Nazism that they attributed to the demands made on Germany at the Versailles Peace Conference. After Germany's withdrawal from the League of Nations in late 1933, the secretary of Friends Hall Peace Group wrote,

We are all responsible for Germany's critical position today. Try to get under the skin of the average German and see what it feels like to have your beloved country humiliated, your pride dragged in the dust, through the vile terms of the Versailles Treaty.[17]

Mutual understanding and reconciliation with Germans is the theme of Philip Gibbs' *The Cross of Peace*, reviewed by Pat for *Friendship* in November 1934. A French officer, Armand Gattières, billeted with a German family during the occupation of the Rhineland, falls in love with the household's daughter. Pat writes how after Armand becomes a history teacher back home in France, 'he watched the seeds of disaster sown with the Versailles Treaty, growing and budding with their inevitable fruit'. Armand is ostracized by the local community for encouraging his pupils to make friends with young Germans, and his wife leaves him. Pat appreciates the novel because ordinary people are not blamed for the hostility between the European powers.

The reader understands how German youth fled to Hitlerism as a way out of misery and hopelessness and in revolt against injustice. One comprehends the fear and distrust of the French and the injured pride and bitterness of the Germans... When the book is laid down, one feels that the only thing to do is help 'to create a new order in the world – the comradeship of youth across frontiers'.

Here Pat is citing the objective of the Youth Section of the No More War Movement.

Joseph Gorman, the secretary of the Walthamstow branch of the No More War Movement taught Pat how to campaign for peace. 'Exhibit a Peace Poster in your front window at home'; take some leaflets away from the branch meeting and 'accidentally' leave them on the bus seat (in Pat's case, her commuter train); help build a library of newspaper cuttings relating to peace and war to use as quotes at public meetings – 'for example, how newspapers build the war atmosphere and serve as the mouth piece of armaments firms'; make sure newsagent and libraries stock books and journals in favour of no more war, by going in to ask for them. Pat was also instructed about how to debate. Should she find herself defeated in an argument about pacifism, she should bring the experience to the next branch meeting for them to find a good answer to use 'in the friendliest way' at the next opportunity.[18]

Notes

1 Article by Violet Palmer in *Friendship*, September 1932.
2 See Martin Freeman, ' "An advanced type of democracy"? Governance and politics in adult education c.1918–1930', *History of Education*, 2013, 42, 1, 45–69.
3 Walter Spradbery, *Friendship*, October 1932.
4 Jonathan Rose, *The Intellectual Life of the British Working Classes*, New Haven, 2001.
5 *Wayfarer*, October 1931.
6 John Horner, Interview with Louise Brodie.
7 *Friendship*, January 1933. Later known as 'Harry' Parsons, he was to become the *Daily Worker*'s business manager.
8 *Friendship*, February 1932.
9 *Friendship*, April 1933.
10 'Board of Trade examination results', *Liverpool Journal of Commerce*, 24 June 1933.
11 *Western Daily Press*, 12 April 1933.
12 Interview with Louise Brodie.
13 Walthamstow branch of the NMWM, *Friendship*, January 1934; NMWM call to action quoted in Richard Overy, *The Morbid Age*, London, 2010, 219.
14 Martin Ceadel, *Semi-detached Idealists: The British Peace Movement and International Relations, 1854–1945*, Oxford, 2000, Chapter Nine.
15 Read the poem at www.oxfordreference.com/display/10.1093/acref/9780191826 719.001.0001/q-oro-ed4-00010379. Accessed 16 October 2023.
16 Vera Brittain, *Testament of Youth*, London, 2011, 640.
17 *Friendship*, November 1933.
18 *Friendship*, February 1934.

6

'THE COMING STRUGGLE FOR POWER'

John's memoir refers to his unemployment as 'yet another lesson in capitalist economics'. The experience decided him that while serving on the *Hardwicke Grange*, he would read about the origins of capitalism. In a pamphlet written ten years after that voyage, he recalls how he had bought in Liverpool a copy of John Strachey's recently published *The Coming Struggle for Power* that then circulated among the other deck hands, certificated officers obliged like him either to sail before the mast or go hungry: 'The slump had taken our livelihoods, had turned our years of study and enthusiasm to mockery, had doomed millions of people all over the world to misery and want'. He wrote how he and his shipmates learned from Strachey about the meaning of Fascism and monopoly capitalism, 'It put the feet of more than one member of that ship's company on the road to socialism'.[1] It was one among the books that John afterwards burnt in 1991 on the collapse of the Soviet Union. I find a second-hand copy of a later edition.[2]

Strachey was a professional journalist and easy to read. The first part introduces the concept of the market and describes the rise of capitalism. Strachey explains how the Industrial Revolution divorced the worker from his means of production, exemplified by the handloom weavers who were 'not dispossessed in any visible way by the Lancashire mill owners'. Rather, they lost their livelihood because the new mass-produced cloth undercut the price of their handloom product. I underline Strachey's felicitous phrase – 'Once again a relationship between people disguised itself as a relationship between things'. Strachey then discusses the causes of the Great Depression – the 'capitalist crisis' – at its peak when he published his book in 1932 – and considers the solution of the neo-classical economists, namely the reversion to red-in-tooth-and-claw capitalism, by removing all constraints that prevented

DOI: 10.4324/9781032671352-7

FIGURE 6.1 John (centre) with shipmates on the SS *Hardwicke Grange*, 1934 (family album).

market equilibrium such as workers' social security or a minimum wage. But because these 'market restorers' had little chance of having their proposals accepted, the booms and devasting busts would continue until the abolition of a dysfunctional capitalism.

This explanation was good enough for John. Like his hero, William Morris, John showed little interest in advanced economic theory. His eyes glazed over when I told him of my travails with neo-classical economists who dominated the British ministry for development aid when I first worked there in the 1980s. Capitalism for John was a moral issue because it destroyed hundreds of millions of lives. On this final voyage to Buenos Aires he was shocked to see anchored in mid-stream idle vessels that had been chartered as floating warehouses for Argentina's unsold grain, their crews sent home as DBS (distressed British seamen) and the ship owners bankrupt. Meanwhile Argentinians were going hungry, the country's stock of wheat mixed with heavy tar as fuel for railways' locomotives, a substitute for the Welsh coal, the country could not afford to import. Thus, Strachey comments on the global depression, 'The abundance and super-abundance of everything which men need is only matched by the destitution of half mankind'.[3]

Worse yet for John was to hear the stories of the starving, unemployed men he met in the Buenos Aires docks, recent immigrants who had come to Argentina to work on the railways and construction sites that now lay idle. John writes how his conversations with 'los desocupados' made a further chapter in his socialist education. Soldiers at the foot of each ship's gangway stopped them begging from the crews. But the soft-hearted young soldier assigned to the *Hardwicke Grange* looked the other way while the unemployed gathered around the stern from where hung a basket of waste awaiting the daily rubbish collection. Amid the buzzing of a myriad of flies, the ship's galley boy would take the empty cans proffered to him by hungry men and cram them with a repulsive mess, the leftovers scraped off from seamen's plates. 'God help them!' writes John, a heartfelt expression of anger at people's distress from systemic injustice; now an old man, still angry about what he had seen and heard in Buenos Aires half a century earlier.

The penultimate part of *The Coming Struggle for Power* introduces Lenin's concept of imperialism as a 'distinct global regime' wherein the capitalist empires compete against each other to gain monopolistic power over the entire world. This is the final stage of capitalism that aided by the disaffected working class will collapse under its own contradictions. Already, 'One hundred and sixty millions of men and women … have taken the road to communism. They have leapt out of the kingdom of necessity towards the kingdom of freedom'. Terrified that the workers in other countries will follow the Soviet example and 'hard-pressed by the rivalries of the competing empires', the capitalist powers are using 'new and far more violent methods to maintain then system'. Hence Fascism – 'a desperate expedient only resorted to by the capitalist class in face of the most urgent danger from the workers'.[4]

Strachey concludes by looking at communist society in its 'transitional stage' in the Soviet Union. Unlike capitalism's system of wage slavery that compels workers to produce goods or commodities at the behest of the capital-owning class, workers collectively own the means of production in the Soviet Union. 'Those functions of the State which consist in the regulation and planning of things, of the control of nature will long persist ... but those which consist in the coercion of persons will disappear'. Strachey hastens to add that after the revolution in Britain, the transition to communism will be easier than it had been in the Soviet Union that had to start from a very low economic base that meant prioritizing the production of capital goods over consumables. Here, Strachey is referencing Stalin's First Five Year Plan (1928–32) that concentrated on developing heavy industry at the cost of consumption goods. Strachey does not mention how the plan's success required hard currency to import machine tools from Western Europe and secured by exporting Soviet wheat grown on the newly collectivized farms.

At around the time John started writing his memoir, he told me a black joke about the first Five Year Plan. On visiting a collective farm, a furious Stalin discovered the land had been left unploughed. The anxious manager nervously explained he had done his best to implement Moscow's instructions to mechanize the farm: ' "We shot all the horses, Comrade Stalin". The only problem', John chuckled bitterly, 'is that they hadn't yet received any tractors. So there was a famine ....' The often chaotic and sometimes bloody business of collectivization and the liquidation of the kulaks contributed to the famine in the Soviet wheat lands in 1932–33. Another contributory factor was the export of Soviet wheat. It not only increased hunger at home but also contributed to the collapse of the global wheat markets in which John was a bit player.

When John signed his apprenticeship indentures at the end of 1928, Houlders, his employers, had been optimistic about the year ahead. With a record harvest underway in South America, they anticipated an increase in the region's wheat exports – and thus a greater demand for cargo tonnage.[5] Houlders were initially correct. Both northern and southern hemispheres having enjoyed a bumper wheat harvest, Canadian dealers tried to keep prices high by releasing only a small part of their stocks, thus deciding importers to switch to Argentina's cheaper, lower-grade crop. The *Orange River* continued to carry Welsh coal to fuel Argentina's British-owned railways, returning with wheat to make bread for Britain's workers. That is until mid-1929 when the Canadians realized their pricing stratagem had failed and dumped their stock onto the global market, with a resultant sharp drop in global wheat prices. The consequent collapse of agricultural credit markets in grain-producing countries contributed in turn to the general shrinkage of credit following October's Wall Street Crash.[6]

Houlders were now scrambling around to find freight for their homeward-bound vessels.[7] Sir Frederick Lewis, the great shipping magnate and chair of Furness Withy (with a fifty per cent stake in Houlders) described 1930 as 'the most troublesome and difficult year through which in my recollection shipping has ever passed'.[8] It was to get worse. In 1933 Argentine wheat was selling at just a third of its price in 1929,[9] by which time there was a great famine in wheat-growing regions of the Soviet Union. In 1930, the Soviet Union had contributed to the global wheat glut by selling some of its crop for foreign currency. The harvest that year had been good but then, despite two successive bad harvests, the Soviet Union continued exporting wheat at double the initial quantity for smaller returns. Silence, lies and statistical jiggery pokery obscured the terrible reality: there was very little wheat back home to feed those who had grown it. Wheat exports contributed to the famine of 1932–33 and the death of millions of Soviet citizens.[10] Meanwhile the British Communist Party's *Daily Worker* denounced the British government for the new Ottawa agreement that gave preference to trading with countries in the British Empire, putting at risk the jobs of British engineering workers who made the machine tools exported to the Soviet Union.[11] Houlders' shareholders were as keen on free trade as the *Daily Worker*: imperial preference, they argued would be bad for British workers. Restrictions on importing chilled meat would push up domestic food prices.[12]

In *The Coming Struggle for Power* John Strachey argues that because continuing with free trade would expose Britain to competition from the younger, more vigorous economies of the United States and Japan, the ruling classes would inevitably choose imperial preference 'at the expense of the rest of the world' and thus cause the next imperialist war, that may be the last because in 'every great, capitalist empire, there is an increasingly exploited, dissatisfied, insecure and unemployed working class which is becoming ever more rebelliously inclined'.[13] In the next imperialist war, an organized and mobilized working class will not fight to protect capitalism but instead will fight for their own class.

> There is no force on earth which can long prevent the workers of the world from building a new and stable civilization for themselves based on the common ownership of the means of production. The realization of this new stage in the history of mankind is not in doubt.[14]

The inevitability of this outcome makes strange reading in a post-modern world where, except among religious fundamentalists, grand narratives have disappeared. Yet what a marvellous inspiration for a serious young man with a ruined career and witnessing misery all around him.

Notes

1 John Horner, 'A book that has in influenced me', in ed. Percy Allott, 'Books against Barbarism', pamphlet, London, 1943, 18.
2 John Strachey, *The Coming Struggle for Power*, New York, 1935.
3 Strachey, 102.
4 Strachey, 265.
5 Mr Frank Houlder's speech, *Times*, 11 January 1929.
6 G.P. Marchildon, 'War, revolution and the Great Depression in the global wheat trade, 1917–39', in eds. Lucia Coppolaro and Francine McKenzie, *A Global History of Trade and Conflict since 1500*, London, 2013, 142–62.
7 *Times*, 20 January 1930.
8 *Times*, 16 January 1931.
9 Marchildon, 148.
10 S.G. Wheatcroft, 'Towards Explaining Soviet Famine of 1931–3: Political and Natural Factors in Perspective', *Food and Foodways*, 2004, 12, 2–3, 107–136.
11 *Daily Worker*, 22 August 1932.
12 *Times*, 13 January 1933.
13 Strachey, 295.
14 Strachey, 395.

7

'MARX FOR YOU AND GOD FOR ME'

It was a few weeks into his fire service training when John joined a great crowd in Hyde Park to greet the Hunger Marchers from Britain's distressed, industrial areas. The marchers were protesting at the lack of jobs, the iniquities of the Means Test and the low levels of state assistance. The *Daily Worker* welcomed them with a cartoon: the capitalists, who had cheered them as heroes when they had marched to war in 1914, were howling at them when they marched for bread.[1] Owen, the younger son of Fred Parsons from Friends Hall, afterwards wrote in *Friendship*, about his reaction to the Hyde Park rally. Soon to graduate from university, he was lucky enough not to be forced to toil over a machine nor bring up his children on a pittance. Nevertheless, he would be 'broken and thwarted' by the capitalist system and 'My fight is their fight and my allegiance is to them'.[2]

How might John Horner have reacted to Owen's commitment to the working class? John who had so wished to go to university and whose Merchant Navy career had been destroyed by the slump, thought himself lucky to be training as a fireman. In today's language, might he have wanted to remind Owen to check his privilege? It seems not. John was perhaps thinking of Owen when in a letter to *Friendship* the following year, he quoted from the Communist Manifesto, 'The conditions of the existence of whole sections of the middle class are threatened. The working class is thereby supplied with fresh elements of enlightenment and progress'.[3] On the other hand, in a subsequent letter to *Friendship*, John warned off other middle-class enthusiasts from telling the working classes how to rise up. If they only looked, they would find already among them the workers making the new world that these enthusiasts dreamt of.[4] The crowd's welcome to the Hunger March was John's first experience of the emotional

DOI: 10.4324/9781032671352-8

energy generated by thousands of strangers assembling to confirm the justice of their common cause. In his autobiography, *I Believed*, onetime communist, Douglas Hyde describes his feelings that day. 'I looked back down the line of marchers stretching as far as the eye could see. Their challenging, threatening banners, sailing along above their heads, brought tears of hope and excitement to my eyes'.[5] John's own memoir explains how he had naively expected the Hunger March to be the principal topic of conversation at next day's mid-morning break on the fire service training course. Not a bit of it; his fellow trainees were chewing over Saturday's football results and only a few shyly accepted one of the pamphlets John had brought back from Hyde Park.

Most new recruits to the London Fire Brigade had transferred seamlessly from the Royal Navy and according to John 'were accustomed to perpetuating the tradition of the disciplined, uniformed service they had just left in the enclave of the disciplined, uniformed LFB'.[6] The custom of recruiting firemen from the Royal Navy had resumed after an interruption at the end of the First World War when the government had obliged the London Fire Brigade to absorb over nine hundred demobilized men, many of whom had served on the Western Front. These were 'the hungry thousand' that were to be the changemakers in the Fire Brigades Union whereas John's fellow recruits were a younger, more cautious, conservative bunch.

John treated the training as a challenge, 'to excel, show off, to prove that the "working navy" as they gratuitously called my former profession, was equal to [theirs]'. He was taught to use every kind of ladder, to handle ropes and lines, how to lower his class mates out of windows and crawl through smoke-filled tunnels, and learnt to rely on others when jumping out of second-floor windows into a canvas sheet they held out for him. The six months' training ended in a written examination wherein he excelled. 'My success', he writes, 'had hardly been the result of any excessive intellectual display on my part'. All he had to do was to learn off by heart the London Fire Brigade's 'Question and Answer Book', the equivalent to Nicholl's 'Viva Voce Guide', studied at nautical school. In both cases, 'the closer to the actual text, the better the answer and the higher the number of marks'. Rote learning was the antithesis of Friends Hall's liberational pedagogy that encouraged student-led, active learning and self-expression but John liked to show off. I imagine he must have equally excelled in Communist Party classes that used a similar question-and-answer approach, such as –

Question – Who are the Masses?
Answer – They are the politically inactive majority of the working class. [7]

Having done so well, John was summoned to the presence of the London Fire Brigade Deputy Chief Officer. The splendidly named Sir Aylmer Firebrace told him he was to be attached to Southwark Fire Station, London Fire Brigade Headquarters, meaning he was on the fast track for promotion.

John studiously observed life and culture in the London Fire Brigade and the fireman's brass helmet epitomized for him its hidebound traditions. Its high, decorated comb, allegedly modelled on those worn by the French presidential guards at the Elysée Palace, was polished daily and after every fire, rendering the crown dangerously thin from generations of elbow grease. On retirement, a fireman handed in his helmet to be fitted with a fresh head harness for a new recruit. John's head was so large that his helmet had to be elongated through the insertion of a brass strip so that he appeared to be wearing an inverted coal scuttle. The LFB's five top officers, on the other hand, were issued with made-to-measure silver helmets: promotion into the senior ranks was John's only recourse from looking absurd for the rest of his working life.

Firemen worked ridiculously long hours, alternating each fortnight between fifteen-hour night and nine-hour day shifts. On night shifts, lights were dimmed at eleven and the fully clothed firemen stretched out on trestle hammocks above the appliance room. When a fire call came with the lights switched on and every bell set ringing, they were expected to instantly jump up and use a pole to go down to the appliance room where drivers were already revving up their engines. On his first night shift, John did not sleep for fear of waking to have forgotten his assigned appliance or how to slide down the pole. 'Don't worry, young Johnny, if the bells go down, just follow me', an ex-submariner, one of 'the hungry thousand', had kindly whispered to him. In later life, a recurrent nightmare in times of stress was to slide down the pole and not find his boots.

On his first day shift things took an odd turn. He was told to report to the house of one of the senior LFB officers, a 'silver helmet', who lived on the fire station grounds. The silver helmet's batman-fireman opened the door and introduced John to the cook. ' "Very well", said Cook. "You can start in the nursery – scrub the floor, then wash along the passage outside and by that time I shall have finished in the kitchen, and you can clear up after me and then scrub this floor" '. An astonished John turned round and went back to his station officer to tell him that, from what he had learnt at training school, scrubbing a nursery floor was not among a fireman's duties. It was then explained that each new recruit was in turn given this task. Although the station officer concurred that he could not make it an order. John's refusal to scrub the floors in a senior officer's house gave him an early reputation as a 'bolshie', a term used in the Royal Navy 'to describe even the most modest form of independent behaviour outside the accepted norm of the lower deck'.[8]

The start of John's fire service training had coincided with Ben Bradley's release from prison in India and return home to Walthamstow. Bradley was a famous communist and ardent anti-imperialist and received a rapturous welcome. He then immediately took the lead in organizing a Walthamstow contingent to greet the Hunger Marchers on their arrival in Hyde Park.[9] As with the many other communists known to John, Bradley is missing from the memoir. The *Daily Worker* described him as 'tall, heavily-built, browned by the Indian sun'.[10] A later photo reveals a serious, man with sharp, deep-set eyes, possibly someone who rarely smiled. Revolution was serious business. The Communist International – Comintern – had sent Bradley to India in 1927 as a secret agent to assist local comrades foment trade union militancy and he was one of three Britons among twenty-seven arrested and eventually found guilty of criminal conspiracy to end British rule in India.[11] During their long and high-profile trial in Meerut, the defendants had been lodged together with no restrictions on reading material. They studied and discussed so much Marx and Lenin that one of them, Sohan Singh Josh, was to describe their prison as 'Meerut Jail University'.[12] So, Bradley gained the equivalent of a degree in Marxism to become Walthamstow's most important communist in a town with a long socialist tradition.

When teenage John visited with his father his brother Charlie's grave in Queens Road Cemetery, he may have spotted, as I did, the gravestone of Jack Williams, friend and comrade of William Morris – 'Pioneer, Comrade, Socialist, Died November 4th 1917, "Those that fight for freedom undertake/ The noblest cause Mankind can have at stake"'. In 1920 Jack Williams' comrades helped found the Communist Party of Great Britain and Bradley soon joined the Walthamstow branch.[13] Party membership reached its nationwide peak during the General Strike, only to shrink after Comintern in Moscow ordered comrades to cut themselves off from the broader labour movement, and to treat members of the Labour Party as capitalist stooges. Yet the relations with Labour in Walthamstow do not appear to have completely ruptured and the local party branches worked together when campaigning for Ben Bradley's release from an Indian jail.[14] Once back home, Bradley soon became secretary of the British branch of the League Against Imperialism, in charge of the Communist Party's Colonial Department at its head office in King Street. As a full-time Party official, he would have been a committed and tireless worker, earning a pittance.[15] His name frequently appeared in the *Daily Worker*'s announcements of forthcoming events: general meetings on the colonial question as well as specific anti-imperial struggles – the Negro Forum, the Irish Republican Congress; the situation in China.[16] And, of course, he gave frequent talks about India, a topic of much concern to Friends Hall. Bradley's anti-imperialism would have resonated with John's South American experience, and I imagine them discussing how British financiers extracted Argentina's wealth, aided and abetted by the local elite who bought Harrods' silk shirts while unemployed workers starved on the wharves of Buenos Aires. Yet John had not yet fully made up his mind about his commitment.

With job security and a regular wage, he began to consider how he should lead his life. Like Pat, he had joined the No More War Movement and was probably attracted by the argument of its Quaker general secretary, Reginald Reynolds, who had explained in *Friendship* how war was an imperialist strategy for the exploitation of colonial peoples.[17] Yet to be anti-war was by itself not enough. Who could guide him? With many Gandhian enthusiasts at Friends Hall, Gandhi's non-attachment to individuals and the discipline of his ascetic life may have influenced John's search for an all-encompassing belief system. He signed up to lectures on the Eight-Fold Path held weekly at the Buddhist headquarters in London. 'Many find comfort in the peaceful philosophy of the East', commented *Reynolds News*. 'Some are attracted by the atmosphere of tolerance, which forbids any dogmatism or compulsion'.[18] But the lectures gave John little guidance, and he writes he gained greater comfort by exploring the City churches where he was introduced to Bach by the organist practicing in St Lawrence Jewry. He did not try to pray.

He then discovered stoicism. Epictetus warned him of too close an attachment to any object or person that might threaten a man's wholeness and accordingly, he gave away his most precious things to people he hardly knew. A clerk at London Fire Brigade Headquarters received a delicate model of a four-masted barque, that 'a gentle old sailing ship man' had carved specially for John; and his precious two volumes of Whymper's *The Sea*, he left with a fireman from another watch. 'In the confused tortures of an immature personality seeking to find and establish itself, I even, masochistically, gave up my love'. For months he avoided meeting Pat, something relatively easy to achieve with night shifts every other fortnight when there were no evenings together, while off-duty weekends were rare.

They appear to have spent their summer holiday separately: the Palmer family album shows Pat in August 1934 at Peacehaven with her Elliott cousins while John was probably tramping the English by-ways with Joseph Gorman from the No More War Movement. In *Friendship*'s monthly gossip column, 'Seen and Heard', Pat's sister Violet had reported John and Joseph as a comic duo in a skit about Chicago gangsters: 'They were altogether too much for most of us, as dressed in pink and crowned with flowers, they tripped around the pile of corpses'. In that same issue, Joseph was advertising a 'Peace Hike, for enthusiastic pacifists with a *purpose*', a fortnight in August on the Pilgrims Way: 'Roll up friends, and help to infuse Pacifism with Pep!'[19] John bought a pocket guide book to the Way and twenty years later was to point out to me the section he had tramped. Perhaps it was while hiking with Joseph through southern England's by-ways that John sorted out his confusion. His memoir rarely provides dates, but it may have been on returning from this hike that

Finally I overcame the doctrines of the enemy Epictetus and we came together again. My sweetheart, long suffering, having endured so much, demanded one evening in the Forest, that I pitch the volume of Epictetus from which I was quoting into the bushes and leave it there. This I did and in this way, she set me on the road to sanity.

Jung and Freud are notably absent from John's extant library that otherwise encompasses history, travel, philosophy, politics, science, poetry and the arts. John mocked psychoanalysis and would have objected to speculation about how ascetic non-attachment such as Gandhi's might be motivated by fear of loving and losing. Instead, his adventure in asceticism is explained as immaturity. 'I hadn't grown up. Happy enough in the half deck, in the focs'le and the station watch room, I was ill at ease in the world of the civvy'. Or, more accurately, perhaps he was ill at ease with women? Possibly even scared by the thought of sex. For four years after his seventeenth birthday, he was to scarcely meet a woman. Once back home from sea he was soon immersed in another, totally male environment: the London Fire Brigade replicated in almost every detail the closed world of bonded masculinity experienced at sea. Pat used to say that she had had several boyfriends before John. But she may have been his first – and only – girlfriend before they married with his term of endearment for her neither 'sweetheart' nor 'darling' but 'mate'.

Pat and John's courting was public knowledge, Violet's a secret discovered by Pat. On the way home from work one evening, she glimpsed her sister at Liverpool Street Station kissing a fellow student and aspiring poet, Reg Latham. Reg and his wife lived in Chingford, a fifteen-minute train ride beyond Walthamstow. The Palmers were to move there in summer 1934, perhaps persuaded by Violet of the advantages of Chingford's cheaper rents. After an evening's committee work at Friends Hall, she and Reg could travel together by themselves on a late evening train back to Chingford.[20] The Palmers' new home in Epping Way was just a few minutes from the Forest's dense canopy of oaks and beeches, ideal for lovers' rendezvous. When she was dying in 1994, Pat recalled an evening sixty years past when John cycled over from Walthamstow at the end of a warm summer's day and how they had strolled together through the Forest to spend the night on Pole Hill, high above Chingford. At dawn, they woke to eat the marmalade sandwiches that Pat had thought to bring and as the sun rose behind them, they looked westwards over the Lea Valley toward the City and the great dome of St Paul's, high above all other buildings. 'Do you remember?' she asked John. He held her hand tighter. 'The best breakfast we ever had', he said. Pat had taught him attachment. And it seems that having committed himself to Pat, he was able to settle upon his world view.

The Walthamstow branch of the No More War Movement was struggling to cope with the division of opinion among its Friends Hall's membership. Was it defensible to kill a relatively small number in order to protect a revolution to eradicate capitalism whose otherwise inevitable wars would slaughter many millions? And what should be the response to the threat of fascism that, unless firmly resisted, might seize power in Britain, as it already had in Germany and Italy, and after which the fascist states would destroy the Soviet Union and the prospects of a communist world peace. Communists should not be tempted by pacifism argued Palme Dutt, the British Communist Party's leading theoretician: a communist's duty 'implies above all a determined political and ideological fight against pacifism'.[21]

Back in the spring of 1934, a thousand recruits a week were joining the British Union of Fascists when Reg Latham's father warned *Friendship's* readers that, however absurd its adherents, fascism was too serious to be laughed at.[22] But if anyone at Friends Hall had indeed ever found the Blackshirts funny, they would have changed their minds in June when at a mass indoor rally at Olympia, fascist stewards brutally and violently ejected hecklers from the meeting. 'I witnessed scenes of great brutality such as I had never thought to see in England', wrote the Reverend Dick Sheppard, who was soon to found the Peace Pledge Union.[23] Most of the hecklers had been communists, deliberately dispersed among the ticket-holders to give the impression of spontaneous, individual interventions; many on the Left admired them for their bravery. After Olympia, some leading non-communists cooperated with the Communist Party to establish a national Coordinating Committee for Anti-Fascist Activities that attracted a wider group of sympathizers to the Party, including John. When duty shifts allowed, he attended the open-air meetings of the Communist Party in Walthamstow High Street while his mother feared for his safety when he heckled at the meetings of the British Union of Fascists on Church Hill. In his interview with oral historian Louise Brodie, he mentioned also attending the talks given by Hyman Levy, the distinguished mathematician, and Communist Party member. These were probably Levy's 'Free Marxist lectures at the William Morris Hall' held every Friday evening in the summer of 1935, as advertised in the *Daily Worker*.[24] Known for his warmth and kindness, Levy was later described by the *Daily Worker* journalist Alison Macleod as 'an enchanting talker and a lecturer of genius [who] had done a great deal to mislead the young'.[25] With Friends Hall closed for the summer, the Friday evening literature class students, including Pat and John, may have found Levy's talks a satisfactory substitute for Fred Parsons' take on Shakespeare.

John's favourite spot for reading the recommended communist literature was a bench in a quiet corner behind the disused horse stalls in Southwark Fire Station's appliance room. Among the books listed in his memoir are John Reed's *Ten Days that Shook the World*, Emile Burns' *Handbook of Marxism* ('*Das Capital* by easy stages!') and Palme Dutt's *The Rise of Fascism*.[26] He regularly bought the *Daily Worker* from an 'old class warrior' outside Liverpool Street Station, leaving it on the mess room table until an outraged and patriotic former Royal Navy man 'condemned it to a more lowly use'. Friends Hall's Warden, Arthur le Mare, was meanwhile worrying about communism's evident attraction for his students. He did not disagree with the Marxist analysis of the current world system nor with the abolition of capitalism but opposed the use of violence to achieve these ends, warning that armed revolution in Britain would lead to devastating civil war. Communism's message might appeal to the 'idealism and hopefulness of youth but, without critical judgement and reference to principles, such enthusiasm may serve only to produce chaos'.[27] But John had been warned by Strachey in *The Coming Struggle for Power* about how people like Arthur, misled the workers 'by the disingenuous pacifism of social democracy' and how unless the workers fought for their existence, 'the imperialists would plunger the world into universal war [and] a new dark age of perpetual conflict'.[28]

As the sisters discussed these dilemmas with their lovers, Violet and Pat began to move apart politically. Reg believed with Arthur that violence was never justified. In his poem 'The Pacifist' he wrote,

> I cannot judge mankind, can only keep
> Faith with the living dream in my own mind.
> Hold to what reason and what seeming right
> Compel the heart's allegiance.[29]

John shared Reg's hatred of violence. During his fire service training, he had taken a full part in all the physical exercises, except boxing because he could not bear to see men fighting. The only time in his life he was to remember hitting a man was in a heated argument about the Spanish Civil War.[30] Yet, by adopting communism, his and Pat's pacifism became contingent. The Communist Party had established a front organization, the British Anti-War Movement, which would have attracted them.[31] Pat greatly admired the left-winger Ellen Wilkinson who urged that the pacifist resolution, 'Do no let your sons go to war', be changed to 'Do not let your sons go to war in the interests of big business and capitalism'.[32]

In November 1934, Joseph Gorman had reported in *Friendship* the year's achievements of Walthamstow's No More War Movement; over fifty members had at various times attended the weekly study circle – 'from steadfast Pacifists to red-hot Communists … everyone has become more cheerfully tolerant'. It was wishful thinking. Internal disagreement was causing No More War branches to fold across the country, including it seems in Walthamstow – as indicated by the Movement's subsequent disappearance from the columns of *Friendship*. Instead, Arthur le Mare had started the new year of 1935 by articulating his vision of a socially concerned and non-doctrinaire Christianity that differed from communism in the Quaker's reliance 'upon the divine seed of goodness in every human heart'.[33] Violet and Reg were soon to join the new, definitively pacifist, Peace Pledge Union and began regularly attending Quaker Meetings for Worship.

Ben Bradley had a younger brother, Len, likewise communist and like Ben, absent from John's memoir. Len was to become a cause celebre when his influential position on Walthamstow's Trades Council was one of the cases that allegedly influenced the Trades Union Congress leadership in 1935 to issue the 'Black Circular' banning Communist Party members from representing their unions on local trades councils.[34] Len may have been interested in coaching a bright young local comrade about how to strengthen the Party's presence in the Fire Brigades Union. First of all, however, John had to learn about the practicalities of trade union organization. When Charlie Horner was on night work, John offered to take his father's dues to the weekly meeting of the Walthamstow branch of the Labourers' Union.

The doorkeeper came to know me and would let me stand at the back of the hall but the proceedings were largely incomprehensible and I would soon quietly excuse myself. The school boy enthusiasm of the General Strike days was but a memory and the shame of my own strike-breaking at Villa Constitución still haunted me. I therefore set about in earnest gaining trade union experience.

In 1934, the total membership of the Fire Brigades Union was 2,307, of which 1,700 served in the London Fire Brigade (LFB).[35] London's unpaid branch secretary was Sam Randall, one of the 'hungry thousand' who had joined the London Fire Brigade in 1919, after serving as an artilleryman on the Western Front. John first met Sam soon after Labour had won control of London County Council, which militant FBU members believed was the opportunity to negotiate shorter working hours. 'Sam Randall visited Southwark Fire Station and listened politely to us chatterers', writes John, 'among whom I was learning to become one of the most talkative and that, as some of my elders were quick to remind me, with hardly a "dogwatch" of service'. Sam then organized a London branch meeting in Conway Hall where John first met Percy Kingdom, the Union's general secretary. The same age as John's father, Kingdom was sixteen when he had joined the Royal Navy and after his standard twelve years of service had transferred to the London Fire Brigade in 1912. He had taken charge of the Union in 1929 following the death of the FBU's first general secretary. John was to remember Kingdom as 'slow in movement with heavy eyelids and jowl', speaking briefly but 'always to the point'. He was 'dour and somewhat morose'; and despite a reputation as a courageous champion for his members, he never visited them at their fire stations. At this first meeting with Kingdom, John writes how he was wise enough to listen and learn. Yet, he could not resist making known his political views and the Silver Jubilee provided the opportunity.

The twenty-fifth anniversary of King George the Fifth's accession to the throne in May 1935 was to be a splendid affair to celebrate the nation's and the Empire's progress. The day itself would be marked with a service of thanksgiving at St Paul's Cathedral, a chain of bonfires blazing from hilltop to hilltop across the kingdom, and nationwide street parties on a special bank holiday. Prime ministers from the dominions arrived in London. The *Times* reported that before embarking on a flight from Salisbury, the prime minister of Southern Rhodesia had broadcast to the settlers' children, telling them that when they had last celebrated a royal jubilee in 1897, they had only recently occupied their country. The Empire had achieved its present greatness, he said due to efforts of great will and character, today typified in King George the Fifth who 'represented to all his subjects the pattern of what an English gentleman should be'.[36] The Empire's 'jewel in the crown' was to be embodied at the Jubilee by the Maharajas of Jammu and Kashmir, Bikaner and Patiala, who would escort the royal carriage on its journey from Buckingham Palace to St Paul's Cathedral. The *Daily Worker* had a field day with the Maharajah of Patiala's extravagant lifestyle and his reputation as a sexual predator; its cartoon, published on the day of the ceremony, shows the imperialist pageant as a merry-go-round of maharajas. Draw back the curtain and the Empire is exposed as a blood-sucking capitalist vampire under whose wings Kenyans are flogged and a maharaja cheers on British troops tear-gassing Indians demanding independence.[37]

With high voltage cables from movie cameras for the first time inside St Paul's Cathedral, an experienced fire prevention officer was to be posted inside the Cathedral during the royal service, assisted by two firemen. Southwark's station officer was disagreeably surprised when John objected to the assignment on the grounds of republicanism and atheism. Although prepared to concur with John's objections on the grounds of religion, the republican argument was deemed unacceptable. He therefore instructed him to join a firemen's brigade of honour to salute the royal cavalcade when in mid-morning it passed by Cannon Street fire station on its way to St Paul's. After that, he could go off duty for the rest of the day. It was a clever inducement. Friends Hall students were celebrating the Jubilee bank holiday with a ramble in Epping Forest and Pat was disappointed John could not join her. This new arrangement would allow him to change out of his uniform and run for a train in time to meet Pat in Epping and walk back with her to Chingford. He surrendered.

Firemen when on duty, customarily gathered together for tea and biscuits in groups of five known as tea-boats. John's included a skilful comic artist, known to his mates as 'Lurcher'. On hearing of John's apostasy from republicanism, Lurcher's merriment, writes John, 'bordered on the ecstatic'.

Lurcher displayed on the wardroom's mantelpiece a cartoon of John: his right hand was waving a large Union Jack as the Royal Procession passed, while his left hand, hidden behind his back, held the *Daily Worker*. Not everyone found it funny. The Union's London secretary, Sam Randall, told John he had been stupid; he doubted the Union could have helped were the station officer to have reported him for insubordination.[38]

In August 1935, Pat and John holidayed in the Lake District, where Fred Parsons loved to walk. It may have been Fred who encouraged Pat to write for *Friendship* a full-page article about her visit, entitled, 'I said it on the mountain stairs. A student's glimpse of the Lake District'. The quote is from a hymn by Lucy Larcom, then much favoured by Quakers –

> I said it in the meadow path
> I said it on the mountain stairs
> The best thing that any mortal hath
> Are those which every mortal shares.

Pat wrote,

> If you attend the Evening Meeting and sing the hymns, you will know what I said on the mountain stairs, or rather what I thought. My Guide and Companion would tell you that usually I said, 'Are we nearly at the top?' or 'Do we really go up that one?'

Pat had climbed nothing steeper than Epping Forest's Pole Hill prior to this holiday, and John may not have realized what he was asking of her.
Their first evening had been dull and misty and

> when we left our grey stone farmhouse and wandered along the valley I felt I had never known silence before. The great grey hills stood up on every side, closing out all the noisy world and the only sounds were sheep and their funny, black-faced lambs. 'Up Rosset Ghyll, over Eskhaus, up Scawfell Pike, and down into Eskdale tomorrow', said the Guide and Companion. I looked and thought it was time for bed.

They walked for a week and slept each night at a different farm house; after scrambling up Scafell, they climbed Helvellyn, John with a thirty-six-pound pack on his back. 'You who have visited Switzerland may not call these mountains', Pat wrote, 'but you cannot and would not deny their beauty or solemnity'. They read together Wordsworth's 'Prelude' but disliked Grasmere, 'that gave us the impression of being the home of many retired majors'. In Rosthwaite, they saw from a newspaper placard that Hitler

FIGURE 7.1   Pat walking in the Lake District (family album).

had said something but did not tell what 'and we were determined not to know until our return'. It was in fact about Hitler who marked the fifteenth anniversary of the founding of the Nazi Party by attacking the Church: 'All the pious people', said Hitler, 'Who think they have monopoly of Heaven's blessing should be made to realise that we would not be where we are if we did not have Heaven's blessing also. What we are, we are not against, but, with the will of Providence'.[39]

Then home to the re-opening of Friends Hall after the summer break. Professor John MacMurray, well-known for his wireless talks on topical cultural and moral issues, spoke to Fred's Sunday class about his recently published book, *Christianity and Communism*. Despite his sympathy for Marxism and the Soviet Union, MacMurray asserted religion's importance for individual and collective well-being.[40] After the talk, John returned with Pat and Violet to their home in Chingford and stayed all evening arguing with the Palmer family. In next month's *Friendship*'s gossip column, 'Seen and Heard', Violet wrote how it was midnight before the advocate of communism [John] – still communist – was encouraged to go home by the family who still preferred Christianity. If only, she wrote, we could combine the best of both worlds, as in this limerick –

If we could but combine the two
As John MacMurray wants to do,
With Marx for me and God for you
And Good for the enlightened few –

Adding, 'No prize is offered for a last line though the author's inspiration failed her here. "We shouldn't be in such a stew" is perhaps rather an anti-climax'.[41]

Dispatched home by the Palmers to Boston Road, John had promptly drafted a riposte to MacMurray's talk. Among the Horners' small bundle of surviving papers is the carbon copy of the letter that Pat had typed for him. Published in the same November issue of *Friendship* as Violet's limerick, his letter is categorical. 'Communism', he writes, 'is avowedly atheistic; although some Christians like MacMurray have a social conscience, organized Christianity is uncompromisingly reactionary'. John cites two long passages from Lenin, including, 'We must not allow the forces waging a genuinely revolutionary economic and political struggle to be broken up for the sake of opinions and dreams that are of third-rate importance and which are rapidly losing all political significance'. He had decisively thrown religion into the dustbin of history. Despite his affection and respect for Arthur le Mare and Fred Parsons, their pacifist Christianity had not convinced him. John was a communist.

Notes

1   *Daily Worker* (DW), 27 January 1934.
2   *Friendship*, April 1934. Owen kept his pledge. An obituary comments on a long legal career: 'He vented his hatred of the capitalist system in vigorous prosecution of workmen's compensation and damage claims'. *Socialist Lawyer*, 1986, 1, 2.
3   John Horner, letter to *Friendship*, November 1935.
4   John Horner, letter to *Friendship*, May–June 1936.
5   Douglas Hyde, *I Believed, The Autobiography of a Former British Communist*, London, 1952, 50–51.
6   John Horner, 'Recollections of a General Secretary', 286.
7   'The Elementary Course of Party Training', 1926. Marx Memorial Library (MML), YF 184.

8 'Recollections', 292.

9 *DW*, 18 February 1934.

10 *DW*, 11 August, 1934.

11 LHA/ CP/IND/BRAD/02.

12 Marc Matera and Susan Kingsley Kent, *The Global 1930s, the International Decade*, London, 2017, 166.

13 There were three delegates from Walthamstow at the Communist Unity Convention, www.marxists.org/history/international/comintern/sections/britain/subject/unity_convention/delegates.htm. Accessed 19 February 2022.

14 *DW*, 7 February 1933

15 'Dedicating their lives for a pittance' – Raphael Samuel, *The Lost World of British Communism* London, 2006, 55.

16 *DW*, 7 March 1936; 3 November 1934; 18 December 1934.

17 Reginald Reynolds in the special peace issue of *Friendship*, May–June 1933,

18 *Reynolds News*, 8 April 1934.

19 Announcement in *Friendship*, July 1934.

20 The Palmers new address, *Friendship*, September 1934.

21 Cited in Nigel Copsey, 'Communists and the Inter-War Anti-Fascist Struggle in the United States and Britain', *Labour History Review* 2011, 76, 3, 184–206 (186).

22 *Friendship*, May 1934.

23 Martin Pugh, *Hurrah for the Blackshirts!: Fascists and Fascism in Britain between the Wars*, London, 2013, 157.

24 *DW*, 11 June 1935.

25 John Stewart, 'Hyman Levy', *Oxford Dictionary of National Biography*, Oxford, 2004; Alison Macleod, *The Death of Uncle Joe*, London, 1997, 85.

26 Thanks to Kevin Morgan for suggesting that John is probably referring here to Palme Dutt's *Fascism and Social Revolution*, published June 1934 and reissued in 1935.

27 *Friendship*, October 1934.

28 John Strachey, *The Coming Struggle for Power*, New York, 1935.

29 W.R. Latham, *Poems*, (privately published) 1990.

30 Terry Segars, 'The Fire Service: A Social History of a Uniformed Working Class', PhD thesis, University of Essex, 1989, 204.

31 Martin Ceadel, ' "The first communist 'Peace Society' " The British anti-war movement 1932–1935', *Twentieth Century British History*, 1990, 1,1, 58–86.

32 *DW*, 6 July 1934.

33 *Friendship*, January 1935.

34 See *DW*, 22 August 1935.

35 'Annual Report for 1934', *Firefighter*, 1935.

36 *Times*, 22 April 1935.

37 *DW*, 6 May 1936.

38 'Recollections', 298.

39 As cited in the *Ballymena Weekly Telegraph*, 17 August 1935.

40 The talk was published in *Friendship*, November 1935.

41 John Horner, letter to *Friendship*, November 1935.

8
HAMPSTEAD

'Through the big beeches which cover the slopes of the valley, the sun splashes the shadowy depths with mellow golden pools. There is a strong autumn smell of the forest loam, and a silence that can be listened to'.[1] Thus, an extract from Brimble's *Epping Forest* that was to be Pat's birthday present to John in 1950, and a souvenir of their courtship. Although chilly for the time of year, the early afternoon sun occasionally popped out from behind the clouds. The fallen leaves were starting to obscure the smaller, fainter paths but the newly-wedded couple's familiarity with the Forest's topography allowed them to steer their way by well-loved landmarks: the clumps of birch and beech, the open spaces and boggy bottoms, these last to be avoided as September that year had been exceptionally wet.

They had chosen to start their life together where they had first met and loved. There are no photographs from their wedding at Epping registry office on Saturday the third of October. The previous year her brother, Eric, had inveigled Pat into a bridesmaid's role in a posh church affair. The formal group photograph in the Palmer family's album shows her placed between the bride on one side – 'all dressed in white' and staring haughtily at the camera – and, the bride's bank manager father in a formal morning suit, on the other. Eric is like Charlie Chaplin, in baggy trousers with white spats. The bride's mother sports pearls and furs and stares gloomily at her shoes. Pat, lovely in a long dress, probably made by her mother. She holds a dusky, autumn bouquet to contrast with the bride's voluminous, trailing white lilies. There is a slight twitch to Pat's lips. Is she dreaming of how different *her* wedding will be from this pathetic, petty-bourgeois pretentiousness? Or just rather gratified with how the soft, dark velvet folds of her dress become her height and colouring?

DOI: 10.4324/9781032671352-9

Photos of her when a young woman indicate Pat's interest and pleasure in how she dressed. A post-war picture shows her in a well-tailored, dark, woollen pin-striped costume, the fitted jacket showing to advantage her tall, slim figure. Considering the wartime clothes rationing, and the Horners' modest income, this may have been the same costume she had had made for her wedding day. Either Violet or her mother would have made the blouse that Pat wore with a brooch at the neck. I imagine her favourite beret squashing down her curls – and, of course, walking shoes for the forest's autumnal mud. John's wedding gear would have been his off-the-peg suit, worn at the FBU Conference earlier that year. As they enter the forest at Bell Common, I see him stuffing his tie into his pocket along with the stiff, shirt collar his mother would have lovingly washed and starched for him. And although he tells us he refused to own a hat, his memoir notes a pre-nuptial haircut.

With his father-in-law out of work for months, John paid his and Alice's return bus fare on the wedding party's Green Line coach journey. Pat's leaving home meant one less income for the Palmer household, from now on solely dependent on Violet and whatever Alice made from dressmaking. (It must have been a relief when, a few months later, Violet found her father a job with the Peace Pledge Union managing its literature department). No one but their parents had been invited, but John's Uncle Arthur had insisted on coming. From the registry office, the wedding party crossed Epping High Street to the 'Cock' where John and his uncle paid for a couple of rounds. After which, the newly marrieds left to walk by themselves through the forest to Chingford Station. Pat copied into her commonplace book, A.L. Morton's poem 'Brilliant Wind', in recollection of that ramble.[2] A decision had to be made about how to spend the rest of the weekend. They had chosen their wedding day to coincide with one of John's rare, forty-eight-hour leaves; he had come off duty at nine o'clock that Saturday morning and was due back at work on the Monday morning. Sunday, the fourth of October 1936 was thus to be their one full day of honeymoon – that is until the fascist leader Oswald Mosley had announced that was the date he was marching his Blackshirts through London's East End. The newly marrieds' duty was to join their comrades in stopping Mosley's march, as ordered by the *Worker*, 'Throng the streets in protest!'[3] Yet, could they not remain romantic for some moments yet? As Morton's poem suggests. Let reason wait until the Monday morning? Their forest stroll decided them. They would forget the world's troubles and give the day to themselves.

Married quarters at fire stations were a relic from the London Fire Brigade's era of continuous duty. With their allocation administered centrally at Southwark headquarters, John could keep an eye open for upcoming vacancies. He had secured them a flat above West Hampstead Fire Station: two small rooms and a tiny kitchen. The bathroom, shared with their next-door neighbour, provided constant free and hot water and was

John's first experience of domestic, indoor plumbing. Positioned where West End Lane takes a sharp right to climb up to Finchley Road, the station was set back from the traffic and shaded by a large pine tree, while its upper floors had a pleasant outlook onto the bushes and trees of West End Green.

The flats are now offices and the pine tree long-since gone, but there remains an agreeable, welcoming feel. In 1936, the only access to the flats was through a small wicket gate cut into the great red fire doors. 'To the unaccustomed', writes John, 'it was always a shock when faced with the great brass bound radiators of the escape and pump just eighteen inches from their face'. When they arrived early Saturday evening from Chingford they found waiting for them a pile of congratulatory telegrams from friends denied a wedding reception. Embarrassedly, they squeezed their way past a self-appointed committee of welcoming firemen to scuttle up the narrow stairs to Flat Five. In the night Pat must have had to stop her husband leaping out of bed when they were woken by the bells going down.

FIGURE 8.1   West Hampstead Fire Station today (Wiki Commons).

Sunday morning, they wandered up to Hampstead Village, treated themselves to lunch in a café at the far end of Heath Street, then back down the hill to their new home. John remembered never having been so happy.

No more Buddhism, no more Epictetus. Marx was still around but he could wait a week or two. When Mosley and his bully boys, with their massed escorts of police were defeated at the Battle of Cable Street, the Horners were not there…. we were on our honeymoon.

As convention required, Pat had given up her job on marriage, thus leaving them dependent on John's wages, sixty-seven shillings and sixpence a week (around the national average). The *Highgate and Hampstead Express* was advertising bedsitting rooms in Belsize Park at between twenty and thirty-six shillings a week, meaning that without their subsidized rent of eleven shillings and seven pence, they could never have afforded their little flat in such an attractive part of London. They furnished it from their small savings and with the money from John selling some of the books he had acquired by browsing in St Paul's Churchyard – 'A folio Milton, a macabre early seventeenth century Manual of Surgery with scores of beautifully executed anatomical drawings … and other curious bargains, garnered for no more than a few shillings'.

Among their early purchases for their new home, I imagine a small folding table, a couple of arm chairs and some framed cheap prints from the Old Masters, possibly those recalled from my childhood: a Dutch courtyard scene by de Hooch, Van Gogh's fishing boats and Vermeer's milkmaid. Above the mantelpiece, they hung a frameless, hexagonal mirror. One late spring morning John snapped Pat's reflection in the mirror as she applied her make-up. Next to her is a large clock, their wedding present from his tea-boat chums at Southwark Fire Station. It shows five minutes past nine, when John would not normally have been at home, having either just started or ended a shift. Thus the photo (too faint to reproduce) must have been taken on a rare weekend off, the vase of tulips, also reflected in the mirror, celebrating the occasion. As followers of William Morris, the Horners aspired to create a home that contained only what was beautiful or useful. Unlike the windows of their neighbours, theirs had no net curtains that required frequent washing. They had nothing to hide and although Pat was proud of her new status, she had no intention to be a slave to housework. Their aesthetic sensibility acquired at Friends Hall was to help the Horners move with relative ease among Hampstead's upper-middle-class literati, artists and intellectuals. Where they differed from their friends was in their attitude to extra-marital sex. Pat's Elliott cousins in Finchley were fairly relaxed about it; her older cousin Vera twice divorced. But respectable Walthamstow strongly disapproved. 'The political bohemianism of the Hampstead of the 1930s was a world away from Friends Hall', writes John. The Horners were to stay obstinately monogamous.

Marriage had brought Pat her liberty. No more commuting to the City to take dictation and type tedious business letters. After having squeezed past the fire station's great, gleaming appliances and through its wicket door she emerged into West End Lane, with its shops, excellent public library and buses to Baker Street and the West End. Then, a short walk up the hill to Finchley Road transported her to an imaginary 'abroad' where the Jewish refugees on the pavement spoke a foreign language and shopped for exotic food. She peeked into bakeries to sniff the cinnamon and admire the dark rye bread and apfelstrudel, and, encouraged by the *Daily Worker*'s women's page, experimented with continental recipes: 'If no oil or garlic can be found or the flavour not liked, fat and onions can be substituted'.[4] And, being Pat, she would have pondered over how it must feel to be forced to leave your home and come to a strange land. A Hampstead resident she came to know well was the communist poet Marjorie Battcock, who wrote about a refugee's experience.[5]

John's memoir indicates that Pat was already a member of the Communist Party when they moved to Hampstead.[6] There they already knew two local comrades, Fred Parsons' sons. The older, Douglas was married to Olive Franklin who came from the same banking family as the communist film-maker Ivor Montagu and, like Ivor, Olive devoted her income from stocks and shares to fight capitalism. Having settled into a large house in tree-lined Perceval Avenue, her money allowed Douglas (now calling himself Harry) to run, for a pittance, the communist-controlled Labour Research Department; Olive meanwhile chauffeured the Party's leader, Harry Pollitt, to meetings. The Horners would have been closer to Fred Parsons' younger son, Owen, whose final appearance in *Friendship* dates from June 1936 when he gave a provocative talk to the Sunday Evening Fellowship: 'Pacifism's Dead! Reach for your Gun'. Owen had just been articled to W.H. Thompson, a solicitor friend of his father's from when they were both conscientious objectors in the First World War.[7] Owen had probably encouraged Pat and John to follow him to Hampstead where he was a neighbour of a rather unusual communist sympathizer, a retired army major, recently returned from a long visit to the Soviet Union. Major Hooper is the only Hampstead resident mentioned by name in John's memoirs, wherein he is described as a shy man who used to come for supper at the fire station. 'If at any time, I was tempted to unburden myself of political misgivings or philosophic doubts, the Major would snap, " here's no sin but ignorance, no devil but fear. Make sure of your facts and don't be afraid" '.

John's fire service shifts meant he was less involved in the life of the local Communist Party than Pat who scandalized her neighbours, also firemen's wives, when she let young men into her home while John was on night shift.

On one occasion, writes John, 'the lady over the way had to step across the young man who was trying to retrieve the copies of the *Daily Worker* he had dropped on the staircase'. It was the era of the Popular Front when communists reached out to the broader political left to oppose fascism. With a Conservative member of parliament and a Tory-dominated local council, Hampstead's Communist Party campaigned for the Labour candidates, most of whom were on the left of their own party and some even secret communists. Many of them, like Marjorie Battcock, had the advantage of a university education, enjoyed by less than two per cent of the population, and, embarrassed by the shortage of working-class comrades, Party members parodied Fred Astaire's song:

> We joined the Navy to see the world …
> We joined the Party to meet the workers
> And who did we meet? The bourgeoisie.

Not every comrade was middle-class. The local Party leaders, whom John's memoir typically avoids mentioning, were like him: self-educated, working-class men whom the Marxist theoretician Gramsci would have described as 'organic' intellectuals, to distinguish them from the Party's self-referential, middle-class intelligentsia. The Party branch secretary, David Michaelson, was a young garage-hand, poet and short-story writer who published highly accessible, popular science articles in the *Reynolds News*.[8] Michaelson's classes in dialectical materialism would have provided Pat with the homely analogy of scrambled eggs that she later used to teach Marxist theory to her daughters. First, the thesis – the milk, eggs and butter together in the saucepan. Then the anti-thesis when the saucepan is stirred over heat and the ingredients collide with each other. Lastly, synthesis: milk and eggs have disappeared to reveal a new creation – scrambled eggs.[9] A photo of Michaelson in the Marx Memorial Library shows a thoughtful, serious man, a half smile on his pleasant face. I imagine he would have been a good teacher.

The older, flamboyant Pat Dooley was a full-time Communist Party organizer for St Pancras and Hampstead: former miner, ardent Irish nationalist and journalist, Dooley was a tall, striking figure, locally famous for speaking against fascism from a soap box on Parliament Hill. Known for mentoring younger comrades he taught them a fundamental rule that brings to mind John's own manner of public-speaking: 'First put your audience in a good humour, then smite 'em. And don't forget the collection!'[10] Long after leaving Hampstead, John stayed in touch with Dooley.[11] Perhaps it was from him that John learnt to sing the Republican ballad, 'Kevin Barry' with an emotional intensity that made his listeners cry.

The last in the trio of Hampstead's communist leadership was John (E.W.) Darling, who organized Hampstead's Tenants Defence League, fighting against unjust evictions and rent increases in the working-class streets of West Hampstead. The local police found Darling irritatingly evasive about his position and responsibilities in the Communist Party but believed him to be secretary of Hampstead's Young Communist League and principal instigator of organized heckling at Whitestone Pond where every Sunday fascists held an open-air meeting and abused Jews.[12]

Welcoming students back to Friends Hall after the summer break in 1936, Arthur le Mare wrote of 'a world torn with the violence of warring parties and peoples, wherein the minds of men are shadowed by fear of another, more terrible war'.[13] Even were they to have remained in Walthamstow, I doubt that at such a moment Pat could have justified spending her evenings studying English literature and psychology. In Hampstead she must have registered for the autumn course of evening classes organized by the Communist Party and advertised in the *Daily Worker*: Dialectics on Monday; Working Class History on Wednesday and Political Economy on Friday.[14] Then in the New Year there started up a Hampstead group of the Left Book Club, one of hundreds across the country that met monthly to discuss the Club's latest publication. Hilda Utting, a young married woman the same age as Pat and secretary of the Hampstead group, explained the Club's purpose in the local newspaper as 'to help in the terribly urgent struggle for world peace and a better social and economic order … The Hampstead Group is extremely enthusiastic and a lively discussion follows the speaker's address at each meeting'.[15] In July that year, the group organized a meeting in Hampstead Town Hall with four hundred participants, where Pat would have heard a speech from the club's founder, the publisher Victor Gollancz, who explained that the Left Book Club was 'trying to give knowledge to people which would help to stem the tide of Fascism'.[16]

From its broken spine and worn cover, A.L. Morton's *A People's History of England* seems to have been the most frequently read volume among the Horners' Left Book Club collection. Morton was a poet, historian and admirer of William Morris. Lines from Morris' *A Dream of John Ball* appear on the history's title page: 'Ill would Change be at Whiles, were it not for the Change beyond the Change'. I imagine John reading the history in a quiet corner of the fire station while waiting for the bells to go down. Morton diverges from the usual English histories of that time that were largely concerned with kings and the battles they won; Morton is more interested in how medieval wars were financed and the economic and social impact of changes to military technology. John's pencil marks Morton's analysis of the War of the Roses when the ruling class of nobles took a suicidal course of action, 'A situation characteristic of an age on the edge of a great social transformation', Morton writes, analogous to the 'blind and suicidal impulse driving the bourgeoisie to-day towards war and Fascism'.[17] The narrative continues with the growing strength of the bourgeoisie, sixteenth-century venture capitalism and the origins of Britain's imperial expansion. Exceptionally, John uses red pencil to underline, 'But it was in Ireland which was the first important English colony, the place where they learnt all the tricks of governing subject races'.[18] Then onto the English Civil War and Morton's conclusion (the pencil hard at work) that despite all their faults, the bourgeoisie were the historically progressive class of their time, and 'they could not fight for their own rights and liberties without also fighting for the rights and liberties of humanity as a whole'. John underlines a petition that a group of women presented to the Commonwealth government, unless – the thought occurs to me – perhaps Pat also had a pencil.

During the day, Pat dedicated herself to Spain. The Marx Memorial Library's collection of Hampstead's Civil War ephemera indicates what kept her occupied –

* Hampstead Spain Week, 1937;
* Screening of the 'Defence of Madrid' in West Hampstead;
* Hampstead Spain Week, 1938;
* Winter Relief in Spain, at Hampstead Town Hall;
* Mass Protest against Bombing at Whitestone Ponds;
* Milk for Spain dance at Hampstead Town Hall;
* String quartet for Spanish Relief;
* Left Book Club rally for Spain;
* Give us money for the Hampstead ambulance;
* Spanish Relief show at the Everyman cinema;
* Ambulance for Spain dance;
* Hampstead collects food;
* Spanish Medical Aid Committee meeting at Hampstead Town Hall;
* A Food Lorry from Hampstead;

The Spanish Civil War had started in July 1936 when an army revolt led by General Franco attempted to seize power from the left-wing, democratically elected government. Germany and Italy instantly supplied Franco's forces with munitions and airplanes, thus helping the insurgents make rapid territorial gains. The British and French governments having committed themselves to non-intervention, resisted calls to allow the export of arms to the Spanish government. By the time the Horners moved to Hampstead, Madrid was under siege from Franco's army and shortly to experience aerial bombing from German planes. As Germany and Italy treated the Spanish Civil War as a trial run for a wider European conflict, so the Soviet Union supplied the Spanish government with tanks and weapons. Young men from France, Britain and the United States volunteered to join the International Brigade

FIGURE 8.2 Flyer for Hampstead's Spain Week, 1938 (Marx Memorial Library).

to fight alongside the Spanish Republic's forces. The war dragged on. People died; many children went hungry.

It was women, largely middle-class, comrades who took charge of Hampstead's practical support to the Republican cause, Marjorie Battcock pre-eminent among them. She drew upon a wide acquaintance in Hampstead's literary and artistic circles to establish a Hampstead branch of Medical Aid for Spain to which Pat devoted herself as a full-time organizer. Battcock was relentlessly energetic: a frequent correspondent to the local press, as soon as the first bombs dropped on Madrid she was writing about air raid protection (ARP) for Hampstead; after the Nanking massacre, she initiated a Hampstead boycott of Japanese goods; in 1938 she was secretary to Hampstead Peace Council, protesting to the Colonial Office over the shooting of sugar workers on strike in Jamaica.[19] Pat stuck with Spain. In February 1937, with the capital still in government hands, Franco's troops tried to cut the main road between Madrid and Valencia at the point where it crosses the Jarama River. Here, Alexander Tudor-Hart, a surgeon and one of the founders of Medical Aid for Spain, ran the medical unit attached to the Republican army. Under incessant bombardment, Tudor-Hart operated on seven hundred wounded men brought in over a five-day period. George Green had been a cellist playing at Lyons Corner House until he drove an ambulance to Spain with supplies for the Jarama medical unit. Pat would have read his account –

> Here the surgeon, unsterile probes by candlelight the embedded bullet. Here the ambulance-driver waits the next journey; hand tremulous on the wheel, eye refusing to acknowledge fear of the bridge, of the barrage at the bad crossing...Here the sweet smell of blood, shit, iodine, the smoke-embittered air, the furtive odour of the dead.[20]

That same month, Pat copied into her commonplace book a quotation from William Lloyd Garrison, the nineteenth-century American abolitionist:

> On this subject I do not wish to think or speak or write with moderation. No! No! Tell a man whose house is on fire to give a moderate alarm; tell him to moderately rescues his wife from the hands of a ravisher; tell the mother to gradually extricate her babe from the fire into which it has fallen – but urge me not to use moderation in a cause like the present ....[21]

Apart from its leaflets, no records survive from the Hampstead branch of Medical Aid for Spain but a full-time volunteer like Pat would have organized the printing and distribution of leaflets and the door-step collections of funds. Perhaps working from Marjorie's spacious Chalk Farm flat, she would have used the Battcocks' phone to book venues for public meetings and Marjorie's typewriter to write letters requesting well-known people to speak at these meetings. It was probably Marjorie who suggested that interested organizations join together into Hampstead's Friends of the Spanish Republic for a week of events in May 1937, with Pat a backroom organizer. Perhaps it was Pat's idea that Sybil Thorndike, whom she had admired since the school performance of *Medea*, be asked to christen the ambulance for Spain bought with the money Pat had helped raise. Before her marriage, Pat had been hesitating whether to abandon her pacifist convictions. In May 1936 she had clipped out from her parents' *News Chronicle* a dialogue between the newspaper columnist and his wife about the fate of their baby should war break out 'I don't want you to protect us by killing other men's wives and children', declared his wife.[22] If that were what Pat felt then, the Spanish Civil War, changed her mind. John's memoir refers to her participation in London's 'monster demonstrations' demanding arms for Spain. If need be, you had to fight to save the world for peace.

From the summer of 1937, Pat either switched to or worked additionally for a new organization, the Dependents and Wounded Aid Committee that supported the International Brigade's British battalion in Spain, run by another local communist, Charlotte Haldane whose revolutionary fervour had earnt her the epithet, 'hot Lottie'. As with Medical Aid for Spain, the supporters included well-known people across the anti-fascist spectrum, including J.B. Priestley and the Duchess of Atholl, whom Pat remembered meeting. But, while the Party liked to appear just one of many in a broad-based progressive alliance, it ensured there were communists in key organizational roles and Charlotte Haldane in turn checked that everyone who worked at the office of the Dependents and Wounded Aid Committee in Litchfield Street was a Party member.[23]

When Franco was winning the war in Spain and Hitler had marched into Austria, the Hampstead contingent for the 1938 May Day rally in London's Hyde Park brought together the local branches of the Labour, Liberal and Communist Parties, the Peace Council, Young Communist League, Independent Labour Party, Left Book Club, Tenants Defence League, Cooperative Women's Guild and Friends of the Spanish Republic.[24] Pat would have had her choice of who to march with! The *Daily Worker* reported the rally as London's largest May Day turnout since 1926 (the year of the General Strike). After the shrill note of a bugle sounded above the clamour of London's Hyde Park calling for a moment of silence, 'tens of thousands of men, women and children raised their voices to pledge unalterable opposition to Fascism and War and their resolve to defend Freedom and Peace'.[25] The *Daily Herald*'s front page news that same morning was Goering's threat to France and Britain: don't try to interfere with Germany in Czechoslovakia.

As the government began defensive preparations for a war it was still trying to avoid, the flats above West Hampstead Fire Station were converted into quarters for the new, volunteer Auxiliary Fire Service to be mobilized in case of war. Pat and John would in any case have had to move out to a larger place: they were expecting a baby in December and had already left for Walthamstow by the time of the Munich Crisis. Pat clipped out and kept a newspaper photo of the air raid protection trenches dug during the crisis on Hampstead Heath, where she and John had used to 'walk secure in a high, leaf-hung path' (from 'Brilliant Wind'). By December, Spain was close to being lost to the fascists and the Dependents and Wounded Aid Committee organized a welcome home for the last British contingent of the International Brigade. In a five-minute film of the evening's event, Ivor Montagu's chiaroscuro effects of bright light and dark shadows capture the emotion of the crowd waiting at Victoria Station to greet the proud men coming home defeated, leaving behind them over five hundred comrades who had given their lives for a democratic Spain. Now in her ninth month of pregnancy, Pat could not attend but at 1.22 minutes into the film, I glimpse John's young, solemn face, hatless in the crowd, on a cold, winter evening.[26] The future was bleak and he was shortly to become a father. Perhaps it was that same evening while John was out that Pat made what was to be the last entry in her commonplace book, this time her own reflections –

> Removed for a little from the tiny part I play in fighting for a new order,
>   Well fed, well housed, encircled by great love,
> let me not forget those other women,
> Heavy as I am, who are not removed from the grim struggle.
> Hungry and cold they bear their burdens…to be born alive or dead in
>   war-torn Spain or China, or country-less from Nazi persecution –
> Or living in misery even here in England,
> I can do almost nothing because of this, my baby
> But because of him, I must not forget.

Notes

1 J.A. Brimble, *London's Epping Forest*, London, 1950, 127.
2 For 'Brilliant Wind', see Christian Høgsbjerg, 'A.L. Morton and the Poetics of People's History', *Socialist History*, 58, 2020. Available at https://core.ac.uk/rea der/334594909. Accessed 16 October 2023.
3 As advertised in the *Daily Worker* (*DW*), 2 October 1937.
4 *DW*, 13 October 1936.
5 The poem and a biographical note about Marjorie Battcock can be found in ed. Catherine W. Reilly, *Chaos of the Night: Women's Poetry and Verse of the Second World War*, London, 1984, 12.
6 John's memoir refers to Pat organizing Party meetings in their flat. Overall in the UK, the proportion of women members in the CPGB hovered around fifteen per cent in the inter-War years (Thomas Linehan, *Communism in Britain, 1920–39, From Cradle to Grave*, Manchester, 2007, 97).
7 Owen was articled to Thompson in 1936. See Steve Allen, *Thompsons, A Personal History of the Firm and its Founder*, Pontypool, 2012, 96–97.
8 Warwick MRC note about David Michaelson.
9 For Michaelson's lectures on dialectical materialism, see *DW*, 8 November 1938. For the scrambled eggs, see Rosalind Eyben, *International Aid and the Making of a Better World*, London, 2014.

10 Dooley's obituary in the *Irish Democrat*, March 1958; 'We mourn a fighter and a friend', *The Newsletter* 2, 41, 22 February 1958.

11 See *The Irish Democrat* (edited by Dooley), March 1945.

12 NA/MEPOL/2//3095.

13 *Friendship*, September 1936.

14 DW, 10 October 1936.

15 Letter to the *Hampstead and Highgate Express*, 26 June 1937.

16 *Hampstead and Highgate Express*, 3 July 1937.

17 A.L. Morton, *A People's History of England*, London, 1938, 139.

18 Morton, 199.

19 Japanese Boycott, *Reynolds News*, 23 January 1938.

20 Quoted in Jim Fyrth, *The Signal was Spain The Aid Spain Movement in Britain 1936–39*, London, 1986, 62. Green was to die in the final action of the British battalion in September 1938.

21 Dated February 1937.

22 *News Chronicle*, 14 May 1936.

23 The reference to 'hot Lottie' is from Andy Croft, 'The Young Men are Moving Together', in eds. John McIlroy, Kevin Morgan, Alan Campbell, *Party People, Communist Lives: Explorations in Biography*, London, 2001, 169–189 (186); for the office in Litchfield St, see Fyrth, 215.

24 *Hampstead and Highgate Express*, 7 May 1938.

25 *Daily Herald*, 2 May 1938.

26 www.youtube.com/watch?v=Lr4EMeSWLfg. Accessed 15 May 2023.

9

'PALE PINK' AND 'DEEPER RED'

The evening he welcomed home the International Brigade, John was on a nine-to-five schedule on a four-week driving course. He was preparing to re-take the technical qualifying exam for promotion to sub-officer, having failed the first time by just one per cent. Jim Bradley, his best mate in the London Fire Brigade, believed management had rigged the results because of John's trade union activism and his reputation as a communist sympathizer. John may have first come to senior management's attention in 1935 when he refused the honour of protecting St Paul's from fire during the Jubilee service; or perhaps it was a year later when he was one of twenty-seven delegates to a one-day annual conference of the Fire Brigades Union where he had spoken in the debate on international affairs.[1] During the twelve months preceding that FBU conference Mussolini had invaded Abyssinia while Nazi Germany had contravened the Versailles Peace Treaty by sending troops into the demilitarized zone of the Rhineland. Britain and France's failure to respond to these aggressive moves was encouraging Hitler to quicken his preparations for war and for the first time in the FBU's seventeen-year history, they were to discuss matters beyond firemen's parochial concerns.

Delegates had been asked to approve a convoluted and wordy resolution from the Executive Council that opposed absolute pacifism while proposing that democratic governments 'should not fail to take all reasonable and necessary co-ordinated steps to safeguard the interests of Peace and Democracy'.[2] Harold Gibbs, the assistant general secretary, had moved the resolution in an extraordinarily long and rambling speech. The speeches from the floor were equally muddled and verbose until the turn of the conference's youngest delegate to speak. John then proceeded to exhibit the essential qualities of a communist leader, summarized by historian Ralph

DOI: 10.4324/9781032671352-10

Samuel to be clear.[3] Regretting that the 'pious' resolution had not taken a more concrete form, John suggested it be rephrased to identify the steps which the FBU should take. Perhaps he had been coached for his speech by Ben and Len Bradley, Walthamstow's seasoned communists. He may have attended London District organizer Ted Bramley's classes in public speaking where he would have been told you were insulting your audience if you spoke unprepared.[4] 'Communism', writes Ralph Samuel, 'took youngsters and turned them into orators, organizers and reasoners'.[5]

The conference photograph shows 'F. Horner' looking at the camera with the confidence of the other, older firemen delegates.[6] He is sitting next to his mentor, Sam Randall, the powerful secretary of the Union's London Branch Committee that represented over half the FBU's two thousand, five hundred members. The conference proceedings had confirmed for John what Sam had already told him: this tiny union was beset with political and personal rivalries. For the first time since becoming general secretary in 1929, someone had stood against Percy Kingdom in his annual re-election and although Kingdom had easily won the vote, his foreword to the conference report made clear his discontent: No position at the head office was technically permanent,

> yet in practice there is usually no question of change while such officers are giving good service. It is not the desire of the members, I am certain, that officers who have possibly given their whole life to the service of the Union should be rejected by some passing whim or that there should be spasmodic change.[7]

John's speech at the annual conference was followed by his election to the London Branch Committee. He was then taken aback when his tea-boat chums enquired whether he had already packed his bags. 'You've gone and got yourself on the Committee. They don't have Committee men in Southwark'. Yet, even before this, John's personnel record points to management concerns. When earlier that year he took part one (educational) of the qualifying exam for promotion to sub-officer, he had failed to secure first place by just 0.25%, an absurd fraction of a percentage point, not used in the exam results of the other candidates. Had the marks been slightly massaged to prevent him coming first? He may have been unaware of possible shenanigans: his memoir recalls only examiners' congratulations on his excellent English paper for which the records show he received 93%. He would not have known someone had written on his file, 'We know that Horner is exceptional'.[8] Exceptionally unsuitable for fast-track promotion? John's tea-boat chums in Southwark were saddened but not surprised when he was told he would be transferred from London Fire Brigade Headquarters in Southwark to Euston Fire Station. It seems that management had decided to 'localise the infection', writes John, by assigning him to the same watch as a fellow London Branch Committee member, the notorious 'Red', Jim Bradley, the son of the Fire Brigades Union's founder. 'Undemonstrative as he was, Jim did not hide his pleasure at my joining him'. Like Sam Randall, Jim was a war veteran who had joined the London Fire Brigade in 1919, his distrust of authority shaped by his experience on the Western Front. He was less than enthusiastic when invited to a meal in the flat above West Hampstead Fire Station to hear Major Hooper talk about the nature and challenges of leadership that so intrigued John Horner.

John's opinion about the poor quality of the FBU leadership is evident from two questions he asked the following year at the 1937 conference. In the morning: had they discussed with other public sector unions the transfer of their firefighter membership to the FBU? According to the conference report, Kingdom appeared not to recall John's name, referring to him as 'our friend' and rudely brushing the question aside. Then, in the afternoon, 'With great temerity, in view of my experience this morning', ironized John, had the leadership considered joining forces with other public sector unions to make joint representation to government on matters of common interest? This time, they remembered his name. Harold Gibbs, the Assistant General Secretary, replied to 'Brother Horner' that they had occasionally tried it but had learnt, 'Whenever we have had to get anything, we have had to move on our own'.

John also supported a resolution that the union organize an educational scheme through the National Council of Labour Colleges to teach firefighters how to wage the class struggle. He said,

> It has been my very bitter experience to listen to my brother Trade Unionists decrying the efforts and demands put forward by the London busmen in an attempt to reduce their working week …. They do not understand that when one section of the working class moves forward, whether it be the London busmen or the Haworth miners or the Beardmore engineers, it helps them with their [own] demands on the London County Council.

As with his previous question about coordination with other trade unions, John was stressing workers' solidarity.

The education resolution had been proposed by a fellow Marxist, Harry Short from East Ham fire brigade whom John had met at the 1936 conference. He appeared to be 'deeply read in the Marxist classics', was 'a surprising person to be found in the Fire Service …. His receding hairline revealed a noble forehead' and he envied Harry's 'beautifully cultivated voice', compared with John's cockney glottal stops and diphthong vowels. Harry's resolution was heavily defeated; John failed in his bid to be elected to the Union's Executive Council; Harry Short was voted off it.[9] As the Union's treasurer, Chick Merrells was to phrase it at the 1938 conference, it seemed the membership was divided between the 'pale pink' and the 'deeper red'.[10]

While making no progress in influencing FBU policy, John continued to damage his career prospects. During Hampstead's borough elections in 1937, he and a certain Harry Webb went out 'chalking' one evening in West Hampstead, with Pat keeping watch to alert them should a policeman appear. From her look-out post, she could see John 'in earnest conversation with a passer-by' and thought he was doing a good job canvassing. But the passer-by was a plainclothes police sergeant who told the magistrates how he had seen one man chalk 'Vote' and the other man, part of the word 'Labour'. When asked what they were doing, 'Horner had said "What has it got to do with you?"' Each was fined ten shilling with five-shilling costs.[11] His offence came to the attention of the London Fire Brigade. Summoned before a senior officer, he was told, 'Use your loaf, laddy, keep your head down, keep your nose clean'. 'All these were admonitions', he writes, 'to which I had been regularly treated by well-wishers in my three years of service, but alas, admonitions which I had persistently neglected'.

London firemen were disappointed by the Labour-run London County Council's refusal to reduce their weekly working hours from seventy-two to sixty. It would mean recruiting more firefighters and Herbert Morrison, the Council's leader was cautious about increasing local government rates. It seemed to the FBU that Morrison cared more about retaining the middle-class vote than improving the conditions of LCC workers.[12] John was among the union members pressing Kingdom to be a tougher negotiator. He writes how he had discovered the ability to articulate what he sensed was in the minds of FBU members and 'without recourse to demagogy, I could translate the colloquialisms of a messroom dispute on Union issues into what I felt were a set of cohesive logical arguments'. Kingdom's response was to be brusque to the point of rudeness.

> Here was a man, a founder of the Union, old enough to be my father... It was hard to listen patiently to a youngster with less than four years of experience who, happened to have the gift of the gab. 'That bloke would sell sand to an Egyptian, stair-rods in a bungalow' were among the less uncomplimentary remarks on my newly found aptitude ... On one occasion as I sat down after criticising his handling of affairs, Kingdom sat grimly silent, his eyes hooded. I was near enough to hear the Chairman urge him to reply, 'You'll have to say something, Percy' and I heard also the old timer's response of 'Fuck him'.

He was popular with the 'Hungry Thousand' but many of the Union's older, ex-Royal Navy members were less keen about John Horner, which may explain his absence from the FBU conference in 1938. According to a contemporary account, he failed to be re-elected to the London Branch Committee, whereas in the Union's history, *Forged in Fire*, John writes that he had lost patience with the trivialities of the Committee's agenda and had decided not to stand again.[13] Whichever the case, he and Pat were expecting a baby and he may have been paying more attention to the damage his activism was doing to his career prospects. Having failed by just one per cent the technical exam to qualify for promotion to sub-officer (the equivalent of a sergeant in the police force), he tried to put Jim Bradley's suspicions to one side; he had given a weak answer to the question on the internal combustion engine and so accordingly registered for a fire brigade driving course prior to re-sitting the exam. Shortly after the Munich crisis, he was thus transferred from Euston to Clerkenwell Station as trainee driver and was either lucky or had arranged it to suit him, when he took the course in December, meaning no night shifts during the last month of Pat's pregnancy.[14]

Christmas 1938 was one of London's coldest on record. He needed a shovel to dig a footpath through the snow drifts to reach Walthamstow's maternity hospital where their daughter, Carol, arrived on Christmas Day. Joy soon turned to terror when within hours of her birth, he was told that Pat was likely to die. There was a family history of an over-active thyroid from Graves' disease – Violet (and to a lesser extent Alice) had the typical bulging eyes – but Pat appears to have shown no symptoms until just after the delivery when a 'thyroid storm' threatened to kill her if not immediately treated. She would have died, had she not given birth in a new and well-staffed hospital run by a Labour-controlled local authority and at the forefront of many developments in midwifery. The young mother eventually came home with Carol to the flat they had rented on Church Hill Road overlooking the great trees in Walthamstow's old churchyard. She was now suffering from chronic Graves' disease, manifested by nervousness and irritability, mood swings and constant fatigue.

Despite having been deeply affected by the baby's arrival and by the threat to Pat's life, by early Spring John was back in the thick of Union's politics, debating the FBU's response to the Auxiliary Fire Service. A trickle of volunteer firefighters had been coming into fire stations for training and practice since early 1938 and that summer's FBU conference had criticized Kingdom for ignoring the potential threat of the AFS to diluting regular firemen's pay and service conditions. After the Munich crisis, the trickle had become a flood when over twelve thousand volunteers joined the London Fire Brigade's Auxiliary Service, outnumbering the regulars by six to one. Old hands were appalled. Fire stations overflowed with clerks and shopkeepers playing at firemen; there were even women auxiliaries learning 'to man' the telephones and drive the pumps.

Other than when training them, the regulars refused to talk to the auxiliaries and denied them access to their billiards rooms, kitchens and mess rooms. The masculine chumminess of the ward room had disappeared forever. John remembered, 'There hung a cloud of unarticulated fear at this assault on their professional standards and livelihoods'. Yet, still Kingdom offered no strategic response to the auxiliaries whose lower pay, poorer quality uniform and minimum occupational injury payments threatened to destroy the FBU's achievements. To John it was evident that the only way to save the Union and safeguard its members' pay and conditions would be to make common cause with the auxiliaries. He broke ranks to chat with a couple of City gents in the AFS to find out whether given the chance, they would join the FBU and assisted by these new friends, he facilitated informal discussions between Clerkenwell's auxiliaries and its regular firemen. As such conversations spread to other London stations, Jim Bradley and Harry Short, who believed this dialogue between regular and auxiliary firefighters could become nationwide, suggested that an advocate for rapprochement should oppose Kingdom in that year's annual election for general secretary. Although the challenger would be unlikely to win, it would impel Kingdom to do something about the Union's existential crisis. As the leading protagonist of bridge-building between the regulars and the AFS would Horner agree to Randall and Short nominating him as a candidate?

It was April 1939. He had just re-sat the technical examination for promotion to sub-officer and this time had passed eighth out of the sixty-nine successful candidates.[15] Provided he kept his nose clean, he could envisage a career into the upper echelons of the London Fire Brigade. Meanwhile, a sub-officer's salary would be welcome. The rent for their Walthamstow home was higher than that for their flat in West Hampstead and they had the extra expense of their little daughter, now four months old. Should he gamble with this security? Run the risk of defeating Kingdom to find himself elected into a job subject to annual re-election? 'As always', he writes 'I took my problems to Pat'. She encouraged him to stand, said she had never envisioned him spending his working life as a fireman. She was prepared to take the risk should he win.

Immediately after his nomination, the LFB headquarters transferred him without notice to Holloway, a small fire station on the LCC perimeter.[16] Crucially, Holloway lacked Clerkenwell's access to the LFB's telephone communication network that John had been using for his conversations with Union members. 'I had not thought', he writes, 'that my activities had been so closely observed'. Nor had he anticipated the general secretary's reaction to John's nomination. Fifty-nine years old and in poor health, Kingdom decided someone else would have to fight Horner. He informed the astonished Executive Council that he would not let his name go forward for re-election and was taking immediate sick leave until the expiry of his notice. He nominated his assistant, Harold Gibbs, to replace him. Kingdom then reminded the meeting that following the contested election of 1936, the Executive Council had changed the rules to require EC approval of candidates' eligibility in elections for paid union officials. On that basis, Kingdom proposed that Horner's candidacy be rejected because of his inexperience. Horner had failed in his one attempt to be elected to the Executive Council and 'It was elucidated that though Horner had been elected to the Branch Committee on one occasion, he had been defeated in election for such committee since then'. Horner was no more qualified for the post of general secretary than any other London fireman. Gibbs, on the other hand, had been employed by the Union for seventeen years and was qualified to stand for election because he had been 'closely connected' with Union business.[17]

Sam Randall was in a difficult position. In 1936, he had proposed the rule change requiring the Executive Council to vet a candidate's competence and was now reminded of what he had then said about the risk of electing someone unsuitable. But although not disputing John's inexperience, 'there was a feeling in the [London] brigade that he should be allowed to stand'. Yet, not every Londoner on the EC agreed with him: Randall took exception to Brother Curtis' objecting to John's candidature because of his rumoured Communist Party membership. Political beliefs, said Randall, should not disqualify a candidate to which Curtis replied such a principle did not apply to communists who prioritized their party's over their union's interests.

Despite a conflict of interest, Gibbs had not withdrawn from the meeting and now intervened: Should the nomination be approved and Horner subsequently elected general secretary, rather than serve under him he would immediately resign as assistant general secretary. Kingdom then formally moved to disqualify Horner's nomination to which the Executive consented by seven votes to three. Kingdom and George Hayes, the more junior assistant, voted against Horner's candidacy while Gibbs now had the common sense to abstain. Three of the other five votes against Horner came from Executive Council members in the London Fire Brigade. The meeting then confirmed Gibbs as general secretary Elect pending formal confirmation at June's annual conference. Gibbs in turn nominated the third, most junior official, George Hayes, to replace him as assistant general secretary. It all seemed wrapped up. John writes,

> The circular to members of these unexpected changes was signed by the new general secretary, Mr Gibbs who thoughtfully sent me a copy for my personal use. What little I knew of Harold Gibbs convinced me that as general secretary he would be a disaster. A pleasant enough man, he was completely dominated by Kingdom's powerful personality and had seldom

been allowed to speak in public. There was no evidence that he had ever expressed an independent point of view.

Kingdom's manoeuvre outraged John's London supporters. Without access to the LFB switchboard, he cycled from station to station stirring things up while an emergency meeting of the London Branch Committee voted to instruct all the London members on the EC to endorse John's eligibility as a candidate. With the FBU in turmoil, it must have been Randall who asked the London Trades Council to sort out the mess. Its secretary, Bob Willis met with the Executive Council in an emergency session and after a heated debate, the EC confirmed that Horner, as well as Gibbs, was a qualified candidate for the post of general secretary and that Harry Short and George Hayes (the second assistant) were both eligible candidates for Gibbs' former post of assistant general secretary. Kingdom having already departed and the two remaining officials both being candidates, Willis took charge of the election process.[18]

Two days after the London Trade Council had posted out members' ballots to fire stations, the Fire Brigades Union met in London for its scheduled one-day annual conference. Infuriated by Kingdom's attempt to stitch up the election in favour of Gibbs, Conference approved the London Branch Committee's emergency motion to disallow the union's paid officials from voting rights on the Executive Council and from nominating each other for office. Announcing that they took this as a vote of no confidence and 'bidding the President goodbye, Gibbs and Hayes walked out of the building', John writes 'to play no further part in the Union's affairs'.

He had been damping down a fire in a timber yard when Willis phoned Holloway Fire Station with the news that John had been elected general secretary of the Fire Brigades Union. 'Have your dinner and get away home', said the friendly station officer, after giving him the message. Next morning John went see Willis who showed him the election report he was sending to the Union's president, Gus Odlin. John's memoir does not mention by how much he had won, and the election report must have been burnt along with most other FBU records when its head office was destroyed in the Blitz. It is likely that most of John's votes came from the London Fire Brigade and the neighbouring suburban brigades. Then, 'along with much comradely advice about "not getting too close to the reds"', Willis gave John the keys to the FBU's one-room office in City Road. He cycled there straight away, propped his bike against the red-brick walls of the Leysian Building and climbed the stairs to the third floor. He had to push the door open against the post that had piled up on the other side. Inside was a large table, on which lay dusty papers and Harold Gibbs had left his typewriter uncovered. The air was stale. He wondered whether to open the window but decided against it. He locked the door and cycled home to Walthamstow, to Pat and their baby. It was the eighteenth of June 1939.

The London Fire Brigade had immediately put John on a week's special leave, pending the termination of his five years of employment and so he handed in his oversize helmet, his boots, axe and spanner.

> Fire tunics, fine Melton cloth with woollen lining I made over to an old seafaring comrade who later put them to good use on the North Atlantic convoys. Brigade coat I kept and wore in the freezing winters of the war.

He then returned to City Road to start his new job.

> I had not the slightest idea what to do. There was no filing cabinet in the office and it seemed, even to my unprofessional eye, that the filing system was in any case somewhat primitive. The office possessed a single typewriter but I couldn't type.

There was some cash in the safe, but he had never been inside a bank, let alone handled a cheque or studied a balance sheet. He would have to seek the advice of his father-in-law who as a failed businessman would know about these matters. Meanwhile, he could have the room tidied up. A cleaner he had met on the stairs agreed for two shillings to sweep the floor, wash the windows and generally remove the accumulated grime and dust. Best to pay her from his own pocket. As he waited for her to finish, the phone rang. It was an anecdote that John enjoyed telling. 'Should I answer it? Should I betray my presence? I picked up the receiver and affecting a high-pitched voice that I hoped that the caller would mistake for that of a woman receptionist, answered "Fire Brigades Union" '. The speaker explained he was from the office of the town clerk of Dagenham; he had been calling for several days but had not managed to get through and wished to have a word with the general secretary. In a falsetto voice, John asked the caller to please hang on. 'After what I deemed an adequate pause for the general secretary to conclude some urgent business, I introduced myself – in a deep baritone'.

He was to discover that the Union's Executive Council of serving firemen so abhorred the idea of employing women in any capacity connected with the fire service that when later that week they met their new general secretary in an emergency session, they agreed to his request that a typist be recruited, provided it was male. Pat's father, Geoff, had meanwhile advised that the Union's accounts should be professionally audited prior to John accepting any financial responsibility and the Executive Council reluctantly agreed to this further additional expenditure. But alarmed that the Union was now in the hands of such a young inexperienced man, it voted to put John on one year's probation with a reduction in the general secretary's salary until his re-election in 1940. Harry Short's election as assistant general secretary had meanwhile brought John great comfort. He was sharing an office with a colleague with much greater knowledge about the Union than he, including arcane matters such as Fire Brigade pensions, the subject of the telephone call from Dagenham Council. And the newly appointed typist, Mr Matthews, was able to provide complete office support in answering the phone, establishing and managing the filing system, taking minutes and keeping the accounts. Nevertheless, the disruption consequent to a new set of staff meant no post-conference annual *Firefighter*. John sent instead a circular letter to the Union's membership:

> In the coming years it may well be that the working-class organisations in this country will be put to the severest of tests. It would be folly to fail to recognise that this Union of ours may also be tried to the utmost.[19]

The *Independent*'s obituarist, Sally Holloway, was to describe John's election as a 'coup d'état' but in an era when in many trade unions delegates to annual conference cast a block vote based on the collective decision of their branch meeting, the Fire Brigades' Union's election procedures were remarkably democratic.[20] FBU members completed individual ballot papers at their fire station that the branch secretary then posted to head office to be counted.[21] There was a high turn-out in elections: over eighty per cent of the membership had voted in 1937's elections to the Executive Council, and sixty-five per cent in 1938.[22]

John's surprising elevation to leadership of the Fire Brigades Union had in fact resulted from Kingdom's manoeuvring to have Harold Gibbs appointed unopposed. Gibbs had never been a fireman and a more credible candidate may well have beaten the young John Horner who had no experience of running an organization and was too deeply Red for many members.

Yet, notwithstanding John owing his victory to contingency rather than conspiracy, this does not preclude the possibility of the Communist Party having encouraged, perhaps even coached him in his bid. In the 1930s, the Party's strategy was to get communists into leadership positions. According to the instructions of the Communist International in Moscow: 'A struggle must be carried on for every elected trade union post … those elected to trade union posts must work as communists'.[23] *Every elected post* – even perhaps in a tiny union like the FBU? In which case, Len Bradley, the local trade union leader in Walthamstow's Communist Party, may have encouraged John to challenge Kingdom for the general secretary's job.

Inside the FBU, Sam Randall and Harry Short were more Red than Pink but do not appear to have been close to the Communist Party; John tells us that Harry belonged to the Independent Labour Party that was deeply suspicious of communists for receiving their orders from Moscow; nor does John ever hint that Randall was a communist or fellow traveller. As for Jim Bradley, he had little standing in the Union other than being the founder's son and unlike Randall and Short, had never been a delegate at the Union's annual conference nor served on its Executive Council. Jim may well have had communist sympathies but his anti-authoritarianism would have kept him on the Party's fringes and John appears to have valued him more as friend and confidant than strategist and coach. And when directly asked by historian Terry Segars, John was to insist there were few if any Communist Party members in the Union before the war.[24] This may well have been the case: Len Bradley's experience with the TUC Black Circular in 1935 could have decided him to advise the young John Horner not to apply for a Party card.

Willie Thompson's history of the British Communist Party, *The Good Old Cause*, cites John's election to the FBU to exemplify how the Party regained lost ground within the trade union movement.[25] Yet, whereas Labour's *Daily Herald* had briefly reported John's election, the *Daily Worker* surprisingly ignored it, despite the considerable space it devoted to industrial matters and its routine reporting of a trade union's change of leadership.[26] Does this mean that even if John had been coached by Len Bradley, the Party's industrial organizer, George Allison, had disregarded this tiny, public sector trade union, insignificant compared with the mainstream sectors of mining, transport and manufacturing where the communists focused their efforts? John's union was of course a minnow compared with that of his communist namesake Arthur Horner, the leader of the South Wales miners. Yet FBU members belonged to a uniformed civil defence force clearly destined to play a key role in the impending war and John's election was certainly a bonus for the Party that by the summer of 1939 was encouraging communists to join the Auxiliary Fire Service.[27]

The *Worker*'s first ever mention of the Fire Brigades Union came a month after John's election when Charlotte Haldane announced an FBU donation of fifty pounds to the International Brigade's Dependents' and Wounded Aid Committee.[28] The Union's donations to good causes had until then been five pounds or less; this comparatively, extraordinarily large donation indicates the new general secretary was sufficiently settled into his position to make a bold decision – and with Lottie's help to have the *Worker* notice his union's existence!

Notes

1   *Firefighter*, 1936.
2   *Firefighter*, 1936.
3   Ralph Samuel, *The Lost World of British Communism*, London, 2006, 125.
4   Samuel, 109.
5   Samuel, 136.

6 *Firefighter*, 1936. Unless John attended the previous year's conference as an unlisted observer, his memoir mistakenly refers to 1935 as the date of his first conference.

7 *Firefighter*, 1936.

8 LFB personnel records LMA/ LCC FB/STA/03/028.

9 *Firefighter*, 1937.

10 The phrase, paler pink' or 'deeper red' was probably already common currency in the LFB when Chick Merrells used it at the FBU Conference in 1938 (see *Firefighter* 1938, 12).

11 *Hampstead and Highgate Express*, 4 December 1937.

12 Annual Conference Report, *Firefighter*, 1938.

13 For the two accounts see FBU EC Minutes 3 May 1939 at the Modern Records Office, MSS.346/1/1/2 and 'Recollections of a General Secretary', 305.

14 LMA/ LCC FB/STA/03/028.

15 LMA/ LCC FB/STA/03/028.

16 LMA/ LCC FB/STA/03/028.

17 FBU EC Minutes 3 May 1939. From the annual conference reports, it seems that Gibbs had been employed by the Fire Brigades Union since 1922, and first elected to his post from 1936.

18 London Trades Council Minutes 25 May 1939, LMA/AC/3287/01/025; Horner's memoir.

19 Cited in *Firefighter*, March 1940.

20 For trade union elections, see Paul Smith et al., 'Ballots and union government in the 1980s', *British Journal of Industrial Relations* 1993, 3, 3, 365–382.

21 See the discussion at the FBU Conference in 1938, *Firefighter*, 1938, 21–22.

22 As reported in the annual issues of the *Firefighter*. The figures for 1939 are unavailable due to there being no *Firefighter* that year.

23 John McIlroy, 'Restoring Stalinism to communist history', *Critique*, 2013, 41, 4, 599–622 (611).

24 Terry Segars, *The Fire Service: A Social History of a Uniformed Working Class'*, PhD thesis, University of Essex, 1989, 219.

25 Willie Thompson, *The Good Old Cause*, London, 1992, 63.

26 *Daily Herald*, 19 June 1939.

27 See Bob Darke, *The Communist Technique in Britain*, London, 1952, 73.

28 *Daily Worker*, 13 July 1939.

10

CLOSE TO DEATH, AUGUST–SEPTEMBER 1939

On the tenth of August 1939, Londoners experienced a trial blackout. A *Daily Worker* reader wrote,

> Watching the movements of the powerful searchlights and the airplanes hovering overhead my thoughts turned to Spain and China where these instruments have been, and are being, used in the slaughter of masses of people. Can't we stop it, before it is too late?

Pat's growing ill-health kept pace with the deteriorating international situation. Too feeble to walk far without assistance, she mostly stayed indoors with baby Carol. Despite the joy in their child, they could not hide from themselves that Pat was weakening. On the fifteenth of August, John took Pat to an appointment with a specialist at St Bartholomew's (Barts) Hospital. On the bus, they read the news about the previous day's meeting between Hitler and Mussolini at Berchtesgaden. At Barts, Pat was told she would be admitted immediately, pending an urgent operation to remove her thyroid gland but she protested she wanted to go back to her baby. Reluctantly, they let her go on condition of total bed rest; a letter would be sent to her with the date of the operation. That same afternoon, they moved to her parents' house in Chingford. By nightfall, all was organized. After John shut up the little flat, they were never again to live in Walthamstow.

Because the house in Epping Way had only three bedrooms, Mavis must have moved in with Violet. It was her fifteenth birthday and Pat was sorry to have spoiled her sister's celebrations. But their moving to Chingford had made things easier for her mother, no longer having to shuttle back and forth between home and Walthamstow. With Pat bed-bound, Mavis became baby

DOI: 10.4324/9781032671352-11

Carol's principal carer. Her cheerful and affectionate youngest daughter was Alice's comfort, while her eldest continued to be a worry. The warm evenings would have been tempting Violet once more into the forest to meet Reg Latham. The affair no longer a secret from the family, Alice fretted that Violet, now in her early thirties, had little prospect of a husband or home of her own. Possibly in a vain attempt to stop seeing him, Violet had stepped down from *Friendship*'s editorial committee, but they soon came together again. Friends Hall may have had its suspicions about them confirmed when soon afterwards Reg published in *Friendship* a love poem that alludes to his meetings in the forest. Alice would not have been overmuch concerned about the immorality – nor, for that matter, what the neighbours might have thought. After all Violet's favourite Elliott cousin, Vera, was already twice divorced. Alice was upset, however, by Reg's treatment of Violet, and by his reluctance to separate from his wife, despite many promises that he would do so. Reg's indecisiveness infuriated Geoff, while John was astounded that Pat's sister could love such a timid, dithering individual, who in Violet's absence was the subject of John's jokes.

John writes,

> Harry Short was not yet married and while the work began to pile on us with two new brooms at head office, he readily accepted that I should spend every evening with my wife. And every evening when I went into her bedroom, I could see that she was literally fading away.

Major Hooper came over from Hampstead to see how she was doing and to tell them he had been called back to his regiment for active service. He still thought the war wouldn't happen, that Chamberlain would sell out again, as he had at Munich. They discussed the British government's slow and reluctant response to Stalin's offer of a military pact with France and Britain, and how Chamberlain had let the negotiations drag on through the summer. On the seventeenth of August, the *Daily Worker* had urged the British government to speed up its protracted negotiations. Opinion polls showed most people approved of a pact with Russia and, from the backbenches, Churchill spoke strongly in favour. Chamberlain was however still hoping peace could be preserved through some compromise with Germany over Poland without having to make a deal with communist Russia. In any case, Chamberlain believed the Red Army would be useless should it come to fighting Germany.

Yet, even Chamberlain was surprised when Stalin eventually concluded Britain had been negotiating in bad faith. On the twenty-third of August, Moscow and Berlin announced a non-aggression pact and, worse, a trade agreement promising German weapons and machinery in return for Soviet raw materials.[1] The Communist Party leader, Harry Pollitt, privately told the Party's central committee that it left a nasty taste in his mouth.[2] Now there was no obstacle to Hitler's invasion of Poland. Parliament rushed through an Emergency Powers Act, placing the United Kingdom on a wartime footing. On the twenty-fifth, the family celebrated Pat's twenty-seventh birthday while fearful that should her thyroid not be removed in time, she would not make it to her next.

For Alice, the only relief was that the Emergency Powers Act brought an abrupt end to one of Geoff's rash ideas, the Peace Pledge Union's (PPU) pirate radio station. Every Sunday evening that summer, he had been illicitly broadcasting appeals from a team of young pacifists asking listeners not to fight. He broadcasted each week from a new location to hinder the Post Office engineers from tracking him down. When asked by the *Daily Herald* about the PPU's suspected involvement, he cheekily replied,

> We like to be credited with a certain amount of common sense [and] we should obviously not make these illegal broadcasts and admit to them. I have heard some of the transmissions, and must say that the sentiments expressed are similar to our own.[3]

John admired his father-in-law's initiative and anti-authoritarianism but disagreed with his and Violet's absolute pacifism. With Britain now on the verge of war, he believed, like the Communist Party leader Harry Pollitt, that to stand aside 'while the fascist beasts ride roughshod over Europe would be a betrayal of everything our forebears have fought to achieve in the course of long struggles against capitalism'.[4]

The Monday after her birthday, Pat received a letter from Barts, not, alas, with the date for her operation but about its indefinite postponement. In anticipation of mass casualties from the expected aerial bombardment, all new admissions had been cancelled. Meanwhile, she was to lead a quiet life, 'In bed if possible. Uninterrupted rest and freedom from worry was essential'. On the Friday – the first of September – a depressed and exhausted John locked the door to the union's tiny office in City Road. That afternoon the BBC had announced that all auxiliary firefighters were to report to their stations bringing with them a blanket and food for two days. Regular firefighters' leave was cancelled, and a system of continuous duty was imposed of 48 hours on, 24 hours off. No one at London Fire Brigade Headquarters could tell him more.

On the way to his wife and baby in Chingford, he stopped off at Boston Road to check on his parents before the bombs fell. These days, his father was coming home earlier; sixty-two years old and worn out from a lifetime of heavy labour, he had a local, less demanding job, digging holes for telephone poles. John's mother's sister, Mill, had recently moved in with them but when she saw her nephew arrive, she left by the back door without a greeting. She had been on bad terms with him since when, aged fifteen, he had abandoned the Baptist Chapel and she meanwhile had become a staunch Tory and deeply suspicious of her nephew's politics. Dusk had already fallen when John said goodbye to his parents and on the bus to Chingford, he nodded off, waking to find himself in darkness. This time, the blackout was for real. The German army had crossed the frontier, and its air force was bombing Poland. Saturday morning Britain issued an ultimatum: Unless Germany withdrew its troops from Poland by eleven o'clock on Sunday morning, their two countries would be at war. Geoff drove a heavily sedated Pat with Alice, Mavis and the baby to stay temporarily outside London in a cottage in Surrey belonging to Quaker friends. By the time they arrived, the past fortnight's spell of hot weather had broken to thunderstorms and heavy rain.

John spent that Saturday organizing somewhere longer term for the family to live, far, far away from London and the other towns at risk of imminent bombing. The summer before Carol was born, he and Pat had holidayed at a friendly farmhouse in the village of Corscombe, hidden away in a deep, green Dorset valley. There, Alice and Mavis could look after his wife and baby in safety while he concentrated on leading the Fire Brigades Union into its greatest challenge. But it might have been better if John had consulted Alice before rushing down to deepest Dorset.

Very early on Sunday morning, a hired car and driver weaved its way westward through the heavy traffic leaving London before the ultimatum expired. On arriving in Corscombe, John learnt that Britain was now at war with Germany and that the farmhouse could take his family in. By late afternoon, he was at the cottage in the Surrey hills to explain to Alice and a 'drugged and sleepy Pat' his plans to take them to Dorset the following Saturday. Then back into London before that evening's blackout, to see the sky now heavy with barrage balloons. He paid off the driver at Clerkenwell fire station to spend an hour with his former work mates: 'Their undaunted good humour and my first wartime fire service supper helped to cheer me up, for by now I was in need of cheer'. Then, a walk through the blackout to nearby Kings Cross Station for a night train to Bridlington, on the Yorkshire coast. Two and a half months into the job, John was to represent the Fire Brigades Union at the annual meeting of the Trades Union Congress.

He spent the first night of the war, sitting up on a train that slowly chugged northwards. Most of the other delegates had arrived the previous day when while he had been rushing down to Dorset. Fatigued and self-conscious about his appearance, on arrival in Bridlington he bought a pair of suspenders, that, as he wrote to Pat, felt 'darned uncomfortable'. But at least, his socks would not fall down for this first encounter with the massed ranks of Britain's trade union leaders. Nervously, he mingled among the hundreds of delegates waiting for the proceedings to start. Most of them were much older than him and milled around to greet acquaintances while he stood by himself, shy and lonely. Finally, someone who knew him: Bob Willis, of the London Trades Council, who had supervised the union's election earlier that summer, gave him a friendly nod, 'Hello there, you've made it'.[5]

The letter that John wrote Pat that evening shows he may already have had second thoughts about the wisdom of her moving to Dorset. But it still does not appear to have occurred to him that Corscombe was all very well for a summer holiday but its isolation had many disadvantages: far from a hospital, without mains water or electricity and the only toilet a shed at the bottom of the garden – difficult conditions for a very sick woman and a baby.

> I hope that everything is going well with you and that Mummy [Alice] is not working too hard. I think she will like it at Corscombe, although it may be rather quiet at first. That should do you both good however and if you can manage to make the rooms a little more homely with one or two additions you should be quite OK there. Mavis will love it.

Discounting Pat's wretched state of health, he absurdly concludes by hoping she will enjoy walking Dorset's green lanes before the winter sets in.

John's memoir does not tell how and when the unsuitable Corscombe plan was dropped; Alice must have dissuaded him, aided and abetted by the Quaker friends who, having given them emergency lodging, now offered to let them stay longer. When, on the twenty-ninth of September, the government registered the location and occupation of every resident of the United Kingdom, Alice, Carol and Mavis were living in the village of Albury. Mayor Farm cottage had all the advantages lacking in Corscombe: close to a reasonably sized town (Guildford), it was connected to mains water and electricity and easily accessible from London. As for John, the register records him, Geoff and Violet living at the Palmer home, 50, Epping Way. In the standard terminology of the era, Violet has 'unpaid domestic duties', apparently having given up her paid job to look after her father and brother-in-law.

Pat, meanwhile is recorded on the register as on the other side of London, in St Albans, to where much of St Bartholomew's had relocated in anticipation of mass aerial bombing. A hospital for 'imbeciles' had been converted into an emergency surgical unit to receive bomb casualties. But the expected air raids had not materialized. Poland had been brutally divided between Germany and the Soviet, as agreed in their secret protocol, but Western Europe was tranquil. It was the 'phoney war'. The British Expeditionary Force had settled down with their French allies behind the Maginot Line, and the government announced, 'Business as usual'. Barts sent Pat a letter, inviting her to St Albans for her delayed operation.

John was by now driving a Wolseley limousine loaned him by a stockbroker auxiliary fireman, who considered the union's general secretary needed a faster means of travel than bike or bus. He arranged the backseat with pillows and blankets and took Pat to the hospital, she, 'too sedated and sleepy to note the grim corridors which radiated like spokes from a wheel, dark and echoing'. There, part of her thyroid was removed by Geoffrey Keynes (brother of the famous economist) known for his innovative surgical practices and research on the thyroid gland.[6] Pat returned to the Surrey cottage, a well woman, although warned to take it easy for the next three years. John writes,

The heart which under intolerable strain had been threatening to surrender its fight; a metabolism which had produced such body temperatures that a bystander could feel the heat and which was almost visibly consuming the body itself had – as Geoffrey Keynes had promised – all been restored to normality.

FIGURE 10.1   The Horners at the Surrey cottage, late 1939 (family album).

John was taking a week off when a photo was taken of him with baby Carol in his arms, Pat beside him, well-wrapped up in a blanket (Figure 10.1). John's wrinkled socks indicate he has evidently discarded the Bridlington suspenders. I imagine that Alice or Mavis was the photographer; the woman standing behind them may have been their friend, the hospitable Quaker who had taken them in when the family was in crisis.

The evenings at the cottage were used by John to write his first pamphlet, concerning the compensation rights of auxiliary firefighters injured at work. He had brought a typewriter with him, with the intention, he writes, of learning to use it. Or perhaps, he had hoped that Pat would take it from him, which of course she did – 'Before the week was out, she the most competent of secretaries had corrected my grammar, re-phrased the worst of my infelicities and presented me with an immaculate beautifully typed manuscript to take to the printers'. That week was to mark the start of their common project, John Horner the public man.

Almost a year had passed since Pat had written in her commonplace book that having a baby would remove her for a little time from fighting for a new order. She could not have anticipated the permanent loss of the autonomy she had enjoyed in Hampstead that she was to look back on as the happiest two years of her life. John's unexpected elevation from ordinary fireman to trade union leader and her nearly fatal illness had combined to create a different dynamic in their marriage.

Notes

1   R.J. Overy, *The Origins of the Second World War*, London, 2009.
2   Kevin Morgan, *Harry Pollitt*, Manchester, 1993, 107.
3   *Daily Herald*, 22 August 1939.
4   Harry Pollitt, *How to Win the War*, September 1939, cited in Morgan, 1993, 108.
5   Interview with Louise Brodie.
6   'Sir Geoffrey Keynes', *Oxford Dictionary of National Biography*, Oxford, 2004.

11

'IMAGINATION AND DECISION' 1939–40

'In history, as you know', John Horner reflected to Terry Segars, 'there are a set of circumstances that you can't fit together and then, suddenly something happens and everything changes'.[1] John was good at making quick decisions. The day war was declared, he had found a safe place for his wife and baby far from any danger of aerial bombardment. But, having neither consulted those most directly affected nor considered the practical difficulties ensuing from living so far off the beaten track, that his Corscombe scheme had been rejected is no surprise. Yet, almost immediately after that impetuous dash to Dorset, this untested, youthful general secretary was to demonstrate a brilliant decisiveness in carrying through to successful completion an equally madcap scheme, later described as 'one of the most remarkable achievements in the trade union movement'.[2]

His election pledge had been to strengthen the Fire Brigade Union's links with the new Auxiliary Fire Service (AFS). Time was not on his side and before he could develop a detailed proposal, the auxiliaries had been called up: taxi drivers, plumbers, musicians, plasterers, shop assistants, bank clerks, poets and stockbrokers arrived to disturb the regular firemen's set ways. To the even greater disgust of many FBU members, women auxiliaries were employed as telephonists and dispatch riders and some even attempted to 'man' the pumps.[3] The auxiliaries received less pay, had no injury cover and were worse equipped than the regulars to whom they were attached. Hours of duty varied between local authorities, as did their working environment. London's schools, empty of children evacuated to the countryside, were turned into dormitories and 'tiny tots' toilets and washrooms became the auxiliaries' ablution blocks. Elsewhere, the auxiliaries were either overcrowded into

DOI: 10.4324/9781032671352-12

damp, insanitary and chilly makeshift stations or squeezed into the existing fire stations to encounter hostile regulars.

If the auxiliaries were to be recruited into the FBU it would have to be into a new section – at least until conditions had been standardized and the regulars did not see the auxiliaries as a potential threat to downgrading their own pay and conditions. Might a separate section be feasible? At the Trades Union Congress in Bridlington, John had been enraged by the TUC general secretary's censure of the Nazi-Soviet Pact, but now back in London, he thought it politic to seek Sir Walter Citrine's views on recruiting auxiliary firefighters into the Fire Brigades Union. Citrine, having no doubts about the matter, advised John it would be impossible to organize into a single union such a diverse collection of men and women; furthermore, in the absence of instructions from the Union's annual conference, it would be foolish, possibly illegal, to risk the FBU's scarce resources on such a dangerous venture. Citrine was a 'precise, pedantic speaker', writes John, and 'his acerbic description of the AFS is sharp in my memory – "A heterogenous collection of transients"'. Insulted on behalf of his prospective members, John returned to his City Road office to find the printers 'had already delivered the first ten thousand application forms'. It would have been good to have had Citrine's support, but were he not to receive it, he had already decided to go ahead.

With all leave cancelled for all firefighters since the declaration of war, the Union's Executive Council was unable to meet to discuss John's scheme. He therefore agreed with the Union president, Gus Odlin, to consult individually those EC members he could visit in the London area while sending reply-paid telegrams to the others, requesting their authorization to establish an AFS section with immediate effect. His memoir omits their replies but a booklet published by the FBU in 1968 notes that 'the majority' of the EC approved 'the most far-reaching (and incidentally the most irregular decision) ever taken by the Union's leadership'.[4] The historian Victor Bailey gives another version: 'The result of this irregular ballot remains a secret but Horner acted as if he had a mandate'.[5] In an interview with Terry Segars, John said, 'I can't recollect how many replied but I am satisfied in my own mind that enough people replied for us to justify the organisation of the AFS'.[6]

When he came to seek retrospective approval at the Union's annual conference in May 1940, John glossed over the consultation process, describing the situation as acute. 'It brooked no delay', he told the delegates, 'Imagination and decision were necessary'.[7] I remember from my childhood him telling me, with a chuckle, the story of Nelson at the Battle of Copenhagen: On being told that the fleet's commander had signalled him to retreat, Nelson put his telescope to his blind eye, pronounced he could see no signal and proceeded to win a victory.

His memoir is frank about the members' fury when within a week of the war starting, he announced that the Union was recruiting auxiliaries as members.

> Their stations had been taken over; their brigade in which many of them had served for twenty years was vanishing before this invasion and the man they had just chosen as their champion was proposing that the same invaders be given a brotherly welcome into the one remaining stronghold which was theirs alone – their Union.

'Traitor', 'bloody sell-out', were phrases repeatedly appearing in the letters sent to Head Office. He was not helped by the loss of five hundred of the Union's younger members who had voted for him three months earlier but had since been called up as reservists. 'There was nothing for it but for me to bike around the stations and meet the doubters face to face'. It was then that his AFS stockbroker friend from Clerkenwell station loaned him the Wolseley, with its walnut fascia and fittings, 'but to my detractors, the fact that I was coming around in a posh car belonging to one of the AFS was further proof of my subjection to them'.[8]

And it was not only London. Tackling the provincial membership was an even harder task. Still confused about Kingdom's departure, most members outside London had voted for Gibbs. During the coldest winter for years, John and Harry Short travelled across Britain. 'In the black-out, in unheated trains, with timetables all awry, we took the argument for unity across the country'. In Bradford, angry firemen threatened John with a thrashing, but he knew he would bring them around – eventually. It would help if more regulars could be brought into the Union. Many outside London were not yet in the FBU, either because the local authority included them in the police force or they were attached to small fire stations rarely if ever visited by a union official. The EC agreed to appoint the Union's long-standing and popular treasurer, Chick Merrells, as 'Organising Secretary': his task to increase and look after the membership among the regular fire service. By May 1940, the number of regular firemen in the FBU had increased by a thousand to 4,500.

As for the tens of thousands of auxiliaries to be recruited into the Union's AFS section, John writes, 'The EC boldly gave me a free hand in choosing my helpers', omitting that the first man he hired was his father-in-law, Geoff Palmer, who had already given him helpful advice on administrative and financial matters. Geoff's initial job with the FBU was 'inner London organizer'.[9] He was available, energetic, full of initiative and with proven organizing skills; his ignorance of trade unions would have been a drawback but he was adaptable and a fast learner, as evidenced by his success in the Camel Corps after never having previously ridden a horse. Geoff's resignation from the Peace Pledge Union would have relieved Alice from worrying about the illegal radio station and John owed much to his mother-in-law who was taking care of his wife and child. The omission of his father-in-law from among his list of the first FBU organizers may have been because by the late 1980s, when John wrote his memoir, it was no longer acceptable to give jobs to close relatives, especially in the absence of a competitive process.

Next, John hired two Labour councillors, familiar with the inner workings of local government, the firemen's employers: for the north of England, a Bradford trade unionist and mill worker, and for Scotland and Northern Ireland, Tom Murray from Edinburgh, who had fought with the International Brigade. John is disingenuous in his published 'Recollections' when describing Murray 'as a left-wing socialist'. Murray had been the Communist Party's political commissar in Spain and although, like John, a member of the Labour Party, he was also an undercover Communist Party member, that he later freely admitted to.[10] John had made a good choice in Murray who later recounted,

> I said to John Horner…and Chick Merrells 'Look here, give me thousands of membership application forms and I'll go around the stations'. So I went round and just dropped into a station. I said, 'Have you any grievances here or is everyone very happy?' They would say, 'Oh for goodness sake! We're glad to see you. We can't sleep for the mice or rats!' – or this, that or the other. I said, 'How many of you are members of the Union?' 'Oh, we're not members of that'. 'Well', I said, 'I can't negotiate on behalf of non-members. How many of you are there?' 'Oh, there's fifty of us here'. 'Alright, there's a batch of membership forms. You sign up and appoint somebody to be your shop steward and send in the application forms and then we'll deal with your problems'. The result was phenomenal.[11]

Peter Pain, the Union's AFS national organizer, was the last of this first batch of the Union's new, unelected officials, appointed during the first month of the war. A young, left-wing barrister who had joined the AFS, Pain was to become a close friend.

John had the knack of gaining the trust of older men to whom he turned for advice and assistance and unlooked-for encouragement was to come from London Fire Brigade HQ. During the first days of war, none of John's contacts in the senior echelons had had time for him but this was to change in late September when Commander Firebrace was posted to the Home Office and his deputy, Major Jackson, placed in charge of the London Fire Service (comprising the London Fire Brigade and the London Auxiliary Fire Service). Jackson was widely respected in the fire service as an officer who kept closely in touch with all ranks.[12] He had known the FBU's new general secretary from when John had been posted to Southwark Fire Station in

1934 and he now invited him to come in for a chat. Jackson approved the bold decision to welcome auxiliary firefighters into the FBU: it would help unify the new commander's 'motley, ill-assorted, divided and untried command'. He promised to facilitate the Union's work by permitting members' meetings at the fire stations, giving Union officials free access to service premises and allowing time off for members to attend Union committee meetings. And despite Home Office hostility, neighbouring Chief Officers soon followed Jackson's example. By January 1940, out of the twenty-four thousand auxiliaries in the greater London area, twenty thousand had joined the Union.

It may have been Owen Parsons, John's communist friend from Friends Hall, who put John in contact with W.H. Thompson, a left-wing solicitor specializing in trade union work for whom Owen worked. The Walthamstow communist Ben Bradley may have also told John about Thompson, who had been in charge of Bradley's defence at the Meerut Trial.[13] But, despite close links with many communists, including his own wife, Joan Beauchamp, and an enduring friendship with Harry Pollitt, Thompson was independently minded; he was said to have briefly joined the Party but left because it was not teetotal.[14] 'Tall and lean-jawed with the keenest of eyes', John writes, 'he was a somewhat forbidding character on first acquaintance' but was to provide precious guidance when John risked being overwhelmed by the complexity and challenge of the task. 'There were times of self-doubt when my confidence would wane. It must have been with some surprise that WH came to recognise just how raw a tyro I was among trade union officials of his acquaintance'.[15]

Either Thompson or Owen Parsons would have been advising John when the FBU took the lead among the concerned trade unions in seeking Air Raid Protection (ARP) workers' compensation for injury. It was the subject of John's first pamphlet published in December 1939.

> The auxiliary fireman attending to his job in an air raid is par with a bank clerk sitting in an air raid shelter. The man in the demolition squad, whose job is perhaps one of the most difficult and dangerous in ARP work is treated in the same manner as an evacuated civil servant whose hotel might be damaged by a stray bomber.[16]

Back in 1937, John had asked the FBU leadership whether they had considered joining forces with other public sector unions to make joint representation to the government on matters of common interest, and Harold Gibbs, the assistant general secretary had replied, 'Whenever we have had to get anything, we have had to move on our own'.[17] Now John was in charge and determined to prove otherwise. Thompson may have insisted that he got in touch with the other unions with members in the ARP, such as ambulance drivers and the workers who dug out survivors from under the rubble of bombed buildings. Civil defence was the responsibility of the Home Office and in early 1940 those trade unions with ARP members established a Joint Trade Union Civil Defence Committee to make collective representations about their members' conditions. The Home Secretary refused to meet them and only in April, towards the end of the phoney war, were they offered an appointment with a senior civil servant.

The heavy weight Ernie Bevin was the delegation's leader and general secretary of the great Transport and General Workers Union. The official explained to Bevin that ministers were reluctant to recognize unions for civil defence employees in case this gave trade union leaders with dubious political affiliations (meaning people like John) access to sensitive locations. Norway had just been captured by the Nazis and the civil servant reminded Bevin 'that whole areas of the country's administration were easily taken over by the enemy since they had already been undermined by Quisling groups in public administration'. John was sitting behind Bevin.

> At the mention of Quisling, I saw Bevin's great neck redden. The civil servant expanded on his theme. Bevin exploded in a voice which sounded to me like a blunt saw hitting a knotty piece of wood. 'Don't dare mention Quislings and trade unionist in the same breath when you talk to me … It wasn't our lot that sold Norway to the Nazis … It was your [Minister's] lot – just as they would dig the ground from under our feet in this country and sell it abroad if they could get two and a half percent profit'. Adding, 'And tell him this too. Tell him to tell his friend Chamberlain that if he wants to win this war, he will only do it with the help of the Trade Unions'.

Having witnessed Britain's most experienced trade union leader at his performative best, Bevin's working-class assertiveness became a favourite anecdote of John's. 'It was *your* lot', that had mucked everything up.

Once war was declared, the Auxiliary Fire Service had expected to be immediately in action. But Hitler's bombers stayed on the ground. 'Week followed week, and month followed month' recalled a senior fire officer, 'with a hundred thousand fireman and firewomen at action stations and no attack. Drills and exercises, sandbagging and scrubbing … were the sum total of activity'.[18] The general public began to query why the auxiliaries were getting paid for lounging around, and morale was low. Yet, the nine-month phoney war was to give John and colleagues the time to establish the arrangements for the Union's separate AFS section and to start campaigning to improve their conditions of service. By May 1940, total Fire Brigades Union membership had increased more than fifteen-fold. Time to find a bigger office. Many firms in central London had relocated their staff further out and office rents had dropped. The Union moved from its cramped single room in City Road into the spacious second floor of the Chancery Lane Safe Deposit Building. Thompson already occupied a small office on the floor above, the firm itself having moved to High Wycombe at the start of the war. A chat with Thompson, 'could be a real stiffener', remembered John,

> Alone of all trade union officials I had the good fortune to have the sharpest of intellects, the most liberal of minds and the possessor of the widest experience in trade union law, occupying a spare room above my head.

A photo was taken of the Executive Council in the new office's committee room to be published in the new, monthly *Firefighter* that before the war had appeared only annually to report FBU conference proceedings. Thwarted in his boyhood ambition to be a journalist, throughout most of his time as general secretary, John was to edit the paper and write much of the copy. At home, he spread out on the living room's acid green lino the articles, letters, cartoons and photographs for the next issue and with scissors and paste arranged them into an attractive and accessible journal.

With the establishment of a proper office and a journal for union members, it was time to regularize the relationship between the regular and AFS sections of the Union. He planned it as a two-stage process. In late May 1940, three hundred delegates from the AFS membership met in London to approve a representative management structure for their own section of the Union. A week later, the FBU held its annual conference of the regular membership, the first since John's election. He needed a belated endorsement of the establishment of the AFS section along with approval to expand the Executive Council to include AFS representatives. He had to win over delegates from branches still grumbling and who had come prepared to vote 'no'.

John prepared important speeches by jotting the key points down on any available old envelope or book fly. Then having written each point again on separate half sheets of paper, now organized into a logical sequence, he would ask Pat to review the flow of argument. He rarely wrote down a speech in full, nor rehearsed it, relying on his live audience for the emotional response that was to make him a confident and popular speaker. And as he became more acquainted with his union members, so he dropped a habit copied from Fred Parsons of peppering his speech with snippets of Shakespeare.[19] His speech to conference in June 1940 began by establishing the legitimacy of his decision to bring the auxiliary firefighters into the Union. The delegates were reminded how the previous year's conference had approved a resolution to re-examine the relationship between the AFS and the professional, regular fire service. He then spoke of the urgency of the matter: once war had been declared and the auxiliaries had been mobilized, not a moment could be lost. The decision had been taken to save the Union – *your* Union; when the war is over, the auxiliaries will disappear to their peacetime occupations but you will be there, your Union stronger than before. Meanwhile, the AFS are your friends and comrades. Like you, they are keen trade unionists. Working together to win the war.

After the applause had died down, Brother Sumpter was the first to take the floor; he was from John's home town, Walthamstow, whose firemen had been among the most critical about inviting auxiliary firefighters into the Union. 'I was mandated by my branch', said Sumpter, 'to oppose this resolution but after hearing Bro. Horner's speech, I would be compelled to return to my branch and tell them of the very different complexion Bro. Horner has put upon this question'.[20] The resolution was carried unanimously. John had won the confidence of the professional firemen. Like Nelson, he had broken the rules to save the day. Owing to his irregular and prompt decision at the start of the war and due to his skills in organizing and inspiring staff and members, it can be argued that the Fire Brigades Union did more to create a united, efficient fire service than any Home Office action. When three months after their annual conference, the bombs started falling, professionals and auxiliaries had already acquired a shared identity to fight the fires together.

Notes

1 Interview with Terry Segars, 8 July 1975, British Library audio recording.
2 Victor Bailey, 'The Early History of the Fire Brigades Union', in ed. Victor Bailey, *Forged in Fire*, London, 1992, 3–97, 83.
3 Terry Segars, 'War, women and the FBU', in Bailey, *Forged in Fire*, 139–157.
4 'The Fire Brigades Union's Fifty Years of Service', The Fire Brigades Union, London, 1968.
5 Bailey, 'The Early History of the Fire Brigades Union', 45.
6 Terry Segars interview.
7 Conference Report, *Firefighter*, June 1940. Horner's papers.
8 Horner, 'Recollections of a General Secretary', in ed. Victor Bailey, *Forged in Fire*, London, 1991, 312–3.
9 1939 Register, Ancestry.co.uk.
10 Tom Murray in ed. Ian Macdougall, *Voices from Work and Home*, Edinburgh, 2000, 254–332.
11 Murray, 289.
12 G.V. Blackstone, *A History of the British Fire Service*, London, 1957, 402.
13 Steve Allen, *Thompsons, A Personal History of the Firm and its Founder*, Pontypool, 2012, Chapter 11.
14 Allen, 61.
15 Letter from J.H. to John Saville n.d. in HHC/ Saville archives, 'FBU History Part One'.
16 *Yorkshire Post*, 1 December 1939.

17 See Chapter Ten.

18 Blackstone, 403.

19 See for example in his speech to the FBU Annual Conference in 1940 – 'Whatever may be the results of this War, the Fire Service as we knew it in pre-war days has gone for good. Let us hope that the Authorities will take the advice of Hamlet to his mother to "Throw away the worser part of it and live the purer with the other half"'. *Firefighter*, June 1940, 4.

20 *Firefighter*, June 1940, 32.

12

'BOMBED BUT FAR FROM BEATEN'

Following the fall of France, the cottage in Surrey was needed for refugees and Pat and Carol came back to Chingford. They moved into a newly built, semi-detached house, at the bottom of Hawkwood Crescent, a quiet suburban street that curves gently upwards to meet the fringe of Epping Forest where a primary school had recently opened for the children of Yardley Estate's growing population of skilled workers and clerks; once she was five, the school would be perfect for Carol. A further fifteen minutes' walk up to the top of Hawkwood Crescent brought them to a path through oak and beech onto the rolling grassland of Yardley Hill from where Violet's lover Reg Latham had written -- 'To see a sunset from Yardley Hill / Is worth a seven-days journey/ To be still ....'[1] In August 1940, the extended Palmer family living in the neighbourhood celebrated Pat and her sister Mavis' birthdays on Yardley Hill.

The first big air raid came on Saturday the seventh of September, a perfect day of clear skies and mellow sunshine. Pat and John had taken Carol for tea in Boston Road and from his parents' small back garden they saw the fleet of German bombers heading wave after wave towards the East End. John writes, 'My father had sacrificed one of his chicken runs to make an Anderson shelter and as the family went to earth I watched great pyramids of smoke and flame rise into the blue sky over London's dockland'. When the 'All clear' sounded, they quickly left for home where they had invited for supper the FBU president, Gus Odlin, and his wife, who lived in West Ham but were spending the weekend with their married son in Edmonton, the other side of the Lea Valley reservoir. Towards the end of their supper, the bombers returned.

Pat took Carol and Mrs Odlin into a recently built brick and concrete air raid shelter at the junction of Hawkwood Crescent and the main road.

DOI: 10.4324/9781032671352-13

Inside the poorly ventilated, dark and damp shelter, crowded with frightened women and children, Mrs Odlin became severely distressed by the possible fate of her docklands home. When the 'all clear' sounded, John and Gus drove to the top of Chingford Mount, from where they could see the docks ablaze. They tried to imagine how their fellow firefighters were coping with this new and terrible calamity. Once back in Hawkwood Crescent,

> There was some half-hearted talk between us of dashing down to Odlin's station in West Ham, talk which Pat swept aside as mere mock heroics, making it plain that if we were going anywhere it was to take Mrs Odlin, now quiet but exhausted, back to Edmonton.

Next morning, at first light, John drove by himself through the silent, empty streets of Walthamstow and Leyton, heading towards the docks. He knew the way well from his seafaring days: through Stratford, along Angel Lane, past West Ham football ground .... After which, the extent of the devastation made it difficult to find a way. 'The rescue squads and air raid wardens still searching ruins would pause to give a surprised glance at this invader of their battered neighbourhood, trying to manoeuvre his sturdy little Austin over the rubble'. Reaching at last the entrance to the Royal Docks, he found the familiar landmark of the Connaught Arms among the ruins, and in the strengthening light, recognized some of the ocean-going vessels now listing at the bottom of the dock, 'their upper work still visible and smouldering'. Since the first raid from the previous afternoon, hundreds of auxiliary firefighters had been toiling on the wharves alongside London Fire Brigade regulars. With the sun now well up, he watched them damp down the last of the still-smouldering, warehouse fires. 'Now and again someone would call out to me. An officer jocularly shouted across that this was no time for a union meeting'.

Back in Chingford, the Palmers were finalizing their evacuation plans. Violet had been in contact with Arthur le Mare, the former Warden of Friends Hall who had retired to Kirkby Stephen on the northeastern edge of the Lake District and was now the district billeting officer, organizing accommodation for women and children evacuated from northeast England's industrial heartlands.[2] Perhaps it was because Violet had told him she wanted to end her affair with Reg, that Arthur offered her a job that enabled her to move far away from London.[3] He had already found her somewhere to live and now told her he could arrange a billet for her brother Ken's children. It was then that Alice decided that she and Mavis would accompany them.

That evening, the bombers returned, the western sky again lit up by a smoky crimson glow that coloured the full moon blood-red. John was clear about what *he* wanted. 'We agreed she must seek safety for our baby far from London'. He would then be free 'to plunge back into the life of the Service which I had left such a short while before'. Yet where should Pat go? Her mother must have urged her to come with her and Violet but Kirkby Stephen was almost three hundred miles from London – too distant and remote for John to visit easily. She wanted to be as close to him, somewhere he could come for the day or the weekend, as he had when she was in Surrey. They compromised on the city of Oxford, only sixty miles from London and a government-designated evacuation centre. When John drove her and Carol there the next day, they discovered many other families had made the same choice. 'Such were the strains upon available accommodation', writes John, 'that the Classic Cinema was turned into a caravanserai, its auditorium being cleared of its seats while families camped out on its sloping floor'. He helped Pat move into some 'miserable lodgings' and returned to London. It must have been shortly afterwards that she took Carol to a photographic studio in Oxford. (Figure 12.1),

FIGURE 12.1   Pat with Carol in Oxford, 1940 (family album).

She is wearing her best dress, determined to smile bravely in a picture to post to John. Carol at twenty months was an easy-going child, happy to smile at the strange man with the camera. Pat was far from cheerful. Their lodging was so overcrowded and disagreeable that she quickly moved to another that proved equally bad. Recollections of their pleasant stay in rural Surrey decided her to move out of Oxford into the nearby countryside where she would have more space and privacy.

John appears to have asked the assistance of Lord Faringdon, a left-wing peer and Oxfordshire landowner, a strong supporter of the Republican cause in the Spanish Civil War and now an auxiliary firefighter and enthusiastic member of the Fire Brigades Union. A few miles east from Faringdon's country seat of Buscot Park lies the village of Aston where Pat and Carol moved into an ancient, poorly furnished cottage. John's memoir includes encounters with Faringdon in Aston and mentions the village's proximity to William Morris' riverside home in Kelmscott but passes over Pat's experience of Aston which she remembered as the worst eight months of her life. She may have mistakenly believed Aston was in the Cotswolds of which she had happy memories from a pre-war weekend with John near Temple Guiting. But Aston lies in the dreary, broad valley of the upper Thames with none of Temple Guiting's hanging woods and winding streams. As for the cottage, she probably assumed it would be like that in Surrey, a simple farm labourer's home that nevertheless benefitted from piped water and electricity. She was to discover Aston Parish Council did not approve of such amenities, having voted against bringing into the village the mains services enjoyed elsewhere in the district. Pat had to get used to an outdoor pump, learn to cook on a paraffin stove and every evening fiddle with pressure lamps while, as winter advanced, visits to the unheated outhouse at the end of the garden became ever more challenging.[4]

Aston was principally a farming community where, according to Pat, incest was rife, the consequences depressingly apparent through the congenital idiocy that she claimed to be common among the population. Many villagers were fundamentalist Baptists, preaching fire and brimstone, like Amos Starkadder in Gibbon's *Cold Comfort Farm*, whose comic novel she had enjoyed reading before the war. Pat was reminded of how Gibbons' heroine, Flora, had arrived at the farm:

The lantern was lifted higher while Judith steadily looked into her face in silence. The seconds passed. Flora wondered if her lipstick was the wrong shade. It then occurred to her there was a less frivolous cause for the silence which had fallen and for the steady regard with which her cousin confronted her. So, Flora mused, must Columbus have felt when the poor Indian fixed his solemn, unwavering gaze upon the great sailor's face. For the first time, a Starkadder looked upon a civilized being.[5]

The village was not quite so isolated as Pat later claimed. Aston had received Basque refugee children from the Spanish Civil War and in September 1939, an entire primary school from London's East End had been billeted there. Aston's residents may have been unfriendly because of Pat's politics. The 1939 Register shows some employed at the nearby RAF base who would not have been happy when hearing from Aston's shopkeeper that Pat took the unpatriotic *Daily Worker* that was opposed to the war. The damage to her reputation in Aston may have been irreparable after the *Worker* was banned in January 1941 for its divisive messages that Herbert Morrison, the Home Secretary, believed to be undermining people's confidence in the war effort.[6] A toddler and wireless her only companions, she began smoking heavily. The sole variety in the tedium was the weekly bus into Witney to change her library books and treat Carol to an iced bun in the teashop. During the exceptionally cold winter evenings, she huddled over a paraffin heater, worried about John, and wondered where he was sleeping.

When not in a trestle hammock at a fire station, he may have been in his office where he had organized a comfortable arm chair and blanket, with breakfast in an all-night printer's café in nearby Fleet Street. Or perhaps at his mother's, 'I must have been there frequently for someone did my washing'. Or possibly at his father-in-law's, 'For I can distinctly remember the late suppers of tinned pilchards from his store [Geoff] inevitably put in front of me'. He rarely went home to Hawkwood Crescent because it reminded him of his absent wife and daughter. He spent the day in his office and the evenings at fire stations; sometimes he accompanied his members out on a call and lent a hand by helping keep the heavy branch (hose) pointed to the fire. Early on in the Blitz, during a heavy night-time raid, a senior fire officer had met him at a fire and expressing alarm at his bare head, arranged for a London Fire Brigade dispatch rider to deliver a tin hat and service respirator to the office for John's use. Yet, just driving around London was dangerous. One evening, in Charing Cross Road he was caught in a shower of incendiary bombs that luckily proved to be duds, but shortly afterwards, from the scream of its fall and the sound of explosion, he knew a bomb had fallen close by. It had sliced off the top of Soho Fire Station and his crewmates from Clerkenwell were digging for survivors.

With no lights in the blackout, bomb craters and rubble were hard to spot. Harry Short was with him one evening when after calling in at

FIGURE 12.2   Firemen at work in bomb damaged street in London, after Saturday
night raid, circa 1941 (New York Times Paris Bureau).

Bishopsgate Fire Station, they had tried to cross a railway bridge at the back
of Liverpool Street Station during a bombardment. In the pitch darkness of
the blackout, Harry spotted just in time that half the bridge was missing.
After that, John took to cycling, often in the company of the Union's AFS
national organizer, Peter Pain. He remembered telling him 'There's one
good thing about these raids, Peter. They keep our members' minds off
their grumbles'.[7]

Auxiliary firefighters grumbled because of the lack of adequate injury pay
and no burial costs when killed on duty. In a pamphlet, 'The First Twelve
Months', published to mark the first anniversary of the Union's AFS section,
John wrote,

> In that first never to be forgotten weekend of September 7th-8th, our
> members saved London from another Great Fire. All this has been told in
> the Daily Press. What has not been told in the Press is the complete lack
> of preparedness which left men isolated for hours without food and drink,
> which condemned men who been wet through for days to return to their
> stations to turn out again and again in their wet clothes.[8]

Angus Calder describes in *The People's War* how firemen could be cut off to perish in acres of flame:

> Men bent their faces to the nozzles of their hoses, craving the draught of pure cold air which dwelt around the water jet. Yet, for others it was the cold which was unbearable, coupled with thirst and hunger ... the force of the water made the hose difficult to hold and the back pressure made it difficult to keep the branch up.[9]

John's 'front line' visits gave credibility to the Union's demands. 'Eight of our dead comrades delivered to their widows for burial in sacks on a council lorry'; Fireman forced to drink water from the Thames'; 'Seven fires in a night and no change. Uniform damp for days on end'. His pamphlet describes the horror when, 'I found ... that authority had not even been given for the purchase of uniforms sufficient to re-clothe even those men whose uniforms had been ruined'.

Three weeks into the Blitz, Major Jackson organized an off-the-record chat between John and the senior Home Office official in charge of fire service matters. The union's demands were accepted: a burial grant for firefighters dying on duty, more mobile refreshment canteens and for a change of clothing, thirty thousand pairs of postman's trousers with a red stripe down the side. I am reminded of the early days of the Covid pandemic when the doctors' union, the British Medical Association, incessantly lobbied for speedy replenishment of the necessary personal protection equipment for its members for which the government had failed to plan. John Horner would have pointed out that for the public to be effectively protected, public servants must have good trade unions.

Some days before that crucial Home Office meeting, the Fire Brigades Union was to lose its office and John could have lost his life. He had spent the night at Millwall Fire Station on the Isle of Dogs and when early next morning he drove back to central London he discovered his office had disappeared along with much of Chancery Lane. 'Our fellows were still working on the debris and there were many witticisms passed among those men .... when my presence was discovered'. Should he have slept in his office that night, as had been his original intention, the Union would have lost its general secretary. The destruction of their records decided the Union to decentralize the organization immediately by setting up regional offices for the northern and Scottish organizers and a separate office for the London area's AFS section that was meanwhile temporarily located at the Palmers' home in Chingford. A fortnight later, John wrote in a pamphlet, 'The First Twelve Months', 'We are now prepared for any and all contingencies. In a week or so we shall have set up another office in Central London. We are bombed but far from beaten'.[10]

Two hundred planes bombed London for fifty-seven consecutive nights. Then came a pause. On John's twenty-ninth birthday, 5 November 1940, Winston Churchill addressed the House of Commons on the state of the nation,

> The cities of Britain are still standing .... Fourteen thousand civilians have been killed and 20,000 seriously wounded, nearly four-fifths of them in London .... None of the services upon which the life of our great cities depend – water, fuel, electricity, gas, sewage – not one has broken down. On the contrary, although there must inevitably be local shortages, all the authorities concerned with these vital functions of a modern community feel that they are on top of their job and are feeling it increasingly as each week is passed.

Or as John was to phrase it in that month's *Firefighter*, the fire service was in better shape than at the start of the Blitz, because of 'the constant hammering of the men's own union against a blank wall of ignorance and lack of imagination'.[11]

Notes

1 *Friendship*, June 1931.
2 See *Penrith Observer*, 10 October 1941.
3 Violet's account of the job offer, in ed. Fred Parsons, 'An Appreciation of Arthur le Mare', Friends Hall, 1943. WFLRO.
4 'George Wiltshire remembers Aston during the war:' recording by Aston History Society. Evacuated to Aston when a child, Wilshire remembered the shock of a toilet at the bottom of the garden after having been used to an indoor flush toilet.
5 Stella Gibbons, *Cold Comfort Farm*, Harmondsworth, 1938, 49.
6 NA/ CAB-66-14-12.
7 John Horner, 'Recollections of a General Secretary', in ed. Victor Bailey, *Forged in Fire*, London, 1991, 326.
8 John Horner, 'The First Twelve Months', pamphlet, 8 October 1940, 'published by the AFS Section of the Fire Brigades Union, 50 Epping Way, Chingford (Temporary Address)'. This was the home of Geoff and Alice Palmer.
9 Angus Calder, *The Peoples War, Britain 1939 – 1945*, London 1971, 182.
10 'The First Twelve Months'.
11 *Firefighter*, November 1940.

13

'KNOWN TO KEEP STRANGE COMPANY' 1941–43

In May 1941, the Home Secretary, Herbert Morrison, announced the creation of a National Fire Service, a move the FBU had urged and supported. It would clearly be easier to negotiate with a single unitary authority but more than that, John wanted an efficient and effective fire service of which his members could be proud. Morrison had taken over the Home Office during the worse days of the London Blitz and had used admirable speed in the complex task of merging sixteen hundred local authority brigades into a single service. Yet, he had not taken advantage of this reorganization to tackle long-standing injustices in firefighters' pay and conditions. 'Our firemen have had a pretty raw deal, as Mr. John Horner general secretary of the Fire Brigades Union, has convincingly shown this week', the *Daily Mirror*, observed. 'We recommend Mr. Horner's moderate but just criticism to Mr. Herbert Morrison.'[1]

Although annoyed by the FBU's skilful access to the press, Morrison's biggest problem with the union was Horner's suspicious politics. Morrison had long been the Labour Party's most vociferous anti-communist and was alarmed that the personnel in a uniformed and disciplined crown service for which he was responsible, belonged to a communist-run trade union while the country was fighting a war that the Communist Party refused to support. Shortly after becoming Home Secretary, Morrison invited John and the FBU's new president, John Burns to meet him at the Home Office – the first of several contentious encounters that reminded John of schoolboy visits to his headmaster's study: you usually only saw him when having done something wrong. At this first meeting, Morrison decided to ignore John altogether, addressing himself to Burns, the older and wiser prefect and a reliable Labour Party member. Spread out on a table were press cuttings, back issues of the *Firefighter* and copies of circular letters to Union members. Indicating all

DOI: 10.4324/9781032671352-14

these to Burns, Morrison told him, 'The constant harping on of weaknesses, unavoidable in war time … could be construed as attempts to undermine morale and the nation's war effort'.[2] He was giving them a friendly warning, ready to make allowances, he told Burns, for this 'young fellow's inexperience and enthusiasm', while cautioning that John was known to keep 'strange company' that risked the union's standing with the Home Office.

A Labour politician, old enough to be John's father, Morrison had come up through local government and was distrusted by trade union leaders. When Morrison eventually tried to rid himself of the Fire Brigades Union, by creating a fire service equivalent of the Police Federation, John could depend on the support of Citrine and the TUC General Council who obliged Morrison to allow the fire service its own, proper trade union.[3] Labour's most aggressive anti-communist had to agree to a cuckoo in his Home Office nest.

The fire service's rapid expansion in 1939 had provided an excellent opportunity for the Communist Party's strategy of optimizing its limited membership to influence the trade union movement.[4] As late as November 1940 the FBU's Executive Council had voted against sending a delegate to the Communist Party's People's Convention that called for 'a people's government' to end the war.[5] But the Party was soon more in control. Once inside a union, Party members formed 'fractions' that liaised with central Party committees in King Street to develop policy initiatives and influence their unions' elections. These were elements of the 'Communist Technique', as described by former auxiliary firefighter and ex-communist, Bob Darke, whose account includes his experience on the FBU's Executive Council from 1941–45. Darke explains how communists took advantage of the political apathy of the majority to move into all levels of decision-making, occasionally by bending the rules, but mostly by delivering tangible benefits. 'I have listened to good socialist trade unionists, who hold no brief for the Party's attitude in international affairs, swear that they will always support the communists in union matters "because they will always fight for the workers".'[6] As a strategic planner, skilful campaigner, and pragmatic negotiator, John was to be re-elected to office after the war because he delivered for his members, while at the same time he ensured the Union had sufficient numbers of communists in positions of influence to support the Party's policy as directed from Moscow.

Yet Darke's allegations that communist trades unionists did not truly care about the workers and were treated as pawns in the Party's schemes, do not match John's behaviour. His genuine concern for his members' wellbeing is evident from his distress during the first days of the Blitz when auxiliary firefighters' bodies were brought back to their homes in sacks on the back of a lorry; and firemen appreciated John's care during his evening visits to the fire stations, when he set them laughing at his anecdotes and then accompanied them when the bells went down to fight the great dockland fires. They found him a decent man, a good listener, sensitive to their needs, quick to sympathize, often angry about the state of the world, but rarely so with his colleagues.

Darke served on the Executive Council's general purposes committee that had oversight of finances and personnel and his book draws on that experience to show how Party members placed communists in leadership positions.

> In the Fire Brigades Union during the war, I was part of a conspiracy that removed eight national officers who stood in the way of the Communist march to full control. Most of them were wiped out of the way by breaking down their health with over-work … Where the rest fought back we turned on a whispering campaign, accusations of immoderate drinking, of gambling and immorality, of a personal or domestic life that reflected on his standing.[7]

Union historians Terry Segars and Victor Bailey largely concur with the accuracy of Darke's account.[8]

By 1942/3, communists were to be found at every level of the Union.[9] An organizational restructuring to match the new regions of the National Fire Service was an excellent opportunity to appoint or promote some staff, and remove others, Pat's father among the latter. Still a staunch, Lloyd George Liberal, Geoff Palmer had made things easy for them. In the New Year of 1941, he had moved to Birmingham to run a new Midlands area office and it was after that he started having difficulties. The general purposes committee reprimanded him for protesting at their treatment of an eligible candidate for a new organizer position. The minutes provide no details. Geoff had perhaps realized there was a bias against non-communist applicants for jobs with the FBU. He was again reprimanded when he rashly went above the general purposes committee, to appeal to the general secretary when not reimbursed for a traffic fine incurred at work. Regardless of his father-in-law's politics, this last may have been enough to persuade John to take advantage of the Union's restructuring to abolish Geoff's post.[10] At the end of 1941, Geoff left the FBU, to remain in Birmingham with a civil defence job.

Now, some younger FBU officials moved into senior positions, notably as a national organizer Jack Grahl, who later became assistant general secretary. Grahl was from Edinburgh and may have joined the Communist Party in his teens when apprenticed as a plumber.[11] By 1936, he was running what was possibly a Communist Party bookshop in Burntisland, in the constituency of Willie Gallacher, Britain's sole communist MP.[12] Shortly after joining the AFS, Grahl was hired as an assistant to the Scottish and north England regional organizer, the communist Tom Murray, who soon promoted him to run the area office in Newcastle. Grahl was later described by a fellow communist as 'an exceptionally good speaker and extremely knowledgeable'.[13] I suspect that Grahl was to become the Union's unacknowledged 'political commissar' for the Party.

Other than the reference to his keeping strange company, John's memoirs omit his wartime association with the Party leadership. Instead, he concentrates on the FBU's campaigns to improve fire service pay and conditions. In the autumn of 1941, the Union organized a two-month highly publicized nationwide campaign for a 'Firemen's Charter' for the new National Fire Service, including a national minimum wage for all firefighters, regular and auxiliary alike, standardized sick pay and promotion on merit. The concept of a Charter resonated with working-class activists familiar with the history of the British labour movement and the previous century's Chartist campaign. John was to reach even further back into the history that he loved – to the English Civil War – appealing directly to the British people 'to take a hand with us to make a New Model firefighting army'.[14]

In a meticulously organized, campaign, he enlisted public expressions of support from members of parliament and other speakers who were provided with detailed notes of the case to make – 'such a good one that it is bound to impress the public, especially if argued soberly, without exaggeration and with an air of responsibility'.[15] A House of Commons debate on the National Fire Service centred on the right of a uniformed, disciplined force to have a trade union and on the legitimacy of the claims in the Firemen's Charter. Morrison told the Commons he disliked the campaign, and that it was 'certainly calculated to render consultation "more difficult".'[16] An exasperated Morrison told the House of Commons, 'I am aware of the views of the union, but I am afraid I do not agree with them'.[17] But with the public on the FBU's side, he began to give way and agreement was gradually reached on some if not all the Charter's demands.

Relations thereafter became less glacial. Yet Morrison and his Home Office advisers remained suspicious of the Communist Party's sway in the fire service, especially when firefighters had more time on their hands after the Blitz. The FBU encouraged cultural activities: John's old tea boat chum, Lurcher was among the firemen artists who exhibited their work and their social realist pictures are illustrated in *Jim Braidy, The Story of Britain's Firemen*.[18] The Union also ran a centre in Dr Johnson's house off Fleet Street that provided the same mix of talks, literature, music and art that John and Pat had enjoyed at Friends Hall.[19] Leonard Cassini, one of several communists on the Union's Executive Council, arranged the panelled drawing room for chamber music performed by firefighters who in peacetime were professional musicians, while the auxiliary firefighter Stephen Spender gave poetry readings, and George Rudé, later a Marxist historian, lectured on Walt Whitman. Any FBU member could offer a talk and John's was 'Sigurd and Socialism'. Having learnt from Fred Parsons how to be a lively and entertaining speaker, he probably exemplified Morris' socialist message in 'Sigurd the Volsung' by declaiming favourite passages, as for example, where an old man predicts how the new-born Sigurd will become a great revolutionary –

> there rose up a man most ancient, and he cried: 'Hail Dawn of the Day!
> How many things shalt thou quicken, how many shalt thou slay!
> How many things shalt thou waken, how many lull to sleep![20]

Discussion groups were the commonest means for the Party to influence Britain's firefighters. Several hundred such groups met weekly at the nation's fire stations, each led by one of their own number. Music, the cinema or hobbies were discussed but most often the topics were political and according to Stephen Spender they 'tended to become demonstrations of the politics of the Left'.[21]

Following the Soviet victory at Stalingrad, the Communist Party was to achieve its highest-ever membership in Britain, and in 1943 applied to affiliate with the Labour Party. Communists argued that just as the alliance with the Soviet Union was winning the war, socialist unity at home would

FIGURE 13.1   'Fire Station Discussion Group' by Reginald Mills.[28]

secure the post-war peace. At the Labour Party conference in June, the Fire Brigades Union supported a resolution to this effect. The Labour leadership opposed it.[22] Many Labourites admired Soviet central planning and the state control of the economy, its full employment and universal access to good quality education and health services. Yet while desiring all these good things in Britain, they also wanted that which Soviet citizens lacked: parliamentary democracy, freedom of movement and assembly, and an unfettered press. Trade Union leaders, notably Bevin and Citrine, objected to Soviet-style trade unions without an independent voice nor the right to strike. And those with long memories had not forgotten Stalin's pre-war treason trials and the reports of slave labour camps and mass famine.

John chose to ignore such objections and in his capacity as a member of the Labour Party, made the case for affiliation in *Labour Monthly* (edited by Communist theoretician, Palme Dutt).

I was finally persuaded to support this affiliation by observing the role of the communists in the present struggle. In the Trade Union movement I have seen no evidence of their disloyalty. I have seen ample evidence of their earnestness and hard work.[23]

As the FBU delegate at Labour's Conference, John must have heard Herbert Morrison wind up the affiliation debate with an analogy to a piece of fire service apparatus known as 'the dual-purpose appliance' (a combination of escape and pump). Communists, Morrison complained, 'Tell you one thing and they mean another': there were delegates at the conference who claimed to be Labour supporters when it was known, but could not be proved, they were secret members of the Communist Party. 'You can try to do business with crooked people if you like. I won't and I don't believe conference will'.[24] Nor did it. Conference voted against affiliation.

Herbert Morrison correctly suspected John to be a secret Communist Party member. Shortly after the conference, the Party's leadership met in King Street to discuss whether to abolish undercover membership. Harry Pollitt, the Party's general secretary, argued for retention: 'There are people in this country who hold Party cards whom I alone in this Party know'.[25] And because these secret members would have to resign from the Party rather than have their membership made public, they would no longer be subject to Party discipline. 'It was possibly over the younger recruits of the 1930s that Pollitt exerted the greatest influence', writes Kevin Morgan, citing the recollections of middle-class intellectuals, less reticent than John in revealing their communist past. Pollitt's influence may have been even greater over John Horner and other young working-class communists, about whom less has been written. Pollitt had a warmth and sympathy, combined with 'the willpower and sense of purpose ... [that]made people go to talk to him, because he would listen, because he was wise'.[26] Twenty years older than John, Pollitt would have been careful and protective of this impulsive, energetic young man, a skilful organizer and charismatic public speaker. Yet should John have been forced to confirm publicly his Communist Party membership, his influential position, as general secretary of a trade union of uniformed civil defence workers in wartime Britain, might have become untenable.

As it was, Morrison gave Horner the benefit of the doubt and made the gesture of publicly recognizing the Union's contribution to building the National Fire Service. In August 1943, delegates from the regular and auxiliary sections of the Fire Brigades Union met in a joint conference to merge into a unitary organization. They celebrated the occasion in the presence of a jovial Herbert Morrison invited to the conference dinner. Pat was there on her birthday, along with the social reformer William Beveridge, the first woman president of the Trades Union Congress, and several Members of Parliament including Reg Sorensen from Leytonstone, whom Pat and John knew from Friends Hall. 'They heard the Home Secretary make his peace with the firemen's trade union', writes John in his memoir.

> Flabbergasted, we listened to a speech in which Herbert said he was 'proud' of the part he had played in succeeding, to the surprise and perhaps not a little concern of 'some in high places' in sustaining trade unionism in 'Britain's Fourth Arm' in time of war. It had not been easy. Initial 'misunderstandings' had left their mark. 'We had learned from each other – though there was still much to learn.' He made a number if not ill-humoured references to 'this young fella' to whom he had been obliged to give so much valuable advice which had been persistently ignored.

John was too generous of spirit for his memoir to include Morrison's revenge for his having kept strange company. It was Pat who told me how, after the liberation of France in 1944, he prevented John from accepting the French government's award of the Légion d'Honneur for his services to the allied cause.[27]

Notes

1. *Daily Mirror*, 22 May 1941.
2. John Horner, 'Recollections of a general secretary', in ed. Victor Bailey, *Forged in Fire*, London, 1991, 337.
3. See John Horner's speech of thanks to the TUC General Council in 1943. www.unionhistory.info/reports/index.php Accessed 18 May 2000.
4. John McIlroy, 'Restoring Stalinism to Communist History', *Critique*, 2013, 41, 4, 599–622.
5. FBU Conference Report 1940, Horner papers.

6 Bob Darke, *The Communist Technique in Britain*, London, 1952.
7 For Darke's membership of the GPC, see the minutes 1941–43 (MRC/ FBU Additional Exec. minutes 1940–1943, 1150/Box 8 and Box 9); and Darke, 57.
8 Victor Bailey, 'The early history of the Fire Brigades Union', in ed. Victor Bailey, *Forged in Fire*, London, 1992, 64; Terry Segars, *The Fire Service: A Social History of a Uniformed Working Class*', PhD thesis, University of Essex, 1989, 220.
9 Bailey, 65.
10 GPC Minutes, 1940–41.
11 Endnote 101 in Bailey, 93.
12 *Dundee Evening Telegraph*, 31 January 1936.
13 Transcript of John Saville's interview with Enoch Humphries, Hull History Centre UDJS/1/28, FBU History.
14 Cited in Bailey, 58.
15 'Speakers `Notes'. Wellcome Collection, HALDANE/5/1/2/75.
16 *Daily Herald*, 21 November 1941.
17 On the 23 July 1942.
18 William Sansom, James Gordon and Stephen Spender, *Jim Braidy, The Story of Britain's Firemen*, London, 1943.
19 According to John Horner, the house's owner, the press baron, Lord Harmsworth had lent it to the FBU for the war's duration in gratitude for a fire crew having saved the house during the Blitz.
20 See Fiona MacCarthy, *William Morris*, London, 1994, 373.
21 Stephen Spender, 'After the Blitz', in Sansom et al., 48–64 (60).
22 Andrew Thorpe, 'Locking out the Communists. The Labour party and the Communist party, 1939–46', *Twentieth Century History*, 2014, 25, 2, 221–50.
23 John Horner, 'Symposium on Affiliation', *Labour Monthly*, June 1943, 172–173.
24 *Daily Herald*, 17 June 1943.
25 NA/KV2/1041, 27 July 1943.
26 Morgan, 1993, 120–121.
27 'No UK citizen may accept and wear a foreign award without The Sovereign's permission'. https://assets.publishing.service.gov.uk/government/uploads/system/uploads/attachment_data/file/920147/Rules_for_the_Acceptance_of_Foreign_Awards.pdf
28 In Sansom et al., 54.

14

THE CAMPAIGN FOR A SECOND FRONT

Asked by my partner how John might have reacted to the Nazi-Soviet Pact, I explained he probably had no time to think about it; I said he must have been pre-occupied with Pat's illness and his new responsibilities at a crisis moment for the fire service. Later, I realized I was making excuses for him, avoiding the likelihood that, like many other British Communists, he had supported the Soviet Union's decision. I had been trying to wriggle out of discussing John's response to the pact, only too evident from the letter he wrote Pat from the Trade Union Congress at Bridlington in the first week of the war and that included an angry reference to Walter Citrine's tirade against the Soviet Union.

When writing his memoir fifty years later, John had not changed his opinion of Citrine's speech, commenting that much of it was 'devoted to the treacherous duplicity of the Soviet government'. Yet, on reading the transcript in the TUC conference report, I find John's memory at fault. 'Treachery' and 'duplicity' were not words used by Citrine who rather briefly noted the universal astonishment at the Soviet pact with the Nazis: the TUC, said Citrine, had consistently urged the government to conclude an agreement with the Soviet Union. And despite Nazism and Communism employing similar methods, their purposes, aims and ends were different 'and we have all recognised these differences'.[1] It must have been the remark about the Communists and Nazis sharing 'similar methods' that caused John's strong reaction in 1939 and influenced how he remembered the speech.

Initially, the Communist Party had continued to identify Nazi Germany as the principal enemy of the working class. John's next test of faith occurred

DOI: 10.4324/9781032671352-15

two weeks into the war when the Soviet Union shifted from neutrality towards favouring Germany.[2] The shift coincided with the Red Army's invasion of eastern Poland. The *Daily Worker* welcomed the Russian occupation as the recovery of territory that had been part of Russia until 1917. It allowed the population to re-join 'their kith and kin' and liberated the peasants and workers from bourgeois oppression. As the Labour politician Arthur Greenwood wrote in the *Daily Herald*, the Soviet Union's grounds for invading Poland were identical to those Hitler had used as 'excuses for his monstrous outrages'.[3] Instructions soon came from Moscow that Britain's war was not ant-fascist but instead an imperialist war that communists should not support. Rank-and-filers like John were unaware of the rancour and arguments within the Communist Party's leadership; they did not know that Pollitt was objecting strongly to these orders from Moscow and that he persisted in seeing the war as one against fascism. But guided by the Party's theoretician, Palme Dutt, all but two of the Politburo voted for the new line and Pollitt stood down as the Party's general secretary.[4]

Then, in 1940, the Communist Party launched the 'People's Convention', a fantasy that were a People's Government to run Britain, the German people would rise up against the Nazi regime and establish their own People's Government with whom Britain could make a People's Peace. And even should the Nazis remain in power, a People's Government in Britain would by definition no longer be fighting an imperialist but a socialist war against fascism. In other words, the Communist Party would only support the war against the Nazis when and if it were to secure a People's Government. Bearing in mind the popularity of the coalition government, how to secure such a government without armed revolution was a conundrum the Party's leadership preferred not to discuss; 'For the most part', writes Kevin Morgan, 'communists were content to leave these problems until they had to face them'.[5]

In his memoir, *Interesting Times*, the communist historian Eric Hobsbawm admits that the Party's line made little sense and he himself was all for fighting Hitler.[6] In contrast, John's memoir is silent about the Party's policy prior to Hitler's invasion of the Soviet Union. Yet when reminiscing about the war, it seems he never saw himself as neutral but proud, as he wrote at the time, that his members were 'on the front line against Hitler'. Presumably, as a good communist, he had to support the Party line, even when it made no sense, just as good Catholics believe in the Virgin birth. The former communist, Douglas Hyde, who after the war left the Party for Catholicism, writes in *his* autobiography that the Nazi-Soviet Pact did not trouble a trained Marxist – 'The Soviet leaders had a responsibility to the working-class of the world to defend the USSR and could if necessary, for this reason, make an alliance with the devil himself.'[7] John loved the Party and – as I have learnt in writing about his muddle-headedness – strong affection facilitates sympathy for a loved one's predicament.

By late May 1941, Germany's aerial bombardment of Britain had ended, and John brought Pat and Carol home to Chingford. A month later, following Hitler's invasion of the Soviet Union, Churchill declared the Soviet Union to be Britain's ally: 'The Russian danger is our danger, the cause of any Russian fighting for his hearth and home is the cause of freemen in every quarter of the globe'.[8] The Communist Party accordingly executed a third policy flip, abandoned a 'People's Peace' and declared its support for the British government in its anti-fascist war. Hobsbawm recalls how Party members, 'sighing with relief, returned to what they had been saying before the war and re-joined the masses of ordinary citizens'; another memoirist remembers how the new line 'lifted an enormous burden of doubt from the consciences of most Party members'.[9]

John's enthusiasm spilled over into impulsive action, unnecessarily worsening an already difficult relationship with the Home Office. Within weeks of the German invasion, he had called on the Soviet Ambassador, offering to lead an FBU delegation to Moscow to provide advice on firefighting during a Blitz. Mr Maisky cordially welcomed the offer and 'we issued a press statement accordingly'. John was then promptly summoned to the Home Office for a scolding from the headmaster. Morrison 'had not been surprised to be told by the Foreign Office that we had failed to consult them about our so called "mission" for we had thought it unnecessary to consult the Home Office before running along to Mr Maisky ... Exit permits would be withheld'.

The Party leadership meanwhile had quickly reinstated Harry Pollitt as its general secretary. Pollitt had always believed the communists should support the war and from then on the Party campaigned tirelessly to increase Britain's production of war materials – 'Tanks for Uncle Joe'. John accordingly encouraged FBU branch secretaries to link up with local factories for outsourcing work to fire stations.[10] With German air raids now rare, firemen were serving long shifts with little to do other than polish, drill and scrub the floors and many were willing to spend their time more productively through assembling components for radio parts, mortar bomb slings and paddles for RAF rescue dinghies.[11] His less enthusiastic members were also told to get cracking. 'When we talk about productive work for firemen, we mean work for Victory over Fascism and not necessarily work bringing home an extra quid at the end of the week', he wrote in *Firefighter*.[12] He was to regularly remind them of their Soviet comrades' sacrifices to defend Britain from the Nazis.

The Communist Party's other campaign was for the immediate opening of a second front in Western Europe to take the pressure off Russia from the

German onslaught; John's memoir hints that it was during the campaign for the Second Front that he worked closely with Pollitt and as mentioned in the previous chapter, it may have been following the invasion of the Soviet Union that John moved from status of communist fellow-traveller to undercover member. A year after Hitler's troops had crossed the frontier, the Germans were advancing eastwards towards Stalingrad when on Sunday 26 July 1942, the Party organised its first mass rally in Trafalgar Square calling for a Second Front. Pollitt received the loudest cheers but from among the other speakers, John proved himself accomplished enough. This was his first time in three decades of speaking in Trafalgar Square, firstly when in the Communist Party and afterwards for the Campaign for Nuclear Disarmament. Without recourse to Churchillian metaphor, John's short, blunt sentences clarified what was needed and stirred the crowd to action. He had done many public meetings during the Firemen's Charter campaign but now he was speaking on a burning political issue that brought together communists, sympathetic trade unionists, intellectuals and fellow-travelling Members of Parliament.[13] It must have seemed to him that the pre-war Popular Front against fascism had at last borne fruit. Douglas Hyde, then on the staff of the *Daily Worker*, remembered standing on the plinth of Nelson's Column and looking down on 50,000 faces. 'To see the hammer-and-sickle badge openly and proudly worn by almost everyone present, to hear great masses of people singing the "Internationale" and "Soviet Land" was to be carried away with a terrific emotion.'[14]

A photo from the rally (Figure 14.1) shows a relaxed, confident John Horner sitting with other speakers below the plinth, his speech loosely clasped in his hands. Next to him is D.N. Pritt, fellow-travelling barrister who had defended the trade unionists on trial at Meerut, a Member of Parliament expelled from the Labour Party for his communist sympathies. On Pritt's right is Bill Rust, Editor of the (still-banned) *Daily Worker*, a man, writes Kevin Morgan, 'to whose memory it is hard to be kind; from most accounts, Rust is vain, self-important, manipulative, a hypocrite – notorious for his subservience to Moscow'.[15] Some of this is apparent from the photo: Rust ostentatiously chooses to disregard the camera, his notes more important. In fairness, he is chairing the meeting and may be checking the list of speakers, none of whom, incidentally, are women; the young woman next to him is his wife, Tamara, a Russian and a feminist whom Rust had met in Moscow.

Six weeks later came another first when John spoke at the Trades Union Congress. He was seconding Jack Tanner, the president of the powerful Amalgamated Engineering Union, in a motion calling for an immediate Second Front. A similar motion from Tanner and the AEU the previous year had been heavily defeated and in the interim John had worked with Tanner to change trade unionists' minds. A generation older than John, Tanner had been a syndicalist colleague of the great labour leader Tom Mann and was

FIGURE 14.1   Second Front Rally, 26 July 1942 (family album).

widely known and respected in the trades union movement for his grassroots organizing of engineering shop stewards during the First World War. Tanner had been prominent in the founding of the British Communist Party and a delegate to the second congress of the Communist International in Moscow where he had famously argued with Lenin about democratic centralism: as Tanner understood it, the dictatorship of the proletariat should not mean the dictatorship of the Communist Party.[16] Soon afterwards, he had resigned from the Party, while staying in close and friendly contact with Harry Pollitt who probably facilitated John's introduction to Tanner.

From reading his speeches, Tanner appears to have been a dry, unemotional but effective speaker whereas John liked to start by making his audience laugh, as he did in this first speech to the TUC in 1942: if, as the TUC General Council maintained, they should leave decisions about the Second Front to the military, 'then it followed that the entire War Cabinet and the House of Commons should close down'. He then fired up his listeners. 'Agreed, the exact details should be left to the authorities, "but on a matter involving their vital interests the working class cannot deny themselves the right to be there …". If the Second Front were regarded as urgent in May, it is now, four months later, a thousand times more urgent.'[17]

Bob Darke takes a cynical view about the campaign for the Second Front –

Maybe rank and file communists thought that the object of it all was to take war strain off the Red Army. But a far more likely explanation was put to me by one of the National Officers of the Firemen's Union, a barrister [Peter Pain?]. 'You know what will happen, Bob? A Second Front now with the Red Army so powerful will enable the Russians to sweep through Europe and you can well imagine that wherever the Red Army goes, it will stay, and the workers will gain power after the war is over'.[18]

Which is probably what the coalition government feared and why Churchill delayed plans for opening a Second Front. John's speech was well reported in the *Daily Worker*, and he must have felt honoured when two months later he shared a platform with Pollitt to celebrate the twenty-fifth anniversary of the October Revolution.[19] But there are no further reports of John speaking publicly about the Second Front. According to Darke, many FBU members disliked such high-profile political campaigning.[20] Despite the success of the Charter Campaign there had remained unresolved the FBU's dispute with the Home Office over duty shifts. The Union had objected to the nationwide establishment of forty-eight hours on, followed by twenty-four off, first introduced by the London Fire Brigade at the start of the war. It wanted instead, twenty-four hours on/ twenty-four hours off. Once again, John arranged for friendly MPs to ask questions in the House until Morrison replied, 'I can assure hon. Members that I have exercised every courtesy, but I am bound to say that I am getting a little bit irritated at the misrepresentations and undue pressure'.[21]

The Union's failure to win this change came to a head at the conference of its AFS section in Leeds in October 1942. It was a gloomy month, with no end in sight to winning the war and John had a difficult speech to make. Since the fall of Singapore in February, the nation's morale had been low. In September, Mass Observation reported 'war weariness' and increasing 'negative' feelings. October brought no improvement; 'War weariness continued'.[22] John's speech to AFS delegates thus started with the gravity of the general situation since Japan's entry into the war; he spoke encouragingly of the members' contribution to the war effort through their productive work schemes. Then to the problem of the shift system.

It must be frankly admitted that in spite of the nation-wide campaign, in spite of press publicity which far exceeded anything that we had achieved even in the Charter Campaign, in spite of the support of many Members of Parliament, the Minister of Home Security [Morrison] has decided to institute the 48/24 system.

He urged that notwithstanding this setback, it should not mean they slackened their commitment to winning the war; unhappily, as they were well aware, there were Union members who were not pulling their weight. There was too much 'Sunday sickness' and a negative attitude among the rank and file. 'We have got to make them understand what this war is all about.' Grumbling must stop.

> Our duty is to see that, even within what we may regard as the restricting limits placed upon us by the Home Office, our activities and energies are spent in making this Service the hundred per cent, efficient Service which the people of this country and our Allies have the right to expect. Everything we discuss here is over-ridden by the necessity of winning this war.[23]

In May 1940 John had been at the meeting of trade union leaders when addressed by Ernie Bevin on being made Minister of Labour in Churchill's new coalition government. Bevin had said,

> I have to ask you to place yourselves at the disposal of the state. We are socialists and this is the test of our socialism … if our movement and our class rise with all our energy now and save the people of this country from disaster, the country will always turn with confidence to the people who saved them.[24]

And despite the Communist Party's opposition to an 'imperialist war', John had been proud enough when the London Fire Brigade fire boat, the *Massey Shaw*, had ferried troops to safety from the beaches of Dunkirk. He may have remembered Bevin's words when he appealed in Leeds for an all-out effort – however angry his members might be with Herbert Morrison. John was learning that many of them appeared to care more about their sectional interests than saving their country.

Unlike his earlier success at Union conferences – and despite the communist presence in much of the Union – John failed at Leeds to bring the majority around to his point of view. If Bob Darke is right, FBU members may have felt that John had been too busy campaigning about a Second Front to win the Union's campaign for improved hours. Conference voted against the Executive Council and instructed the leadership to continue campaigning over the shift system.[25] The disaffection was not unique to the Fire Brigades Union. Shop-floor militants in the strategic engineering sector disliked the Communist Party's pro-management and pro-productivist position. If it were any consolation for John, even Pollitt's oratory failed to convince the engineers.[26]

Nine months later, the Germans were in retreat in the Soviet Union, the allies had landed in Italy and Stalin was still asking for an immediate opening of a Second Front in France. Once more, the Communist Party required the matter to be debated and voted upon at that year's TUC. John's delight in telling a good story momentarily overcomes his memoir's circumspection about his relations with the Party and he allows Harry Pollitt to make his one and only appearance – in the urinals of Southport's conference hall.

The press had doubted that Congress could be persuaded to depart from its long-held position that 'the time and place of any large-scale military operations on the Continent must be determined not by popular clamour, but by the Allied Governments'.[27] In response, John was selected by the Communist Party leadership to move an amendment to the General Council's resolution urging that the government, 'which in 1942 recognised the urgency of the second front should now implement its pledge'.[28] And although it was unlikely that the amendment would be passed, he believed the debate 'might be the sharpest yet'. This then, was the setting for high drama.

On the morning of the day in which the debate was to take place, the massive form of Ernie Bevin lurched unannounced onto the platform. A member of the War Cabinet, he took his seat alongside Walter Citrine. A while later, the two left the platform together. By the time delegates began to stray from their seats for their coffee or mid-morning drink, wild rumours were circulating that something 'was up'. Bevin's unscheduled visit had added to the speculation. Indeed, it seemed that it had sparked off the rumours ....

Just before the lunch break, Citrine returned to the platform – without Bevin – to tell the conference breaking news about a full-scale amphibian allied operation on the coast between Dunkirk and Boulogne. 'Congress went mad. So, the Second Front was finally on!' No one wanted to leave the hall as cheer after cheer, in which the General Council and Citrine joined enthusiastically, shook the ceiling.

Papers were thrown in the air, hardened class warriors embraced each other. When we finally emerged on the street, the bells of the Parish Church next door, silent for three years since the threat of invasion, were ringing full peals.

And yet ... It was not on the one o'clock news bulletin. 'We told ourselves that perhaps the TUC had been privileged to learn the news before general release'. Or was there a mistake, the 'amphibian operations', no more than a large-scale exercise? What was he to think? John was due to move the

Second Front amendment immediately after lunch. If the news were true, his amendment would be superfluous.

Pollitt would have been watching the scene from the visitors' gallery and it must be assumed John had pre-arranged with him a signal should they urgently need to consult – the venue, the gentlemen's urinals.

> Standing next to me in the stalls was Harry Pollitt .... For a year or so we had been working closely together in the Second Front campaign. I asked him, was this the real thing? Delphic as ever in oracular statements, Pollitt answered, 'Bevin didn't come all this way just to say hello to Citrine'.[29]

Meanwhile, the Conference Arrangements Committee was insisting that the amendment be withdrawn, it having been overtaken by events. 'This was no time for divisions in Congress', they told John. So, after lunch, he stood at the rostrum and told Congress that in the light of Citrine's statement he was withdrawing the amendment. The General Council's resolution was thus approved unanimously with no amendments to be debated and voted upon. As Citrine and the General Council had wished, it demonstrated to the Soviet delegation in the visitors' gallery how the British trade union movement stood united behind its government. And by the evening, John had learnt there was no Second Front; it had been no more than a large-scale exercise.

Next morning, the *Daily Worker* trumpeted its outrage – 'TUC Council Gets Away with Second Front Dodge' – accusing Citrine of having deliberately hoaxed Congress, of preventing a discussion 'of the greatest issue before the British people'.[30] John's memoir disagrees with the *Worker*'s conclusion. 'The most methodical, over-cautious of bureaucrats, punctilious in procedure and detail', Citrine was too straight to indulge in such tricks. So how did he make such a blunder? John's account of Bevin's unexpected visit to the conference hints at Citrine having been fed fake news.

According to Kevin Morgan, Pollitt's biographer, the British Communist Party leadership was obsessed with not disclosing internal differences.[31] Hence, John may never have known of the repercussions of Bevin's hoax, as reported by a state intelligence service mole in Party headquarters in King Street. The Political Bureau had asked Pollitt to account for how the Fire Brigades Union's amendment had been withdrawn without a vote. According to Rust, Palme Dutt and others, it had been a great mistake because it gave the impression of the collapse of trade union support for the Party. Pollitt replied that he took entire responsibility for what had happened and if he said anything afterwards about it to John, the memoir does not tell.[32]

Notes

1   TUC Report for 1939, 290.
2   Geoffrey Roberts, 'The Soviet Decision for a Pact with Nazi Germany', *Soviet Studies*, 1992, 44, 1, 57–78.

3 *Daily Herald*, 18 September 1939.
4 Kevin Morgan, *Harry Pollitt*, Manchester, 1993, 108 ff.
5 Kevin Morgan, *Against Fascism and War: ruptures and continuities in British Communist politics, 1935–41*, Manchester, 1989, 219.
6 Eric Hobsbawm, *Interesting Times, A Twentieth Century Life*, London, 2002.
7 Douglas Hyde, *I Believed, The Autobiography of a Former British Communist*, London, 1952, 68.
8 Winston Churchill broadcast on 'The Home Service Programme' (BBC radio), 9 pm, 22 June 1941.
9 Andrew Thorpe, 'Locking out the communists. The Labour Party and the Communist Party, 1939–46', *Twentieth Century History*, 2014, 25, 2, 230–31; Eric Hobsbawm, *Interesting Times, A Twentieth Century Life*, London, 2002, 163.
10 Victor Bailey, 'The early history of the Fire Brigades Union', in ed. Victor Bailey, *Forged in Fire*, London, 1992, 65 ff.
11 John Horner, *Studies in Industrial Democracy*, London, 1974, 171–173.
12 *Firefighter*, July 1942.
13 For Pollitt's performance at this rally, see Morgan 1993, 131.
14 Hyde, 183.
15 Morgan 1993, 148.
16 The transcript is available at http://libcom.org/library/2nd-world-congress-comintern-syndicalism-party.
17 *DW*, 11 September 1942.
18 Bob Darke, *The Communist Technique in Britain*, London, 1952, 77.
19 *DW*, 9 November 1942; *Leicester Chronicle*, 14 November 1942.
20 Darke, 55.
21 House of Commons, 10 September 1942, UK Parliamentary Papers.
22 Mass Observation File Report 1481.
23 *Firefighter*, November 1942.
24 Quoted in Andrew Adonis, *Ernest Bevin, Labour's Churchill*, London, 2020, 186.
25 Bailey.
26 See James Eade and David Renton, *The Communist Party of Great Britain since 1920*, Basingstoke, 2002, Chapter 3; Morgan, 1993, Chapter 6.
27 *Birmingham Daily Post*, 7 September 1943.
28 *Belfast Newsletter*, 10 September 1943.
29 Pollitt's typical 'Delphic utterances' are overlooked by Pollitt's two biographers, Kevin Morgan and John Mahon.
30 *DW*, 10 September 1943; see also the *Reynold News* of 12 September 1939.
31 Kevin Morgan, 'Communist history, police history and the archives of British state surveillance', *Twentieth Century Communism*, 2019, 17, 67–89.
32 National Archives KV-2-1041. John's memoir notes that much later he read a published account of allied amphibian and air operations in September 1943 between Dunkirk and Boulogne designed to deceive the Germans into believing a major landing on the coast was imminent and thus disclose some of their fighting strength. But the Germans were not deceived – only the TUC.

15

'GO TO IT, HOUSEWIVES!'

By the time Pat returned from Aston in the summer of 1941 all her family had left Chingford. On his appointment as the FBU's Midlands organizer, Geoff had moved to Birmingham where Alice and Mavis joined him from Kirby Stephen. Her brother Ken's house in Chingford had meanwhile been badly damaged by a bomb and the family had moved away. Violet was now living in north London and had resumed her affair with Reg Latham. He had taken advantage of the Blitz to escape from his wife, volunteering as resident fire warden at his City office from where he had written his best-ever verses while London burnt around him. In March 1942, he left his wife and moved in with Violet. On behalf of them both she gave the news in a letter to the secretary of Friends Hall with whom they had shared many happy rambles. 'You will agree that under present circumstances, we must sever our connection with Friends Hall'. They hoped to return one day – 'For you know what the Hall has meant to both of us' and she apologized for 'the difficult situation in which we have placed you all'.[1]

I find no evidence of any reply to this sad, dignified letter: a collective failure by Friends Hall to acknowledge Reg and Violet's contribution to its work. Her letter mentions she had also explained the situation to the Quaker-run war victims relief programme for which she worked, 'So that if I stay, it will be with their knowledge and consent'. Once thus informed, they may have felt impelled to ask her to resign. The hurtful silence from Friends Hall and the loss of her job explains why Violet believed Quakers never forgave her for taking Reg away from his wife. Only Fred Parsons stayed in touch. When Arthur le Mare died later that year, he edited a small booklet of Friends Hall's memories of their former warden and invited contributions from Violet and Reg. Yet when Fred himself died in 1947, and a similar

DOI: 10.4324/9781032671352-16

booklet of appreciation was to be published, Violet and Reg appear not to have been approached. It was hard for Violet. Even in old age she hesitated attending her local Friends' Meeting in Hastings, fearing they would whisper behind her back about her illicit relationship.

When they started living openly together, Violet and Reg became outcastes from the institution and its social circle that had given friendship and meaning to their lives. Pat and John observed with compassion Violet's painful rupture from Friends Hall. It may have marked for Pat her final cutting of ties with the Quaker world to which her sister had introduced her. With Friends Hall having thus treated Violet, Pat no longer had any regrets for that lost world, while the departure of her parents and Mavis to Birmingham helped her make Chingford her own, to lead her life as she wished. She turned to the local Communist Party, another close-knit and dedicated society. Yet, she

FIGURE 15.1   Violet with Reg Latham (family album).

was to find them disappointingly dull compared with the remarkable people she had known in Hampstead. The exceptions were Pam and Frank Freeman, professional artists living in Chingford because of Frank's war-time job at the Lea Valley reservoirs. The Freemans were bohemian off-shoots from the British Raj, Pam's father a mining engineer in Mysore and Frank's the director of the Jamaican department of agriculture. After boarding school and art college, Pam became a stage designer and had met Frank at her local Left Book Club in west London where he was to photograph her painting an Aid Spain mural, unperturbed by the large crowd that surrounded her. Pat admired Pam's upper-middle-class confidence and self-assurance that she herself could never quite achieve. Attracted to Pam's intelligence, grace and kindness, Pat was both intrigued and dubious about the Freemans' rackety lifestyle, typified by Frank spending weekends in a dressing gown and Pam's avant-garde habit of drinking tea out of a mug. Lazier and professionally less successful than Pam, Frank had abandoned tea planting in Assam to join the circle of Eddie Marsh, Chelsea's wealthy patron of poets and painters. Yet, according to his biographer, despite Marsh paying for Frank to study in Paris, Frank had the dubious fame of being his only protégé who failed as a painter.[2]

The day after Pat's thirtieth birthday in August 1942, the government lifted the nineteen-month ban on the *Daily Worker*. She immediately walked round to the newsagent to place a regular order. The first issue, published two weeks later, coincided with the opening day of the annual conference of the Trades Union Congress (TUC) where John was to make his speech about the Second Front. Newsprint was rationed and only 100,000 copies of the resurrected *Worker* could be printed. Ignoring its injunction, 'Pass this to a Friend', Pat folded her copy twice, to fit neatly into the pigeon hole of their writing bureau where it was to remain until after her death. Did her decision to keep this issue reveal a determined optimism despite the *Worker* reporting a renewed attack on Stalingrad? Or that after the war was won, she could show her children this souvenir from the dark autumn days of 1942?

Only in late November did the country's mood finally lift and Mass Observation reported 'considerable cheerfulness and optimism'.[3] The *Daily Worker*'s sketch map of 7 December shows that while the battle for Stalingrad was not yet won, the Germans were now entirely encircled by Soviet troops. The same front page includes a report on another, new theatre of war, North Africa, where allied troops had landed, while page three covers Churchill's weekend speech in Bradford. 'It's been a great month' said Churchill, 'The struggle is approaching its most tense part'. And above all, 'We are engaging the enemy closely and not leaving undue burden to be borne by the Russians who have carried this immense struggle through the whole of this year and a large part of last year'. They are defending their country, he said, as we are ours but 'we are all defending something that is greater than country, namely a cause'.[4] Churchill's cause was to defeat Nazism but for many others there was a further cause: to build thereafter, a better, fairer Britain.

The Prime Minister had been disagreeably surprised when a government-commissioned report into the rationalization of social insurance schemes produced a detailed and inspiring vision of a post-war Britain. This same issue of the *Worker* on 7 December reports an over-flowing and enthusiastic public meeting where Sir William Beveridge explained how, his report's recommendations, if implemented, would eliminate want, disease, ignorance, squalor and idleness: a universal social insurance scheme to guarantee a national minimum income for all citizens in all life crises –sickness, unemployment, maternity, old age, industrial injury, loss of parents or spouse – plus special payments relating to birth, marriage and death. Importantly, the scheme would rely on the government to maintain full employment, provide family allowances and establish a national health service. Beveridge had brought together many ideas already in circulation and, as he mischievously told a *Daily Telegraph* reporter, his proposals 'would take the country half-way to Moscow'.[5] When the Soviet Union and Britain had become allies in July 1941, Eric Hobsbawm recalled how communists had 're-joined the masses of ordinary citizens' but it was in December 1942, that Pat's ordinariness reached its apogee: eighty-six per cent of her fellow citizens shared her enthusiasm for the Beveridge Report.[6]

Despite Beveridge's report going only half-way to Moscow, the *Daily Worker* declared its support – although, of course, 'It leaves quite untouched the private ownership of production and the power of the big capitalist monopolies, which are the basic causes of economic crises'.[7] Nevertheless, an excellent start and all progressive opinion would endorse it while expecting resistance from vested interests – private insurance firms – that must be overcome. The *Worker*'s cartoonist, Gabriel, sketched the 'vested interests' lined up at the bus stop on Beveridge Road away from the worst evils of society. The top-hatted individual leaning against the bus stop, tells the worker that he must take his place in the queue. But the worker has a priority ticket and he's not going to let the vested interests stop him from catching the Beveridge bus. Gabriel's muscular male worker was not the only person happy. So were the housewives, absent from this cartoon.[8]

A firewoman, Mrs Privett opened the afternoon session of a special FBU conference organized to discuss the report. Referring to Beveridge's proposals relating to maternity costs, and the provision of paid assistance to housewives with disabilities, she said that for the first time women were considered as something more 'than a piece of furniture of married life'.[9] Pat was as excited as Mrs Privett that the Beveridge Report recognized 'housewife' as an occupational status with her own rights and needs. As a preliminary to eventual legislation of Beveridge's recommendations, a junior minister in the coalition government was put in charge of drawing up a White Paper. The proposals for family allowances having been accepted, he asked the TUC for their views as to whether these should be paid to the father or mother of the children, noting that, whereas there was less danger of the allowance being misused if paid to the mother, this might undermine the father's sense of responsibility for his children.[10] The TUC concluded payment should go to the mother to reduce the risk of depressing the father's wages that might be the consequence of family allowances. The committee drafting the White Paper was less convinced: a separate income for the wife risked undermining the family.[11]

Although the Communist Party does not appear to have taken a line on the matter, Pat knew what she wanted. She supported the housewives' associations and women parliamentarians who lobbied hard and eventually succeeded in changing the draft legislation so that when family allowances were introduced in 1945, they were paid to the mother. The state's weekly payment re-confirmed her autonomy and her value to society. That is what 'Beveridge' was to mean to her and why she was to so frequently speak about it to her daughters.

Child care did not interest the male leadership of the Communist Party and there was no Party line on how to raise children. Like many non-communist, mothers, Pat had religiously followed Truby King's prescription of by-the-clock breast-feeding and no night feeds. Happily, life for toddlers was not so grim. They were prescribed plenty of play, lots of fresh air and regular, early bedtimes.[12] Carol was later to comment that she wished her mother had not worked quite so hard at bringing her up according to the book.

At the start of the war, women members of the Communist Party had been a small minority and most of them were housewives married to other communists.[13] The *Daily Worker* addressed their home-keeping concerns in a weekly women's page. It would not have attracted Pat. She lacked the manual dexterity for sewing or handicrafts and her interest in cooking was largely utilitarian. Until it was banned in early 1941, other than some articles about how much better was life for women and children in the Soviet Union, the *Worker* had rarely examined women's status in society. Most socialists were suspicious of feminism; demands for women's rights were considered a bourgeois and irrelevant distraction from the working-class struggle. Improvement in women's lives would be a natural consequence of a classless society, as had happened in the Soviet Union where women enjoyed equality with men. All this ignoring the predominantly male leadership in politics and industry and disregarding how Soviet women came home from a full day of work at the factory or collective farm to do the shopping, cooking and cleaning without her husband's help.

FIGURE 15.2   The Horner Family, December 1942 (family album).

It was much the same in Britain, except that until the war, most married women stayed at home.[14] Men's sharing the housework was not an issue for public discussion and John was exceptional in helping when he could. First, the Merchant Navy and then the Fire Service had taught him how to wash the dishes, make beds, mend, clean and polish. On rare weekends at home, he helped with these chores while on Sunday afternoons took out the ironing board and pressed his suit ready for his next trip away from home.

There had been long episodes in Carol's short life when she had scarcely seen her father and even after their reunion in the summer of 1941, paternal cuddles had remained a rare treat, with John so much away from home visiting his membership. The picture of Carol with both her parents was taken around her fourth birthday, Christmas 1942 (Figure 15.2). By now Pat had fully recovered from her near-fatal illness in 1939. That she had been unable to follow the doctors' advice to lead 'a quiet life free from anxiety' is evidenced by the cigarette that smoulders in her left hand as she looks over John's shoulder at their daughter sitting on his lap.

Carol was now old enough to go to a kindergarten allowing Pat to work part-time at the National Institute of Industrial Psychology (NIIP), the first time she had a paid job since her marriage. Compared with the working environments Pat had known before the friendly, egalitarian atmosphere in the institute's offices in Welbeck Street had come as an agreeable surprise. NIIP practised what it preached to its clients. Productivity came from making any job as interesting as possible. The mid-morning coffee break in Welbeck Street brought all the staff together, allowing secretaries to listen to and even ask questions to the researchers as they discussed their work. And the institute's research reports and correspondence were infinitely more interesting than the routine business letters Pat used to type in City offices.

Women's part-time work such as Pat's had become increasingly acceptable to employers, as did work outsourced to home.[15] Although useless at any task requiring manual dexterity, Pat was a good organizer and became 'Production Secretary' for the Chingford Housewives Club, a scheme clearly modelled on the Fire Brigades Union joint production units at fire stations. The Club organized housewives to assemble bolts for clamps for 'multi-airline seats' – payment, two shillings a bag of one hundred completed bolts. Detailed instructions for the assembly process are set out in a document typed by Pat. These instructions are followed by a headline, IMPORTANT. 'This scheme is a cooperative non-profit-making endeavour, having as its sole object the increase of production for the war effort. All workers at the depot will be paid at the same rate as workers engaged on assembly'. It is explained that accounts will be regularly published and that the scheme had the approval of the Ministry of Production. While typing her note on assembling airplane widgets, Pat must have been listening to the wireless because she added an NB: 'Saturday July 10th. News has just come through of the invasion of Sicily. Go to it, housewives, and help our boys to finish the job!'[16]

War-time housewives' clubs came in many varieties. Some were offspring from the government-approved Women's Voluntary Service or were supported by the Ministries of Food or Education; others were grassroots initiatives for housewives 'to make and mend', exchange recipes or make up parcels for prisoners of war.[17] Others were more political: Banstead Housewives Club was organized 'to contribute to the general war effort' and 'to meet from time to time to discuss war problems which seemed to be most troublesome' and they lobbied their council for hot school meals and a nursery.[18] Hammersmith housewives knitted 'for the forces' but also had wider concerns; an invited speaker told them about her work with the Committee for the Relief of Victims against Fascism and, in August 1941, they had urged the borough council to call for 'immediate aid to our Russian allies'.[19] Like Hampstead, Hammersmith had had a vibrant pre-war Aid Spain movement and much of its local organizing depended on communist housewives like Pat who had enrolled less politicized women to provide practical help to Republican Spain and then gradually brought them around to thinking strategically about how to make a better world. These same communist housewives would have been the moving spirits in some, if not many, of London's numerous wartime housewives' clubs that served as the Party's recruiting agents.

On an autumn Sunday in 1941, hundreds of women assembled at the Phoenix Theatre to meet two Russian women flown in from Moscow. The visitors thanked the meeting for its promise of more tanks, planes and guns and for 'the cigarettes, chocolate, soap, toothpaste and balaclava helmets, gloves and pullovers collected and knitted by women in Co-op guilds and housewives clubs all over London'.[20] Along with Mrs Clary of Highgate and Mrs Greenberg of Hackney mentioned in this newspaper report, I imagine that Mrs Horner and Mrs Freeman from Chingford also shook hands with the two Russian women: factory worker, Mrs Galubka and housewife, Mrs Chichaeva.

The Phoenix Theatre meeting was timed as a warm-up to the following week's assembly of the London Women's Parliament meeting for the second time to pass an emergency resolution calling for an immediate Second Front. It also discussed the problems of communal feeding, children being left in danger areas, ineffective mobilization of women into industry 'and the fact that British women should not be demanding better rations for Christmas in view of the awful trials now being suffered by the women of Russia'. Most of Britain's handful of women MPs welcomed the initiative. They addressed the Women's Parliament meetings and brought back to the House of Commons the issues raised there.[21] The press reported the regular meetings of the Women's Parliament and its principal demands: equal pay and day nurseries. Party members were among the organizers and, according to state intelligence, the moving spirit was Tamara Rust (see Figure 14.1) who drafted its published report. In 1944, Rust persuaded the Party leadership to establish a Women's National Advisory Committee and a magazine, *Woman Today*, to which Pat was regularly to contribute.

The Women's Parliament – and presumably Chingford's Housewives' Club – followed the model of the Women's World Committee Against War and Fascism, a pre-war Communist front organization that had attracted a broader group of women. As in Hammersmith and Banstead, the Housewives' Club in Chingford sought to raise political awareness by facilitating discussion about 'troublesome' war problems. Pat was to recall how at one of these meetings, someone made an anti-Semitic remark and others nodded their agreement. A typical comment making the rounds was, 'Hitler did at least one good thing in turning out the Jews' and Pat would have read the *Daily Worker* report of how a Mrs Reuben had brought a successful civil action for assault against her neighbour, Mrs Linden who had attempted to throw pepper in her eyes, 'the accumulation of a large number of incidents in which

Mrs Linden … had made a series of Jew-baiting and pro-Hitler remarks'. Now Pat found herself in a group who were echoing prejudices that had led to the merciless slaughter of women and children in occupied Europe. Surely it couldn't be that her neighbours were unaware of where their words could lead? What to do? How could she bring them to their senses? 'Every worker must make it his serious individual responsibility to see to it that no anti-Jewish statement is allowed to pass without challenge' insisted William Gallacher, Britain's only Communist MP.[22] Yet she feared a direct challenge might make them defensive. Because it was not uncommon at that time to describe people as having a 'Jewish appearance', Pat decided her brown eyes and dark hair might convince the others of her fabricated Jewishness; at the very least it might make them realize that Jews were ordinary people like them. She looked around at the circle of women, 'I think, you should know, I am Jewish', she said.

August the twenty-fifth, 1943, and Pat's thirty-first birthday. The resurrected *Daily Worker* is just a year old. It is grumbling about the meeting between Roosevelt and Churchill in Quebec where they had failed to discuss the Second Front while the *Worker*'s daily sketch map shows the Red Army's advancing to reclaim the Donets coalfield from the retreating German forces. Meanwhile, on page two, 'Engels is exciting': *Anti-Duhring* has been re-printed and the *Worker*'s book reviewer declares it 'One of the most readable of Engels' works'. Pat and John always gave each other a book for their birthdays and that year it was Jane Austen rather than Engels that he gave her.

Page three of the *Worker* reports John's successful FBU fusion conference. That evening, Pat was to be a guest at the closing dinner to hear Herbert Morrison's barbed jokes about her husband, to shake hands with William Beveridge and to meet the first woman president of the TUC, Dame Anne Loughlin. In commenting on Pat's presence that night, John's memoir reflects on the stress and loneliness she had endured while he was building a trade union.

> Separation was then the lot of millions of women and Pat was ever conscious that for many of them it would be separation for as long as the war was to last. She never forgot that for too many it was to be forever. Shortages and rationing were everybody's worry and not to be complained of against the plight of the people in Nazi-occupied Europe and of devastated Russia.

By August 1943, the FBU was firmly established as a unitary organization, Pat was full of energy and the allies were winning the war. The time had come to celebrate. It was probably Frank Freeman who photographed Pat and John at their most relaxed. A hot summer's day somewhere in Epping

FIGURE 15.3   A summer day in Epping Forest, 1943 (family album).

Forest, beside a stream. Pam Freeman would have been keeping an eye on Carol and her own little Sally; she must have smiled at Pat, as if to say, 'Go on, have fun'.

Looking straight at the camera, John lets his right hand move up under Pat's skirt; she laughs, turns away from the camera, tries to push his hand off her leg. Yet, not so embarrassed that she was to throw the photo away. By the end of the year, they were expecting their second child.

Notes

1 Friends Hall Archives, WFLRO.
2 Christopher Hassall, *Edward Marsh, Patron of the Arts*: A Biography, London, 1959, 551.
3 Mass Observation File Report 1481.
4 *Daily Worker (DW)*, 7 December 1942.
5 Nigel Calder, *The People's War, Britain 1939–45*, London, 1971, 609.
6 Robert Mackay, *Half the battle. Civilian morale in Britain during the Second World War*, Manchester, 2018.
7 *DW*, 7 December 1942.
8 *DW*, 7 December 1942.
9 *Firefighter*, March 1943.
10 From official minutes of the meeting cited in Jeremy Colwill, 'Beveridge, women and the welfare state', *Critical Social Policy*, 1994, 53–78 (66).

11 Colwill, 67.

12 Mabel Liddiard, *The Mothercraft Manual*, Tenth Edition, London, 1940.

13 Tricia Davis, 'Women and Communist Party Politics', *Feminism, Culture, and Politics*, ed. by Rosalind Brunt and Caroline Rowan, London, 1982, 85–106.

14 For more about women communists, including several known to Pat, see Kevin Morgan, 'True Sons of the Working Class', in eds. Kevin Morgan, Gideon Cohen and Andrew Flinn, *Communists and British Society, 1920–1991*, London, 2007, 143–184.

15 Penny Sommerfield, *Women Workers in the Second World War*, London, 2012.

16 Typed document among Pat's papers.

17 *Derby Daily Telegraph*, 2 December 1942; *Yorkshire Post*, 30 May 1942; *Worthing Herald*, 12 November 1943.

18 Delegate's report back to Banstead Housewives Club, *Surrey Mirror*, 7 November 1941.

19 *West London Observer*, 20 March 1942; 2 May 1941; 29 August 1941.

20 *Daily Herald*, 20 October 1941.

21 Martine Stirling, 'Women's parliaments in the Second World War', *Women's History Magazine*, 2013, 72, 19–29.

22 Gallacher, William, 'Anti-Semitism: What it means to you', pamphlet, 1943, 23.

16

'DARE TO MAKE IT KNOWN'

Eight months into Pat's pregnancy, Hitler launched a new weapon. When a 'flying bomb' ran out of fuel, its engine cut out. For those below, the silence presaged death. One hit a trolley bus on the main road close to John's mother's, killing thirty-eight people. Another exploded mid-morning near Walthamstow High Street, full of shoppers. London fire crews were busy again and John was out many evenings in a repeat of his Blitz-time visits to emergency fire and ambulance stations. And, once more, Londoners fled their homes, heading northwards beyond the enemy's range. Five-year-old Carol embarked on her third evacuation; this time without her mother, travelling with aunt and cousins to stay with their grandparents in Birmingham. Pat had chosen to remain in Chingford. The strain of the journey, uncertainty about availability of maternity care in Birmingham at such short notice and the overcrowding in her parents' home made the flying bombs the lesser evil.

The first to hit Chingford exploded close to Carol's kindergarten. Four people died and Pat changed her mind, phoned her mother in Birmingham and packed a suitcase. Despite the Government encouraging 'voluntary evacuation' it would be another six weeks before it was to allow the railway companies to put on extra trains to facilitate an orderly departure.[1] Meanwhile, there was chaos. At Euston Station, John carved out a path through the concourse congested with people, all too desperate to leave London to make way for a heavily pregnant woman. On reaching the train, they found every seat taken and the corridors jammed with passengers and luggage. Perhaps the guard might let Pat into his van? They found others there before them, the van tightly packed with standing passengers, apart from one young man

DOI: 10.4324/9781032671352-17

sitting on a box. At John's entreaty, he grudgingly conceded his makeshift seat to Pat for the price of one sovereign, almost a quarter of John's weekly wage. 'So much for the Blitz spirit', Pat was to tell Geoff when she collapsed into her father's arms at Birmingham's Snow Hill Station.

Now safely at his grandparents, the baby refused to leave the womb. Poor thing, they said. No wonder, so stressed by the flying bombs and then by the nightmare journey. Pat declared he was refusing to enter such a frightful world, believing it safer to stay inside her womb. As she had feared, there was no room at the local maternity hospital and she would have to pay for a midwife and an expensive room in a squalid, private nursing home. Three long weeks after the due date, the baby arrived, and not the boy for whom they had already chosen a name. What to call her? Casting around for inspiration, Pat's eye landed on the volume she had brought with her into the nursing home and decided on a Shakespearean heroine, her favourite since seeing a performance of *As You Like It* at Walthamstow High School. She told John her choice in a telegram, requesting he send her a postal order. 'Winter garments must be lined/So must gentle Rosalind'. John made a flying visit to Birmingham to meet his daughter, but Pat was desperate to get back to Chingford, her parents' house too small to accommodate comfortably five adults, three children and a baby. The cousins played together well enough; Mavis described them in a letter to Violet as a 'happy band of pilgrims'. Yet the children's mothers had never liked each other. It needed Alice's tact and Mavis' cheeriness to reduce the chilly tension between Pat and her brother Ken's wife.

There has survived the second page only of a letter from John, dissuading Pat from coming home. The missing page must have described an occurrence that 'amply demonstrates', John writes, 'the wisdom of staying away a little longer. We would be so sorry if you came home and after a bang or so and one or two disturbed nights both you and little Rosalind began to feel the effects'. The 'occurrence' must have been John's near miss from death when a flying bomb fell at the top of Hawkwood Crescent as he was on the way to bed. John's letter to Pat concludes by reminding her of their good fortune, 'We never seem to have any money – but while we have each other, two lovely children and a not <u>too</u> untidy house, we have nothing really to concern us unduly'. Imagine, he tells her, if he were in the army in Burma. Nevertheless, there were concerns, and decisions to make that needed discussing yet too sensitive for him to broach in a letter intercepted and read by the state intelligence services. Should he stay with the FBU and go public about his Communist Party membership – or stand as a Labour candidate in the forthcoming General Election?

By November 1944, the allied victory was well into view. The last German troops had retreated from Soviet soil, pursued westwards by the Red Army;

on the western front, the allies were fast approaching the Rhine. Auxiliary firemen had begun to return to peacetime occupations; and the Home Office spoke of abolishing the National Fire Service, of handing the fire brigades back to local authorities. Now there would be the less exhilarating responsibility of managing the union's re-organization; peacetime shrinkage by the end of 1944 was already underway with the membership down to 42,000, almost half from two years before. It was projected to halve again in 1945 and he would have known his standing in the TUC and his wider political influence would shrink with the reduction.

Five and a half years had passed since John had been pitched into the leadership of a tiny, inward-looking Fire Brigades Union of just over three thousand members. War had immediately disrupted his members' ways of working when thousands of men (and women!) from all backgrounds and social classes had flooded into the fire stations. The auxiliaries had cheerfully questioned cherished tradition and worse, employed on inferior conditions of service, they risked undermining regular firemen's professional standing and conditions of service. Although initially most regulars wanted nothing to do with them within three years John had secured the auxiliaries' full incorporation into a unitary Fire Brigades Union and had won standardized and improved conditions for all, regulars and auxiliaries alike. How had he done it?

Victor Bailey, the union's historian, refers to John's courage, of his 'bravely entering the lion's den' of the regular firefighters, listening to their anger and telling them why they must accept the auxiliaries into their union.[2] Bailey's biblical allusion brings to mind a Baptist Chapel hymn John sang while polishing the family's furniture –

Dare to be a Daniel,
Dare to stand alone
Dare to have a purpose firm
Dare to make it known.

John's success in converting lions into comrades – or brothers – owed much to his sensitivity to the cultural divide between insular, quasi-sectarian working-class regulars and the auxiliary firefighters from a wide diversity of background and social class. He had become a trade union leader after a decade of employment in a disciplined service – first the Merchant Navy, then the London Fire Brigade – where he had learnt not to defer to people in authority unless they demonstrated they knew more than he about the matter on hand: thus, he ignored Citrine's advice to let the auxiliaries fend for themselves. Instead, he had looked for mentors to guide him on matters beyond his still limited experience: Major Hooper from Hampstead on strategy; Thompson on trade union law and workers' legal rights; Harry

Pollitt on campaigning. Later, he came to rely on John Burns, long-serving East Ham fireman and the union's President, to tell him hard truths – as in a photograph of them together taken some years after the war (Figure 16.1).

John was good at making friends and allies within officialdom. He had quickly established a relationship of trust with Major Jackson, London Fire Brigade's Commanding Officer, and with Bevin's secretary in the Ministry of Labour, whose brother had been invalided out of the fire service. 'There came a time', he writes, 'when I would tell Miss Saunders certain thing knowing that the member of the War Cabinet whom she served so loyally, might perchance hear of them'. Friendly and approachable, he listened well; people enjoyed talking with him. When they met again, he would have remembered their face and what they had spoken about – although not so good at recalling their name. Above all, he had fast learnt how to negotiate – the essential skill of any successful trade union leader.

Perhaps his most serious shortcoming was impulsiveness – the flip side to being decisive. And although his Nelsonian turning of a blind-eye had brilliant consequences for the expansion of the Fire Brigades Union, it had

FIGURE 16.1   Taking advice from FBU President, John Burns (family album).

also caused serious difficulties with the fire service regulars; should he have been less persuasive at its annual conference in 1940, the union might have foundered. John would have to learn he could not always rely on charisma to get his way. His increasing self-assurance is exemplified by the evolution of his signature in fly-leaves of his books. In 1934, the signature cautiously squeezes itself into the edge; by 1937, it lays claim to more of the page; in 1942 the signature of a former owner, obliges him to move to a more central position; where thereafter it remains. By 1944, a free-flowing joined-up signature owns the whole page. John is now ready to branch out, to take on other, possibly greater challenges in the wider ambit of British politics.

The wartime coalition government in Britain was drawing towards its end; the country was warming up for a General Election, the first for ten years. The

FIGURE 16.2   'Hands Off Greece' Rally (announcement in *Daily Mirror*, 16 December 1944).

left of the Labour Party was sympathetic to Communist Party calls for working-class unity and despite the Labour Party Conference having rejected its application to affiliate, John hoped the two parties could work together. Historian Andrew Thorpe observes that the FBU was 'particularly persistent' in arguing for 'progressive electoral unity', whereby Communists and Labour candidates would not compete in the same constituency.[3] Several left-leaning Labour Party branches asked John if he would be their candidate, and not just because of his successful leadership of the Fire Brigades Union. He had become known as a lively, passionate public speaker and had made recent headlines by organizing a mass rally to protest at Churchill's dispatching of troops to Athens that prevented Communist-led resistance fighters from forming a new government in Greece; many Labour supporters had joined the crowd in Trafalgar Square at one of wartime's biggest demonstrations.[4]

Although Pat afterwards hinted she had hoped that John might go into Parliament, this may have been what she thought later, after things started going wrong in the Communist Party. At the time, it would have been difficult for them to talk it over at length. 'Pat's cooler judgement and innate good sense saved me from many a blunder', John writes in his memoir. Yet, with her in Birmingham and he in London, how could she advise him, knowing that the security services opened his mail and listened into the telephone?

He may have hesitated to go into Parliament because Labour's tripartite leadership of Attlee, Morrison and Bevin was strongly anti-communist and unless John were to have changed from deeper red to paler pink, his chances of a ministerial post would have been minimal, leaving him to waste his leadership talents on the back benches. It is more likely that Pollitt persuaded him to stay with the FBU: an additional, sympathetic MP would not compensate for the loss of a strong and popular leader in one of the few communist-controlled trade unions. Many of the FBU's leading communists, like Bob Darke, were auxiliary firefighters, due to leave the fire service as it shrank to peacetime staffing levels; and although John's potential communist replacement, Jack Grahl, was respected by the membership, Grahl had never been a regular fireman and might have lacked credibility in an election for the general secretary's post. So if John were not to go into Parliament, was not the time ripe to go public about his Communist Party membership? 'To dare to have a purpose firm/to dare to make it known'?

He was never to provide a clear account of his political history. He told Terry Segars that when first elected as the FBU's general secretary, he was beginning to 'flirt' with the Communist Party.[5] Yet, his letter to *Friendship* shows him firmly committed to the Party from as early as 1935. He may have chosen to remain a fellow traveller on Len Bradley's advice and because of the TUC's black circular in 1934 that banned Communist Party members from representing their unions on local Trades Councils. There was no barrier however to Pat joining the Communist Party and she was evidently active in both the Hampstead and Chingford branches. In a chapter of the memoir excised from his final draft, John explains in a single sentence that he had first flirted with the Communist Party, then became a fellow traveller before finally joining, initially as an undercover member. Hence, a possible scenario is that John was a fellow traveller until July 1941 when Harry Pollitt returned as the Party's general secretary and deciding that John needed a firmer steer than W.H. Thompson could provide, invited John to become a secret member.

In February 1945, the *Daily Worker* published an exchange of letters between Horner and Pollitt; John's is a letter of application to join the Communist Party.

> It seems to me that Labour and progressive unity is more than ever essential. Only a united Labour movement can properly tackle problems that will face the British people after the war, and your party alone seems to be making this its main aim.[6]

Like many British communists, John expected the Party to be a significant partner in his country's socialist reconstruction within a post-war world of peaceful international relations dominated by 'progressive' values. That November, he became a member of the Communist Party's Executive Committee. According to a Special Branch informant, allegedly a close contact of Pollitt, the Party was expecting a rapid expansion in Party membership among trade union leaders and that having thus secured control of the Labour Party, 'the Communist Party had an even chance of being elected to power in the not too distant future'.[7] If John had believed this, he overlooked how many on the left did not want communists as partners.

The politician and journalist, John Strachey had been closely associated with the Communist Party for ten years until breaking with them in 1940. Strachey explained he had 'not abandoned socialism but could not understand how British communists deplored totalitarianism in Germany while ignoring the unquestionable existence of Soviet totalitarianism .... They pretend it is not there'.[8] Did John ever read this? He certainly did not turn Strachey into a non-person. He later chose *The Coming Struggle for Power* as his contribution to a pamphlet published in 1943 wherein leading communists and fellow travellers discussed books that had influenced them. 'After 10 years or so the book may date. Possibly I disagree now with much that I hailed then with enthusiasm. I have since read more penetrating, less superficial analyses of the nature of the coming capitalist crisis', but 'I have kept my copy as one of my favourite books'.[9] It seems that in 1943 John had not been over-bothered by Strachey's remarks that the Soviet Union's citizens were 'paying a frightful price for totalitarianism'.[10]

John's memoir explains he chose 'not to join the class of "45" in the post-war Parliament of Labour's landslide victory', for to have done so would have meant deserting the FBU that was moving into deep crisis with two-thirds of its membership leaving the fire service. There was talk of amalgamation between the public sector unions that had worked closely together during the war, and he may have hoped this would give him the chance of leading a bigger union.[11] But such conversations soon fizzled out, leaving John the difficult task of steering a much-reduced union into choppy, peacetime waters. Without a large membership behind him, he must have had gloomy thoughts about his reduced power to stand up to Herbert Morrison. But he was lucky. Morrison became Deputy Prime Minister in the new Labour Government, to be replaced as Home Secretary by the emollient Chuter Ede from a trade union background. The *Firefighter* rejoiced in describing the new Home Secretary as 'friendly, frank and cooperative' and Ede invited the FBU to sit on the Home Office advisory committee drafting the legislation to return fire service management to the local authorities.[12]

When a year after the war ended, John stood for the first time for re-election as General Secretary, he was opposed by Harry Short, the union's non-communist assistant general secretary who in 1942 had resigned on the grounds of ill health.[13] When they had first met at the union's annual conferences in 1936 and 1937, John had been impressed by the older man's love of books and his knowledge of Marxist theory. Yet, Harry's interest in firefighting seemed slight and, as assistant general secretary, he lacked the energy and flair John looked for in a work-mate and had found in Peter Pain, the union's AFS national organizer whom John remembered with affection and admiration. After Pain returned to his law career at the end of the war, John never again had a colleague who could match his own intellect, energy and warmth.

When he stood against the incumbent in 1946, Short won a third of the votes.[14] It was more than one might have expected, bearing in mind John's standing. Short had possibly attracted votes from members unhappy that John Horner was a self-declared communist. A few months later, Chick Merrells, the union's non-communist assistant general secretary resigned, also on the grounds of ill health, to be replaced by the FBU national organizer Jack Grahl, elected unopposed. Strangely, without their knowledge or consent, both Burns and Short had been nominated as candidates for this post and by the time their names had been withdrawn, it appears it was too late to nominate others.[15] Like his contemporary, Johnny Gollan, the Communist Party's assistant general secretary, Grahl had grown up in Edinburgh and from the photographs of Grahl in the *Firefighter*, he seemingly shared Gollan's 'lean and hungry look'. Bob Darke may have been alluding to Grahl in his description of the union's wartime national organizer as a 'young man so well indoctrinated with Marxism that he used to talk to himself … an ambitious and ruthless man, chain smoker and a bundle of nerves'.[16]

Lonely from the departure of Peter Pain, John more than ever sought counsel and support from Pat, who finally returned to Chingford in March 1945. Her sister Mavis was already ill from viral hepatitis caught while working as a nurse in an isolation hospital, and within months Pat returned to Birmingham for the funeral. Mavis had died on the very eve of the General Election that delivered a massive victory for the Labour Party. The Horners and Palmers were from a class and a generation that kept their grief to themselves; when John's father wept over his son's death, he did it alone among his chicken coops. After Mavis' funeral, a fellow passenger on the train back to London, kindly enquired why Pat was crying. She told him what a lovely, kind and funny girl her sister had been, she spoke of her anger at Mavis' death, how unfair it was that she should die just when peace arrived. When the train pulled into Euston, she thanked him for listening to her, did not ask his name, and went home to her children. 'Only to a stranger who I would never see again could I speak about how I felt', she was to tell me.

The Second World War ended on what would have been Mavis' twenty-first birthday, 15 August 1945. In Chingford, Pat helped organize Hawkwood Crescent's celebratory street party, wondering whether peace would endure. The *Daily Worker*'s postbag reflected her feelings about the recent dropping of atom bombs on Hiroshima and Nagasaki. W. Malcolm from Worcester Park wrote that it was all very well to speculate about the future benefits of atomic power but socialists must respond to its current use as an 'instrument of indiscriminate slaughter'. And 'S.M.G' from London was horrified that the Labour Party they had just helped bring to power, in the belief that 'it was going to deliver liberty and equality, has lent itself to this abomination'. Other letters were more positive. The management and control of atomic power should be given to the new United Nations with a new international police force, suggested one reader, forgetting the fate of similar proposals after the First World War. Could Pat permit herself to be more hopeful this time around? When the leaders of the USSR, the United States and the United Kingdom had met in Yalta in March, they had agreed to guarantee world peace, security and democracy.

Harry Pollitt wrote about Yalta for the *Firefighter*. He emphasized the Big Three's commitment to removing the political, economic and social causes of war, thus allowing full international cooperation to create world-lasting peace and eradicate world poverty. According to his biographer, Pollitt was intoxicated by Yalta's 'Wilsonian platitudes'.[17] Pat and John shared Pollitt's faith in the promise of Yalta and like Pollitt, they were committed to supporting the Labour Government. The FBU's congenial, productive relationship with the new Home Secretary must have exemplified for John the benefits of a unified Labour Movement. He invited Pollitt to meet the FBU Executive Council members to persuade them that the Fire Brigades Union should help revive the campaign for Communist Party affiliation to the Labour Party.[18] In an article for *Labour Monthly*, John is baffled by the Labour Party's resistance to a closer relationship with the Communist Party: the new Labour Government needed all the friends it could get and Communist trade union leaders like himself were keen to help. His union had helped the Labour Party during the General Election campaign, not only with money but through the time and effort of its paid officials; he himself had toured the country in support of Labour candidates. 'Without immodesty, I can say that the prestige of the firemen, particularly in Southern England, was such that they exercised some influence in swaying the electorate in various blitzed towns'.[19] He did not understand how he was welcome to attend meetings at Labour Party Headquarters to discuss election financing, yet forbidden to represent his union at its annual conference. And at a meeting of trade union leaders to discuss the repeal of the Trade Disputes Act, Morrison had publicly attacked Horner for this final effort to affiliate the Communist Party to the Labour Party.[20]

Thus, John sat in the visitor's gallery at the Labour Party Conference in 1946 to witness the defeat of the motion for Communist Party affiliation. It was to be the communists' final attempt.[21] John's *Labour Monthly* article had invoked the pre-war unity of the left when they had fought against Mosley, aided democratic Spain and 'exposed the Chamberlain Government and the Men of Munich', but that was then. Now, was a different time: John was outside and the weather getting cold.

Notes

1 *Sunday Mirror*, 6 August 1944.
2 Victor Bailey, 'The early history of the Fire Brigades Union', in ed. Victor Bailey, *Forged in Fire*, London, 1992, 84.
3 Andrew Thorpe, 'Locking out the communists. The Labour Party and the Communist Party, 1939–46', *Twentieth Century History*, 2014, 25, 2, 241.
4 *Daily News*, 18 December 1944.
5 Terry Segars, *The Fire Service: A Social History of a Uniformed Working Class'*, PhD thesis, University of Essex, 1989, 209.
6 *Daily Worker*, 12 February 1945.
7 Conversation with Malcolm Purdie, 3 October 1945, NA/ KV3-402.
8 John Strachey, 'Totalitarianism' in ed. Victor Gollancz, *The Betrayal of the Left*, London, 1941, 202–203.
9 John Horner, 'A Book which has Influenced Me'.
10 John Strachey, 'Totalitarianism'.
11 *Firefighter*, Summer 1946, 13.
12 *Firefighter*, December 1945; January–February 1946.

13 *Firefighter*, November 1942.
14 *Firefighter*, Summer 1946, 11.
15 *Firefighter*, Autumn 1946, 10.
16 Bob Darke, *The Communist Technique in Britain*, London, 1952, 72.
17 Kevin Morgan, *Harry Pollitt*, Manchester, 1993, 140.
18 In a letter from Philippa Clark at the FBU to John Horner after reading his unpublished memoir, n.d.
19 John Horner, 'Unity, Then and Now', *Labour Monthly*, March 1946, 75–77.
20 Sibley, 96 – 97.
21 Thorpe, 2014.

17

'SLIDING INTO THE DEEP FREEZE'

Within weeks of the war ending, the United States cancelled its lend-lease agreement with Britain and attached hard terms to its new multi-billion-dollar loan to a country bankrupted from war. Labour MPs were horrified. The *New Statesman* believed, 'On matters that most affect Britain today, the United States is nearly as hostile to the aspirations of Socialist Britain as to the Soviet Union'.[1] Payment in dollars on the interest meant fewer imports with less to eat. Her mother regularly posted to Pat parcels of food – a few potatoes, a leek, a couple of carrots – plus sometimes a small, home-made present for the grandchildren. Puddings were restricted to semolina, varied by a change of colour – green, blue, pink, purple, orange – thanks to the little bottles from the Holbrooks factory in Birmingham where Geoff Palmer now worked. Housewife Pat was lucky to live just fifteen minutes from the local shopping parade; when the news flashed around Hawkwood Crescent of a rare consignment of un-rationed ox liver, she ran to join the butcher's queue. Neighbours at three houses up kept chickens and occasionally gave Pat a couple of eggs for the household scraps she had boiled up into chicken feed. Otherwise, she increased the family's protein intake by registering her younger child as vegetarian – less meat but a proportionally greater quantity of cheese for the whole family with enough to make a weekly cheese and potato pie – until the winter of 1946–47 when Lincolnshire's potato crop froze into the ground and queues formed outside the greengrocer.

That winter was so cold that coal froze at the mine heads, meaning frequent power cuts without coke for the boiler to heat the water. John brought down from the loft the old tin bath Pat had used to bathe Carol in Aston during that earlier, dreadful winter of the Blitz. Pat placed the bath in front of the living room gas fire, the room's sole source of light apart from a wobbly

DOI: 10.4324/9781032671352-18

candle stuck into a little-used egg cup. Waiting her turn, eight-year-old Carol waggled her fingers to cast shadows of giant rabbit ears onto the wall to make her little sister laugh. But Pat worried about the younger child's frequent colds and coughs. As housewives struggled to keep their families warm and fed, the *Daily Herald*'s medical correspondent scolded its women readers for not eating properly. With just enough rations to go round, they must break the 'bad old habit of giving Father the biggest helping at dinner'. 'Don't forget', the medical correspondent warns, 'Your headache, overwroughtness, forgetfulness and short temper are likely a result of your being anaemic. You need the protein as much as he does'.[2]

Pat did not need to read the *Herald*'s other caution to housewives that without books their life would be nothing but a dreary round of housework. Never over-fussy about dusting and window-cleaning, at four o'clock each afternoon she abandoned her duties for an armchair with a cup of tea, a rich tea biscuit and the latest, serious novel from Chingford Library. The *Daily Worker* she read with her mid-morning tea and, after the children had gone to bed, the *Daily Herald* and the other newspapers that John brought back from the office.

The *Herald* columnist also urged housewives to have an outside interest and might have approved Pat's secretary-ship of the parent teachers association at Carol's school – if it had not been for her politics, in which case he could have judged Pat's commitment to the school as Communist infiltration. Most of her sparse, free time was given to the local Party branch, to the 'Struggle', that Ralph Samuel describes in the *Lost World of British Communism* as 'the metaphysic of the moment which turned immediate tasks into historic responsibilities and bathed the most banal organizational details in a transcendent light'.[3] A favourite poem of Pat's was 'Say Not the Struggle Naught Availeth', and she liked to quote from memory the second verse –

If hopes were dupes, fears may be liars;
  It may be, in yon smoke concealed,
Your comrades chase e'en now the fliers,
  And, but for you, possess the field.

Nor did she forget how much worse it was for mothers in countries where children went hungry and died from curable diseases. She would have been the author of these lines in John's 1946 article in *Labour Monthly*:

The loss of dried eggs, with all that it means for tired, hard-pressed and under-fed housewives must appear insignificant against the fact that before this summer is over, eighty million people throughout the world will be in the throes of famine.[4]

When spring came and the ice melted across Europe, the Soviet Union rejected an American proposal for aid to all European countries, conditional on their adopting market economies; by summer, relations between the USSR and the USA had so much deteriorated that President Truman was promising worldwide help to any country threatened by communism.[5] Stalin responded by extinguishing democracy in the countries of Eastern Europe within the Soviet sphere of influence. And thus began what was to become known as 'the Cold War' in which none could be neutral, as in the hymn from John's Baptist Chapel youth,

> There's one door and only one
> I'm on the inside, which side are you?

The Fire Brigades Union had already chosen. At its annual conference in June, it approved a resolution for John to take to September's meeting of the Trades Union Congress: the United Kingdom should reduce the size of its armed forces that were spread across an Empire it could no longer afford to keep; at the same time the UK should strengthen trading relations with 'countries with planned economies' (meaning the Communist bloc), that were not subject to Capitalism's boom and busts.[6]

Not all FBU delegates were happy about this: Jack Rogers from Southampton warned of the danger of Britain becoming an 'appendage of the Soviet Union' and worried that the Union's Executive Council was 'dominated by members of the Communist Party'. To this last, the Union's president, John Burns, replied, 'A man's political conviction has nothing whatever to do with his activities in the trade union movement'; and John added, 'It is a gross distortion and an attempt to influence this conference to say that the EC is dominated by communists'.[7] Whereas it was true that the majority of the Executive Council members, including John Burns, were not Communist Party members, arguably their role was as Lenin's 'useful idiots'. Labour Party members were needed on the Executive Council to promote communist-inspired policies at the Labour Party Conference from which communists themselves had been barred. Burns was happy to do so because he believed the Soviet Union meant it when it said it wanted peace.

No proxies were needed at the Trades Union Congress. The Communist Party leadership decided who was to fire the opening salvo on the TUC front of the new Cold War. The Welsh miner's leader, Arthur Horner, was a founding member of the British Communist Party and had recently been elected General Secretary of the National Union of Miners – a confederation of regional mining unions with a total membership of over a half a million, compared with the FBU's puny 20,000.[8] Yet, the NUM was not communist-controlled and Arthur Horner as its president had no mandate to speak against the Labour Government's foreign policy.[9] Hence, the task went to

John, who like Arthur, had a seat on the Party's Executive Committee. Along with the foundry workers and the electricians, John's firemen's union could be relied upon to promote the Party line.[10]

That summer of 1947 was to be the first in a long line of an annual holiday taken in the second half of August so as to refresh John before the TUC where he was to argue doggedly for the Communist Party's policies. They spent their first Cold War holiday on a hill farm above Machynlleth in central Wales. The girls played with the farm's animals that provided them with unrationed milk and eggs; Pat sat by the mountain stream, deep into the crime fiction of Marjorie Allingham and Ngaio Marsh, while John mucked around at his new hobby of painting in oils. Their bohemian friends, the Freemans, had encouraged him to take up painting and showed him some basic techniques. He most enjoyed landscape painting because it took him outdoors.

He drafted his speech in the week after their return from Machynlleth and on the Saturday pressed his suit and packed his case ready for an early Sunday morning drive northwards to Southport. He was to speak in opposition to the TUC General Council's resolution supporting the Labour Government's anti-Soviet foreign policy, as expounded by the Foreign Secretary, Ernie Bevin, to Congress. The *Illustrated London News* reported it as one of Bevin's 'most powerful performances' that 'received prolonged applause'. John's speech reads less convincingly: an irrelevant quote from Dr Johnson followed by a call to resist 'dollar diplomacy' and to trade with the Soviet Union. Despite the amendment to the General Council's resolution having been 'overwhelmingly defeated', he had found Congress to be in a glum mood because of the balance of payments crisis and as he wrote in *Labour Monthly*, the Socialist alternative he had proposed at Southport would in due course 'come to be accepted by our Movement'.[11] Two months later, the new general secretary of the Labour Party, Morgan Phillips, issued a press release warning that communists were planning to sabotage the Labour Government and that '… in recent years, the Communists have gained an influence inside certain Trade Unions out of all proportion to their real strength'[12]. All in all, it had been a horrid and surprisingly rapid change from when the Soviet Union and Britain had been allies and the public had admired the Red Army. In 'He Says', a *Firefighter* regular feature that John would have written, a fictitious, ordinary fireman reflects John's feelings during the early years of the Cold War.

It seems funny to me. Russia, four years ago was OK, 'Saving civilisation at Stalingrad'. Now she is supposed to be threatening our civilisation. I don't get it. This country, not yet anyway, is far from out of the 'jam' from the last war, everyone told to work harder, close the export gap and so on, is now going to start rearming. What for? Berlin? The ghost of Dr Goebbels must be laughing.[13]

The government was meanwhile starting to treat British communists as potential traitors loyal to a foreign, hostile power, and therefore to be monitored for subversive activities. Although MI5 reckoned that out of 8.7 million trade unionists, only 30,000 were communist, it was concerned about their disproportionate influence.[14] Too many trades union executive councils were supporting pro-Soviet foreign policies while provoking 'discontent and social unrest' at home.[15] Because the fire service formed part of Britain's civil defence, the 'strong communist influence' in the Fire Brigades Union was judged a special security risk.[16] John's memoir briefly touches on the surveillance that had begun during the war and, as in Communist Party Headquarters, there may have been a mole in the FBU office.[17] Phone tapping and interception of mail was common and when travelling abroad, his bags would have been subject to 'discrete' searches at UK customs and immigration checkpoints, as Pat must also have experienced in 1948 when with John on her first trip abroad as a guest of the Hungarian government.

East European communist governments designed such trips to cheer up and re-motivate foreign comrades from capitalist countries. Visitors were given an idyllic picture of life under communism while supplied with cultural entertainment, good food and drink. The biggest drawback may have been dull travel companions: in this case, Reg Birch, a militant factory worker of dogmatic opinions. Their visit also coincided with Peter Kerrigan's, the Party's national organizer and the British Communist Party's official delegate to a congress that established the new ruling Workers' People's Party designed to tighten the Soviet Union's grip on Hungary.[18] Above all, Pat relished the relief from Britain's dreary austerity: she enjoyed the people's charm, the beauty of Budapest, drinking coffee with whipped cream and the eating of cream cakes (an indulgence denied her since pre-war Hampstead).[19] But there was also a coal mine to visit while a standard element of official visitors' itineraries was a moonlit cruise on a Danube steamer. As described by another visitor, when their steamer stopped at a riverside village, they were greeted by smiling local dignitaries and taken to the inn where after an aperitif of apricot brandy, they consumed a supper of fish soup and paprika, followed by noodles with sour cream, cheese and bacon, with wine throughout. Out of courtesy to the visitors, the village fiddlers accompanied the meal with 'Auld lang syne', before switching to their own gypsy music. 'It was long after midnight when we left, laden with bunches of lilac taken from the table decorations, and with pressing invitations to return in time for wine harvest'.[20]

John was becoming excluded from the mainstream Labour movement. After officially joining the Communist Party in 1945, he believed it unfair he could no longer represent the FBU at Labour Party conferences but, otherwise remembered that 'to be a communist trade unionist in the early days of peace was acceptable to most in the movement'.[21] Then, in the spring of 1948, the TUC General Council blatantly changed its rules to prevent him from filling a vacancy on the Council, otherwise his automatically.[22] The Cold War had also begun to disrupt the Fire Brigades Union with a fractious annual conference in 1949. A delegate opposing the Union's Executive Council resolution that the FBU affiliate with the British Soviet Society was accused of fascism by another delegate. There were also grumbles about that year's newly established triennial re-elections of the full-time officials: Horner, Grahl and Bagley (all members of the Communist Party) were returned unopposed, the Executive Council having ruled out the nominations of other candidates on technical grounds or because of their lack of experience – this last ironic, considering John's own inexperience when first elected general secretary.[23] The mayor and mayoress of Whitley Bay seem to be the only happy people in the photograph of the FBU leadership at their conference dinner (Figure 17.1).

Above all, the conference was disrupted by Jack Rogers, the Union's (unpaid) area secretary for Southampton. Rogers had already protested in 1947 about communist influence in the union and he appears to have corresponded with Vic Feather, the assistant general secretary of the

FIGURE 17.1   The FBU entertains the Mayor and Mayoress of Whitley Bay. FBU Conference, June 1949. John and Pat (far left), John Burns to the right of the Mayoress, and Jack Grahl at end of the table (family photo album).

TUC after Feather's pamphlet, *The Communist Menace*, found its way to Southampton's central fire station. Rogers then sent a circular letter to all the FBU's area representatives, quoting the pamphlet's warning that communists were seeking to control British trade unionism. Rogers wrote to a colleague in Portsmouth,

> I am not anti-Horner, anti-Grahl or anti-anybody else but I am anxious that our largely non-political membership shall not be seduced by political or industrial opportunists who may be using present conditions ... to trade upon the apathy and indifference of large sections of our membership.[24]

Conference was asked to approve Rogers' three-year suspension from the FBU on the grounds that his circular letter had undermined the confidence of the membership and weakened the Union's negotiating power at a most difficult moment in its history when it was struggling to keep parity with police pay. One hundred and ninety-four delegates voted to suspend Rogers; twelve abstained. Most delegates cared less about their leadership's politics than its energetic efforts to secure them better pay and conditions and many still remembered John's heroic performance during the war and appreciated his successful management of the FBU's transition in the smaller post-war fire service. Nor did the conference object to its Soviet visitors as guests, including Boris Pischikevich, Chairman of the Central Committee of the million-strong Soviet Workers Union. Pischikevich had been made Hero of the Soviet Union in 1943 when serving as a military commissar he defended a bridgehead on the Dnieper River from a German counter-attack.[25] He and John took to each other and in 1950 and 1953 'my friend Boris' was to make return visits to the FBU annual conference while in 1950 and 1954 groups of FBU members toured the Soviet Union.[26]

The communist leadership's hold over the FBU was facilitated by the 'fractions' of Party members who worked locally and regionally to ensure the Union's branches sent delegates to Conference who supported the leadership's policies.[27] Enoch Humphries, for example, had joined the Scottish fire service in 1947 and within a year was a Party member. Communists in Glasgow's fire brigade met weekly at a café where senior comrades led them in discussions about how to change the world. Enoch then graduated to six-monthly UK-wide meetings of the Union's leading communists to discuss matters such as German rearmament and the Cold War. Enoch was probably referring to the FBU's National Advisory Council where communist FBU national and district officials met with the Party's industrial organizers. Enoch told the historian, John Saville how the general secretary was always present at these meetings but the assistant general secretary, Jack Grahl, took the lead and was 'an exceptionally good speaker and an extremely knowledgeable person'.[28]

Grahl was possibly the FBU's main link with Peter Kerrigan, a fellow Scot and the Party's national organizer. Horner's and Grahl's division of labour is evident from the 1949 Trade Union Congress (once again in Bridlington) where John moved two resolutions relating to workers' conditions of service while Grahl criticized the anti-Communist TUC General Secretary, Vincent Tewson, for having interfered in the Jack Rogers affair.

Although the 1949 Congress should have been celebrating the TUC's partnership with a Labour Government that had successfully implemented much of the Beveridge Report, government ministers were struggling with a balance of payments crisis and prices were outstripping wages. Two ministers came to Congress to ask for a continuation of the wage freeze to control domestic demand and thus increase exports. That year's TUC President, Sir William Lawther of the National Union of Miners backed their appeal. A Pathé news clip from Bridlington shows him speaking from a platform of large, elderly, generally overweight members of the General Council. Sir William had gone down the mine when he was twelve, had been imprisoned during the General Strike, supported the Communist Party's failed bid in 1943 to affiliate to the Labour Party and is now ferociously anti-communist. He is a poor speaker. He rarely looks up from his notes as he tells the delegates he had expected attacks from the Conservative Party but not the betrayal of the working class movement by some of its own, the communist agitators who are inciting unofficial strikes to undermine their trade unions' support of the wage freeze. A few loud boos can be heard from various parts of the hall and as the camera pans over the delegates applauding Lawther, it stops momentarily on a man who strongly resembles John and who is not clapping.

Next day's Congress was devoted to attacking communism, both abroad and at home. In the morning, delegates approved the General Council's proposal that the TUC quit the World Federation of Trade Unions that five years earlier it had been instrumental in founding. John was devastated. He was committed to international working-class solidarity, as manifested by the WFTU, whereas his fellow trade union leaders sought to disassociate from an organization heavily influenced by the Soviet Union that had suppressed non-communist trade union movements throughout Eastern Europe. In the afternoon, the TUC turned to home-grown communists: the General Council asked Congress to endorse its warning that communists were successfully manoeuvring for leading positions in trade unions.

That day at Bridlington was noticeable for the strongest assault the British Communist Party had so far experienced in its relations with the trade union movement: all grassroots, unofficial strikes were attributed to malevolent communist influence and some trade unions, including the massive Transport and General Workers' Union announced they were making Party members ineligible for office.[29] The tone of the assault may in part be attributed to the pressure placed on the TUC leadership by a Labour Government anxious to demonstrate its loyalty to the United States to whom it was heavily indebted.

Nina Fishman has argued the war between the TUC and the communist delegates was largely phoney, with the Communist Party leadership anxious that in routine disputes 'communist-led trade unions continued to act within the very British conventions of industrial conflict as distinct from political issues'.[30] Two former communist FBU officials interviewed by Segars separately recalled two occasions in 1954 when Pollitt instructed the FBU leadership to calm down and not press too hard in the union's disputes with employers.[31] Much worse for John than demonstrations of hostility from the TUC was the break-down in international relations and the decline in the Communist Party's popular support, all of which must have decided him not to include these events in his memoir, other than to write 'We were sliding into deep freeze'.

When advocating in 1946 for the Communist Party's affiliation to the Labour Party, John clarified that he identified primarily as a socialist, as did members of the Labour Party, and that the Labour Government needed Communist Party support to successfully implement its election pledge of building a socialist Britain. The Communist Party, he wrote, had a long and proud record of achievement in the British labour movement and 'the communists feel at least as deeply and agree as sincerely as their Labour Party friends about their common objective of a Socialist Britain'.[32] John was no sectarian communist and his passion for working class unity explains his enthusiasm for affiliation. Yet, he could not see nor understand why fellow socialists were suspicious or outright hostile to the Soviet Union. The days his mother had struggled to put food on the table when his father was out of work; the adolescent experience of the General Strike; the men that Capitalism spat out and left to starve on the wharves of Buenos Aires. The Soviet Union was John's hope and inspiration; there, they were already building the new and better world. On the twenty-fifth anniversary of the October Revolution he had written in *Labour Monthly*,

> A new life blossomed for scores of millions of people…The great Five Year Plans, the flight to the Pole, Dnieprostroi, the grand education schemes, the Stalin Constitution …. A hundred million peasants meeting and mastering science… Countries of the old Tsarist Empire held in Asiatic bondage, oppressed, ignorant and poor saw a new world before them.[33]

John never spoke or wrote of 'the masses'. For him, each one of those 'hundred million peasants' was someone whose life had been improved by socialism. On a later visit to Hungary, he describes his encounter with a chimney sweep –

He was wearing a uniform which we could not recognise. We knew postmen, soldiers, police, railwaymen but this man in black with brass buttons and a strange close-fitting skull cap puzzled us. The interpreter could not help, so we went up and asked him. He was a foreman chimney sweep, out on his rounds of inspection! 'Tell him', I said to the interpreter, 'that I am a fireman and that a good chimney fire is always useful to fill in the time. He is one of those who put firemen out of work!'.

His eyes lit up ...[34] With a firm belief in the brotherhood of man, at home or abroad, John took any opportunity to chat with a working man about his life, his job and his hopes for the future, a habit that continued long after he had left the Communist Party.

Notes

1 *New Statesman*, 2 November 1946, quoted in David Kynaston, *Austerity Britain, 1945–51*, London, 2007, 134.
2 *Daily Herald*, 28 January 1947.
3 Ralph Samuel, *The Lost World of British Communism*, London, 2006, 52.
4 Horner, *Labour Monthly*, March 1946, 75.
5 Martin McCauley, *Origins of the Cold War 1941–1949*, London, 1983. The exception was Communist Yugoslavia that struck out independently from Moscow.
6 *Firefighter*, July 1947.
7 *Daily Worker*, 27 June 1947.
8 These figures from the 1947 TUC Report.
9 See for example the discussion in David Howell's review of Nina Fishman's biography of Arthur Horner in *Twentieth Century British History*, 2011, 22,3, 437–41.
10 Willie Thompson, *The Good Old Cause*, London, 1992, 81.
11 John Horner, 'The Southport T.U.C.', *Labour Monthly*, October 1947, 299–302.
12 Cited in Nina Fishman, 'The phoney Cold War in British trade unions, *Contemporary British History*, 2001, 15, 3, 83–104 (89).
13 *Firefighter*, October 1948.
14 Peter Hennessy, *The Secret State*, London, 2002, 99.
15 Thomas Maguire, 'Counter-Subversion in Early Cold War Britain: The Official Committee on Communism (Home), the Information Research Department, and 'State-Private Networks', *Intelligence and National Security*, 2015, 30, 5, 637–666, 261.
16 NA/CAB 130-37 'Security measures against communists and fascists', 26 May 1948.
17 A security service file that perhaps mistakenly found its way into the National Archives, refers to a separate note (not attached) about the FBU 'provided by a number of secret Office sources'. NA/KV3/298.
18 Kerrigan in Budapest, July 1948: LHASC/CP/IND/MISC/23/7.
19 Phyllis Auty, *Scotsman*, 19 April 1949.

20 Derek Walston, *Scotsman*, 1 July 1948.

21 John Saville, 'The Communist Party and the FBU', in ed. Victor Bailey, *Forged in Fire*, 225–228 (226).

22 *Daily Telegraph*, 29 April 1948.

23 MRC/ MSS 346/3/19.

24 Letter from Rogers to Marchmont, 17 December 1948, MRC/MSS 346/3/19.

25 *Firefighter*, July 1949; more about Pischikevich at www.grsu.by/sdgs-2020/item/43236-pishchikevich-boris-tarasovich.html accessed 19 August 2023.

26 'Firemen visit Russia: a report of a delegation sent by the Fire Brigades Union to visit the USSR in November 1950', MRC/MSS.346/4/132; 'We visit the Soviet firemen', 1954, MSS.346/4/228.

27 Saville, 1992.

28 Transcript of John Saville's interview with Enoch Humphries, HHC/UDJS/1/28. See also Humphries, 'Reminiscences of a President' in *Forged in Fire*, 359–385.

29 Willie Thompson, 'British Communists in the Cold War, 1947–1952', *Contemporary British History*, 2001, 15:3, 105–132 (82–83).

30 Fishman, 97.

31 Terry Segars, *The Fire Service: A Social History of a Uniformed Working Class*', PhD thesis, University of Essex, 355.

32 Horner, *Labour Monthly*, 1946, 75.

33 John Horner, 'We Must Fight Together', *Labour Monthly*, November 1942.

34 John Horner, in 'Britons Visit Hungary ', British-Hungarian Friendship Society, pamphlet, 1955, 6.

18

'THE WORLD SHALL YET LIVE
IN PEACE'

FIGURE 18.1   The Horners in their garden in Chingford, July 1949 (family album).

DOI: 10.4324/9781032671352-19

The comrades joked you could always spot Communist households by their gardens, neglected by comrades busy with canvassing and other Party activities.[1] Yet a rare snapshot of the Horner family from July 1949 shows their garden remarkably neat. Pat planned what and where to plant and tasked John with the labour, claiming the exercise would do him good. From the appearance of his baggy old trousers and rolled up shirt sleeves he may not have finished when there arrived the visitor who took the photo. Or perhaps his casual look is deliberate, a mute protest at his wife's petty bourgeois tendencies? Pat is wearing her best, flounced frock, the same worn the previous month when dining with the Mayor and Mayoress of Whitley Bay. The two girls have identical summer frocks made by their aunt, Violet, who had looked after them when Pat was at the FBU Conference.

Their reluctance to look at the camera indicates the visitor to have been a stranger, possibly from overseas: according to an internal communication in the government security services. Horner had 'many foreign connections'.[2]

From the date of the snapshot, the visitor could have been Betty Ambatielos, a British communist married to the general secretary of a Greek seamen's union. That summer Betty had returned to Britain from Greece to campaign for the release of her husband, one among thousands of communists held in Greek prison camps. John's informal leadership of British trade union support to 'the progressive struggle in Greece' had made him a good friend to the campaign.[3] The wartime coalition's military intervention in Greece in December 1944 had extinguished any admiration John once felt for Ernie Bevin, now Foreign Secretary. Saville was to describe the Greek intervention as 'The outstanding public demonstration that the old order had changed not at all and that the Labour leaders in the War Cabinet, Attlee and Bevin in particular, were wholeheartedly with Churchill in his counter-revolutionary actions'.[4] Within weeks of taking the lead in organizing December's Trafalgar Square rally over Greece, John was speaking alongside the president of the All-India Trades Union Congress at a meeting in London calling for immediate Indian Independence. India, said John, was a 'vast prison' with its key in No. 10 Downing Street: 'And the British people must see the key is turned'.[5]

When he joined the Communist Party's Executive Committee in 1945, John was assigned to a sub-committee on UK domestic issues but on re-election in 1947 changed to what most interested him – international affairs, presided over by Rajani Palme Dutt.[6] It involved campaigning against the development of nuclear weapons by the Western powers and their rearmament of West Germany, along with support to struggles for colonial freedom in Vietnam, Malaya, Cyprus, Kenya and elsewhere. As his biographer explains, Palme Dutt understood the Labour Government as playing second fiddle to the Americans 'in an attempt to hang onto global possessions it otherwise could not afford'.[7] This was the tenor of John's speeches at successive annual meetings of the Trades Union Congress where he argued that maintaining a military presence in the colonies brought a direct cost to British workers through their lower incomes and diminished social services.

At the Communist Party's biennial Congress in 1949, John gave the keynote speech on colonial liberation, described by the *Daily Worker* as a 'terrible indictment of the Labour Government for its recourse to every possible variation of the old imperialist tricks ... Phoney constitutions which give no real power to the people' while the reality was 'Shootings, prison sentences, whippings, sedition trials ... slavery and forced labour'.[8] Whereas John was referring to Malaya, an anti-communist could have made identical remarks about Stalinist Russia. The Cold War was fought through cracked mirrors – illusions and delusions.

When Labour MPs on the left wing of their party became more vocal in their anti-colonialism after Labour lost power in 1952, Fenner Brockway established the Movement for Colonial Freedom. John had the FBU sign up as a founding member.[9] He regularly attended its committee meetings and thus came to know future Labour ministers, including Tony Benn, Tony Greenwood and Barbara Castle, all active supporters of the MCF. His closest friend in the House of Common was, however, more to the left than these: the staunch anti-colonialist Julius Silverman. They had known each other since 1940 when Julius was an auxiliary fireman and a city councillor in Birmingham.[10] His local electorate had included an Indian diaspora and in 1945 when he entered Parliament, Julius was already well-known for his long and loyal association with Krishna Menon and the India League.[11] He was also part of a small group of Labour MPs suspected of close association, if not secret membership, of the Communist Party; another was Stephen Swingler, a friend of Pat and John from pre-war Hampstead.[12]

Despite allegations made at the height of Cold War hysteria, these MPs' sympathy for the Soviet Union did not necessarily make them crypto-Communists, let alone Soviet spies. Rather, they admired the idea of an economy designed for the benefit of the workers and sought to reduce the volume of hate speech directed towards what Ronald Regan was later to call 'the Evil Empire'. Their communist friends meanwhile were eager to assist them in influencing others to their way of thinking through 'front organizations' designed to generate public sympathy towards the Soviet Union and its Eastern European satellites. These were modelled on 'Popular Front' organizations from the 1930s, such as Spanish Medical Aid where communists mixed with other left-wing and liberal elements but always with a Party member to keep the organization in line with its founders' pro-Soviet goals.[13] The *Daily Worker* reports John speaking at meetings of front organizations such as the National Council for Civil Liberties, Greek-Soviet Society and the British Soviet Society, compering a concert to mark Poland's National Liberation Day, and chairing a meeting of the British-Hungarian Friendship Society. But his focus was the Party's most important front organization, the British Peace Committee, a subsidiary of the World Peace Council established to convince influential people in the West of the Soviet Union's desire for peace.[14]

The 'Fight for Peace' became central to the Communist Party's agenda after its poor performance in the General Election in February 1950 that had returned a Labour Government with a tiny majority. In the one hundred constituencies where the communists had fielded candidates to stand against Labour (by now referred to as a 'class enemy'), very few voters supported them, and the Party's two MPs lost their seats. Meanwhile, *Daily Worker* sales were declining, with Party membership stagnant. The mood was gloomy at the Community Party's Executive Committee meeting in March that reviewed the disastrous results. From the minute-taker's hand-written notes that have survived for some EC meetings, it appears that John rarely spoke much but on this occasion he attributed the Party's decline in support to its inadequate challenge to the Labour government's wage freeze.

Sometime during the meeting, they broke off for a group picture (Figure 18.2).

FIGURE 18.2   Meeting of the Communist Party's Executive Committee, 4 March 1950 (Labour History Archives).

John Horner is seated at the left end of the third row. On the wall behind him, dominating King Street's lecture hall, a giant-size photo of Harry Pollitt – Britain's Josef Stalin. The man himself (wearing glasses) sits in the centre of the front row. On Pollitt's left is Johnny Campbell, the editor of the *Daily Worker*. Next to Campbell is Peter Kerrigan, a tough veteran from the Spanish Civil War with whom John and Pat had visited Hungary in 1948. On Pollitt's right is Palme Dutt who had secured only 0.3% of the vote in Bevin's constituency. 'Disgraceful' said Dutt: they had to rethink their strategy with 'a new and serious approach to the Peace movement [that would] provide the basis to reach out to enormous numbers'.[15]

A week later, the Soviet-inspired World Peace Council meeting in Stockholm launched a petition for multilateral nuclear disarmament and the British Peace Committee started collecting signatures for the petition.[16] The Chingford branch of the communist-aligned Unity Theatre supported the petition with a float to remind people of the Blitz (Figure 18.3). Amid the ruins, Pat sits on a kitchen chair, tenderly nursing a doll; Carol kneels on the ground beside her mother. Her glum expression might be good acting but is probably due to her fear of being spotted by someone from school. Two civil defence workers stand in the rubble, gazing miserably at this scene of destruction around them while above their heads is a banner, 'Worse than the Last War. Act Now'. Another banner on the side of the float reads, 'Sign the All Britain Peace Petition. SIGN NOW'.

Since Friends Hall, Peace had been important for Pat. The Party's fresh enthusiasm reinvigorated her commitment by drawing to attention the horrors of nuclear warfare, until then little discussed in public. Between May and August, she and thirty thousand other members of the British Communist Party collected one million signatures for multilateral nuclear disarmament.[17] She knocked on doors, pushed leaflets into the hands of shoppers on Station Road, and made speeches from soap boxes. She even told the queue at the bus stop at the bottom of Hawkwood Crescent how a Third World War would destroy Chingford, terrifying her younger daughter, if not her fellow passengers.

While Pat worked locally, John served on the British Peace Committee's national executive. A few weeks into the Peace Petition campaign, the great American singer and activist Paul Robeson, flew into London to give his support. He attended a meeting of the Bureau of the World Peace Council and sang at an open-air concert in Lincolns Inn Fields, chaired and compered by John. The crowd heard Robeson sing in Polish, a lament for the destruction of the Warsaw Ghetto, in Chinese, the national anthem of the new People's Republic of China, and in English, spirituals from the home of his forebears about who had been slaves in North Carolina and as he told his audience,

FIGURE 18.3 Chingford Unity Theatre Supports the Peace Petition, 1950 (Marx Memorial Library).[51]

whose descendants were clamouring for peace.[18] John recalled the concert, in a letter to John Saville –

> Beautiful summer evening, enormous crowd. Great feeling, happy occasion – came collection time. Horner makes appeal – police intervene – police inspector comes to the rostrum and pulls my trouser leg. Orders me to stop using microphone. I carry on with the appeal, explaining my difficulty with the police – money rolled in. Finally police disconnect wires. I carry on with appeal – I ruin my voice for days. Police very angry since their intervention was an enormous stimulant to money giving!

Summoned to appear before the Bow Street magistrates, John pleaded guilty 'to using a noisy instrument for obtaining money', an ancient statute in the bye-laws of Lincoln Inn Fields. John's wartime colleague, the barrister, John's friend, Peter Pain, explained to the magistrates how John had been unaware of the statute. He was fined ten shillings with three guineas costs John writes, 'I consoled myself that where I stood before the Bench, William Morris had taken his place and when the Bench expressed surprise at having a "gentleman" before them, he declared "But I am a Socialist"'. He adds, 'We gave a dinner to Robeson. Pat was his dinner companion. He charmed her'.[19]

The week after Robeson's concert, John pioneered the slogan 'Ban the Bomb!' in a *Firefighter* editorial, written on the anniversary of VE Day.

> Five years ago, the world had yet to hear of Hiroshima. We know now that even before the second world war ended, there were those who were preparing for a third … The hundreds of millions of pounds spent every year on war preparations are holding back social reconstruction in this country. A nightmare haunts civilization.[20]

The challenge to the peace campaign was not the message but its messenger. For anti-communists, 'Peace' had become a dirty word. A hostile British press put it into inverted commas and referred to 'so-called peace campaigns'. George Orwell's observations on the uses and abuses of language for political purposes had become widely known but the Horners had refused to read *Nineteen Eighty-Four* – an anonymous piece in the *Firefighter* later described it as 'a calculated insult to the entire human race'.[21] The British Communist Party had no formal list of proscribed publications, but good communists knew what to avoid. Pat was thus shocked and amazed how when she campaigned for peace, other women might believe she had ulterior, suspect motives. Did these mothers not care about their children's future? Hers was a deeply emotive commitment. She must have been outraged when Labour ministers alleged that most of the signatories to the Peace Petition were bogus.

'For all its protestations of democratic intent and the unquestionable virtues of its own members', writes historian Willie Thompson about the British Communist Party, 'It was all too evidently at the disposal of and entirely guided by a profoundly tyrannical and bloody foreign regime (even if it actually happened to be right in claiming that the USSR's intentions were not aggressive)'.[22] Much of the British public became even more distrustful of the Soviet Union after North Korea's invasion of its southern neighbour in June 1950, although the invasion had come as much as a surprise to China and the Soviet Union as it did to the United States and Britain.[23] When American troops pushed the North Koreans back across the Thirty-Eighth Parallel and then continued up the peninsula to the Yalu River, China entered the war on the side of North Korea and the Cold War became at grave risk of turning hot.

Opinion was divided among FBU members as to the guilty party. Letters poured into the *Firefighter*. If only the USA had not intervened on the side of South Korea, lamented G.J. Jacques from Plymouth, Korea would have been reunited 'under a socialist and progressive government'. A correspondent from Walthamstow took the opposite view: 'In less than a month after annual conference agreed to continue the association with the British Soviet Friendship Society and all the accompanying peace campaign councils, we are faced with than instance of armed aggression by Communist forces'. 'The thing that most appals me', wrote 'Shiner' Wright from Lambeth, 'is the barbarous raiding of the undefended Korean towns by American planes and this being done in the name of the United Nations'; while Ray Milburn from West Hartlepool found the situation farcical: 'On the hand we are affiliated to the Labour Party which ... strongly condemns the Communists as being the "enemy within", yet on the other hand we allow the Fire Brigades Union to be used for Communist propaganda purposes'.[24]

Anti-communist resolutions were sent to the FBU's Executive Council –

> This district committee is alarmed and dismayed by the ever increasing trend ... to subordinate the affairs of firemen to that of Communistic propaganda, and we inform the National Executive that should they persist in this attitude this district committee will not be responsible for the action of their members.[25]

On the first day of the 1950 Trades Union Congress, three FBU branches in Essex told the press of their intention to quit the union because of the 'Communistic activities of the union secretary, assistant secretary and other members of the Executive'.[26] That year, John left the speeches on international affairs to comrades from other communist-led trade unions with a less restive membership and listened to the Prime Minister, Clement Attlee, tell Congress how the communist threat required an increased level of military expenditure. Communist trade unionists were not interested in serving their members, Attlee warned: 'For all the talk about the workers and for all the sham peace propaganda, communism is today, essentially a conspiracy against the liberty of the common people'. John would have been among those who booed when afterwards Arthur Deakin, the General Secretary of the Transport and General Workers Union told Congress, 'We must make a stand now against the attempts of Red Fascists to subject the rest of the world to the foul and filthy philosophy of communism'.[27]

How must John have felt on experiencing such hostility? His cheerful companionability and capacity for hard work kept him on good terms with much of his union's membership. It also helped him make new friends on the left of the Labour Party after Aneurin Bevan's resignation from the Labour government over the cuts in the National Health Service to pay for the Korean War. Yet, his members' reaction obliged John to tone down his public enthusiasm for Peace and the Soviet Union. Articles about banning the bomb and peace campaigns disappeared from the *Firefighter*; a brief notice explained that other priorities had decided the general secretary and John

Burns, the president of the FBU, to cancel their planned autumn visit to the Soviet Union. Preparations were also speeded up for a campaign to challenge the Labour Government's wage freeze to regain parity with police wages and in November, John and Jack Grahl, the assistant general secretary, made extensive visits to local branches in the north and midlands.[28]

It would have been Pat's idea that a female presence might create a more congenial, less aggressive atmosphere at the following year's annual conference: for the first time, delegates' wives were officially invited to the conference. A fuzzy photo in the *Firefighter* shows Pat and some two dozen other women seated to the side of the conference hall. A rare woman member of the FBU was also invited as a special delegate. It was probably also Pat who drafted the wives' letter that John Burns read out to the delegates at the conference's closure.

> The womenfolk expressed their thanks for the hospitality which had been shown them …. They hoped that the delegates, for the sake of their wives and children, would respond to his [John Burns] call for an all-out effort to preserve the peace of the world.

Bro. Burns said that if Conference had done nothing else but to produce that letter, they had done a good job for nothing was possible unless their better halves were pulling with them.[29] Meanwhile, Pat had witnessed the FBU leadership lose the vote on the union's continued affiliation to the British Peace Committee by 10,091 votes to 7,701. Yet, the leadership's manifest commitment to democracy had been appreciated – 'Speaker after speaker had the opportunity of having a go at anyone they could not see eye to eye with', a delegate afterwards wrote to the *Firefighter* while opinions varied about John: 'In spite of our General Secretary not being a Labour man, I consider him to be the finest secretary since the "Docker's KC", Ernie Bevin'. While another writes,

> As a public figure [John Horner] cannot afford to have the stigma of communism on his character…. I believe the members accept Bro. Horner's judgement and guidance but he cannot serve Stalin and the membership, so why does he not end his dream …?[30]

That he had no intention to do so is evidenced by his younger daughter's collection of communist countries' dolls each dressed in her national costume and that John brought her after a trip to Eastern Europe. John's eventual first visit to Moscow was in February 1952 when he led a British Peace Committee delegation to the Soviet Union.[31] The delegation would have experienced what Doris Lessing describes in *The Golden Notebook* as the 'flowery way of visits to factories, schools, Palaces of Culture and the University, not to mention speeches and banquets'.[32] Boris Pischikevich had given him a Soviet-made Leica camera that John now used to photograph ordinary Soviet citizens: a young woman street sweeper in Moscow, a Crimean Cossack, an elderly Uzbek on a collective farm in the Ferghana Valley. Photography now complemented painting as a creative hobby, aided by John Williams, a fellow communist from W.H. Thompson's, who passed onto him his darkroom equipment that John could not have afforded.

By 1954 John was working ever harder for the Party as a member of its National Cultural Committee.[33] Both sides in the Cold War used culture as a weapon. At the start of the Cold War, the Foreign Office had established the secret International Research Department (IRD) to circulate abroad anti-communist propaganda and to promote the works of anti-communist writers (including George Orwell), film-makers and artists but it was soon encouraging sympathetic British media outlets to also use its material.[34] Meanwhile, the Communist Party had established a Cultural Committee to promote communist thinking and Soviet cultural achievements and to oppose the Americanization of British culture.[35] Although John would have already known fellow Cultural Committee member, David Michaelson (a comrade from pre-war Hampstead), his new assignment gave the Horners the chance to mix with writers and intellectuals associated with the Committee. Their socializing found Pat discussing educational reform with Max Morris while

FIGURE 18.4 John Horner with his Leica in Moscow, 1954 (family album).

John talked history with Eric Hobsbawm, Edward Thompson and John Saville.

The IRD became interested in John, not for his cultural interests but for his trade union role. It developed a network of contacts within the trade union movement to undermine 'communist subversion' and had played a role in deciding the TUC to vote in 1949 to leave the World Federation of Trade Unions.[36] And by the early 1950s, it was deliberately spreading false information.[37] Thus, John was to become caught up in a dark web of deceit and counter-deceit.

When Stalin died in March 1953, Pat complained to her children that the popular press paid more attention to Princess Margaret's cold than to the passing of the great leader. His death broke the log jam in the Korean War that ended three months later, the armistice ratified the following spring at an international peace conference in Geneva. The threat of nuclear annihilation had slightly receded. 'There does appear to be a chink in the Iron Curtain', mused the *Manchester Guardian*, with the news in September 1954, of an official parliamentary delegation visiting the Soviet Union. China also was opening up, eager to welcome official visitors from the West and anti-communist Clement Attlee had travelled there in August. Yet, despite this slight thaw, there was no observable change to the TUC's Cold War rituals. Like the Welsh and Scottish miners' communist leaders, John was respected as a good trade union leader, loyally serving his union, 'though their political utterances were not always appreciated'.[38] And by 1954, Congress was wearying of them.

Three years before John had told Congress that Germany was 'the monster that has twice dominated Europe' and that its rearmament risked another war.[39] Now he prepared for his fourth annual motion on German rearmament at a Congress presided over by Jack Tanner from the Amalgamated Engineering Union, the same with whom John had teamed up to campaign for the opening of a Second Front. The 1946 motion supporting the Communist Party's affiliation to the Labour had been moved by Tanner but at the start of the Cold War he had cut all remaining links with the Communist Party and in his presidential address to Congress in 1954 he criticized those trade unions 'who had reached decisions on questions such German rearmament under the influences of emotional prejudices'.[40] Straight afterwards, John disrupted this opening session by jumping to his feet to protest that the General Council's emergency resolution supporting rearmament was procedurally invalid; to which the TUC General Secretary, Sir Vincent Tewson, responded that Congress was 'getting a little tired' of such nit-picking behaviour'.[41] David Low drew a cartoon from the incident displaying the FBU's hosepipe run dry.[42]

At the following weekend's monthly meeting of the Communist Party's Executive Committee, John reported on the achievements of the 85 Party members, delegates at that year's TUC. The EC was pleased that the vote against rearming Germany had almost been won while the FBU's motion and debate on the colonies on the last day, along with the successful vote on the foundry workers' motion on the Rent Act, were thought very encouraging. 'Horner's report', said Pollitt, 'shows the value of our work'.[43] But John could not have enjoyed hearing trade union leader, Arthur Deakin's remarks at the TUC that the FBU was not actually interested in the liberation of colonial peoples but only in 'propagating the foul Communist philosophy to which you adhere'.[44]

Any weariness John might have felt from his punishing schedule of incessant meetings disappeared when in October he flew to China in a delegation of Labour MPs, trade union leaders and a sprinkling of academics, organized by the British-Chinese Friendship Association. They stopped off for several days in Moscow where the left-wing Labour MP, Barbara Castle, celebrated her forty-fourth birthday in what her biographer describes as a 'vodka session'.[45] She and John already knew each other through the Movement for Colonial Freedom and on this trip their acquaintance was to strengthen. When or from which unkind friend Pat first heard rumours of an affair, I do not remember, but if these reached her with John still away, it may explain Pat's skin irritation so severe that it required a stay in hospital during his absence.

The flight from Moscow to Beijing seemed endless as they flew slowly over the Soviet Union, landing to refuel in Kazan, Sverdlovsk, Omsk and Novosibirsk. Regardless of the time of day or night, they were served a breakfast of cognac, caviar, smoked salmon and blinis with cream. On arrival in Beijing, John turned to one of their group, Professor Pulleybank, a historian of Chinese culture from Cambridge University, and asked him to translate a long welcome speech from the Chinese authorities. Pulleybank coughed apologetically, 'I am afraid I can only read Chinese and cannot understand the spoken language', a possibility that had not occurred to John. How much there was to discover!

In an article for *Labour Monthly*, John writes,

On the Dutch airliner out I had read in *Country Life* that, until the coming of the Communists, the Chinese had the deepest respect for their ancient culture and their lovely old buildings. The real fact is that until the Peoples' Government, the magnificent temples, the superb palaces, the Imperial City, all the buildings which gave Peking the name of the City of Northern Peace – were quietly but steadily falling to pieces. It has been left to the People's Government, with loving care, to restore and pre-serve these wonderful monuments of Chinese culture. No country cherishes its treasures as does China.

Out came the Leica for photos of palaces and temples. But mostly he photographed people.

No city is so alive as Peking. We were treading in Mr. Attlee's foot-steps. Back in England he had said that China had a 'population problem', that 'China was going in for quantity and not quality'. For my part I have never seen such children. Perhaps it's their comical haircuts, their fat faces, dark eyes, their lovely teeth and funny little trousers coupled with their completely uninhibited friendliness. I spent my last afternoon in Peking sitting in the sun in the Bai Pai Park, the old Dowager Empress's Winter Palace. The place was alive with strings of singing, laughing children weaving in and out of the old pine trees. Mr. Attlee, I believe, calls himself a Christian. When he made that remark 'quantity and not quality' about Chinese children he never uttered a less Christian word.[46]

The visit had begun with a three-hour meeting with the Prime Minister, Chou en Lai, whose opening remarks concerned the United States' military support to Chiang's defeated nationalist regime in Taiwan. Barbara Castle cabled the *Daily Herald* 'Chou does not want war!'[47] After that, we were to travel four thousand miles in China before we saw Peking again', writes John. Steel works, dams, irrigation schemes: 'The age-old problem of China's rivers – China's sorrows – had at last been solved by people working together in a way never witnessed before on this earth'. They visited villages where they were told of the suffering experienced under 'the decadent, brutal feudalism of the landlord system. As one woman's story was being translated', writes John, 'tears were running down her face as old memories were revived. When these peasants say, "Under the leadership of the Communist Party and Chairman Mao, we have done this or that", they really mean what they say'. And in Shanghai,

After a splendid time with the firemen in their mess room, late for my next appointment, I went to the pole hole doors to slide down the pole. I was immediately restrained – 'You are our guest, Mr. Horner, we must take care of you.' Politeness broke down – down the pole I went and we had a game of follow my leader with 50 Chinese fire-men chasing me down the poles to the appliance room floor.[48]

For *Firefighter* readers he described his meeting with Rewi Alley, an erstwhile fireman from New Zealand who had lived most of his life in China and 'was a deep student of Chinese art and archaeology and a brilliant translator of Chinese poetry'. Rewi Alley lived in one room,

In this world's wealth he is poor. But if friendship, kindliness, deep moral strength and a passionate devotion to the task of helping ordinary people then Rewi Alley is one of the world's wealthiest …. By showing in his own life that people of the most diverse backgrounds can live in cooperation together, he has supreme confidence that he gives to others, that these same people can guarantee that the world shall yet live in peace.[49]

John had returned in such high spirits about his discovery of China and the success of its communist revolution, that it would have been hard for Pat to continue sulking. In March 1955, she was in the *Daily Worker* for her composition of a campaign song for the National Assembly of Women, a communist-sponsored organization. Written to the tune of 'We Love to go a Wandering', the sixth and last verse is her best –

We love to go a-canvassing,
For things are surely wrong,
Come, women, all unite with us
And make our movement strong.[50]

In August they enjoyed a family holiday on the Gower Peninsula, where the sun shone every day. Pat and John followed this with a week's holiday in Venice without the children, as guests of the Italian firemen's union leader. On returning home Pat discovered she was pregnant. She had just celebrated her forty-third birthday and was both sad and relieved when soon afterwards she miscarried. Yet, that month's repair to their marriage was to serve them well in the next eighteen months.

Notes

1 Ralph Samuel, *The Lost World of British Communism*, London, 2006, 36.
2 NA/KV3/298 Minute to DSO Gibraltar about Horner's role in fomenting labour militancy in Gibraltar, 22 June 1951. This refers to an attached fuller note on the FBU compiled 'from a number of secret Office sources' and unavailable in the National Archives.
3 *Firefighter*, Feb–March 1946.
4 John Saville, 'The communist experience, a personal appraisal', *Socialist Register*, 1991, 1–27, (19).
5 *Daily Worker (DW)*, 27 January 1945.
6 LHA/CPGB EC Minutes, March 1948.
7 John Callaghan, *Rajani Palme Dutt, A study in British Stalinism*, London, 1993, 223.
8 *DW*, 28 November 1949.
9 Stephen Howe, 'The Movement for Colonial Freedom, 1954–1964' in *Anticolonialism in British Politics: The Left and the End of Empire 1918–1964*, Oxford, 1993. Oxford Scholarship Online: October 2011, DOI:10.1093/acprof:oso/9780198204237.003.0006

10 Julius Silverman: mentioned in the FBU General Purpose Committee Minutes, 21 December 1942; speaking about the fire service at council meeting, *Birmingham Mail*, 7 May 1940.

11 Silverman's obituary, *Independent*, 24 September 1996.

12 Darren Lilliker, *Against the Cold War. The History and Political Traditions of Pro-Sovietism in the British Labour Party 1945–1989*, London, 2004.

13 Lilliker.

14 Lilliker.

15 LHSAC/ CP/CENT/EC/02: FILE 1: Minutes and agendas, 1950: Notes by George Matthews on the meeting of 4 March.

16 N.J. Barnett and E. Smith, ' "Peace with a capital P": The spectre of communism and competing notions of "peace" in Britain, 1949–1960', *Labour History Review*, 2017, 82, 51–76 (56).

17 Jeremy Tranmer, 'Odd bed-fellows: British Christians and Communists in the Struggle for Peace', *Revue LISA/LISA e-journal* [En ligne], 2011, IX – n°1.

18 *Daily Express*, 2 June 1950.

19 *DW*, 13 July 1950.

20 *Firefighter*, June 1950.

21 *Firefighter*, February 1955.

22 Willie Thompson, *The Good Old Cause*, London, 1992, 114–115.

23 William Stueck, *Rethinking the Korean War*, Princeton, 2013.

24 *Firefighter*, October 1950.

25 *Firefighter*, October 1950.

26 *Daily Herald*, 5 September 1950.

27 TUC Report, 1950.

28 *Firefighter*, November 1950.

29 *Firefighter*, August 1951.

30 *Firefighter*, June 1951.

31 The British Peace Committee visit to Moscow, *Daily Telegraph*, 5 July 1952.

32 Doris Lessing, *The Golden Notebook*, London, 1972, 464.

33 LHA/ CP/ National Cultural Committee papers, 1954–1959.

34 Thomas Maguire, 'Counter-subversion in early Cold War Britain: The Official Committee on Communism (Home), the Information Research Department, and state-private networks', *Intelligence and National Security*, 2015, 30, 5, 637–66.

35 John Callaghan and Ben Harker, *British Communism, A Documentary History*, Manchester, 2011, 164–85.

36 Maguire, 650.

37 Hugh Wilford, 'The Information Research Department: Britain's secret Cold War weapon revealed', *Review of International Studies*, 1998, 24,1998, 353–369 (369).

38 David Childs, 'The Cold War and the "British Road", 1946–53', *Journal of Contemporary History* 23, 1988, 551–572 (560).

39 *Manchester Guardian*, 6 September 1951.

40 As reported in the *Times*, 7 September 1954.

41 *Illustrated London News*, 18 September 1954.

42 *Manchester Guardian*, 7 September 1954.

43 LHASC / CP/CENT/EC/03/08, notes from the EC meeting of the weekend of 11 and 12 September 1954.

44 As quoted in the *Daily Mail*, 11 September 1954.

45 Anne Perkins, *Red Queen, The Authorized Biography of Barbara Castle*, London, 2003,143.

46 John Horner, 'My six hundred million friends', *Labour Monthly*, January 1955, 30.

47 *Daily Herald*, 25 October 1954.

48 Horner, January 1955, 33.

49 *Firefighter*, January 1955.

50 *DW*, 2 March 1955; the song can be found at LHA/CP 'National Women's Advisory Committee'.

51 MML Peace Movement/Chingford Unity Theatre anti-war campaign 1950 CID: 60496.

19

THE CHILDREN'S PERSPECTIVE

Pat had given her each of her daughters smaller versions of her own folk-style blouse acquired in Hungary. A Chingford comrade converted an old blackout curtain into a skirt that Carol was to wear with the blouse and helped her embroider it with the Hungarian colours of red, green and white. Thus attired, my sister stood alongside other communist children on Nelson's plinth in Trafalgar Square, each in the national dress of an East European country. According to Carol's fragmentary memoir, 'Speakers denounced or made an appeal for something I didn't understand then and have forgotten now.... The Press were taking photographs and I was terrified that the next day all my classmates would see how I spent my weekends'.[1] Her fear of being outed had increased ever since our mother took to looping up Carol's plaits in a style taken from *Soviet Monthly*, a magazine illustrated with pictures of Stalin, a jovial man with a big moustache who received bunches of flowers from girls of Carol's age. She recalled, 'I was very aware that nobody else at school had a hair style like this .... I felt it to be a clue, a badge that someone would recognise'.

Anything that might reveal her identity made her anxious. When noticing she had more Russian and Eastern European stamps than did her school friends, she switched to collecting labels of processed cheese triangles from the non-Communist countries of Holland and Switzerland.

When the British Communist Party ceased to exist with the end of the Cold War, Carol was vexed by a collection of memoirs about our generation's experience of growing up in a communist family. None of its contributors appeared to have shared our fear of public exposure. On the contrary, *they* mostly remembered how as children they proclaimed their community identity. According to one contributor 'We took issue with our teachers ...

DOI: 10.4324/9781032671352-20

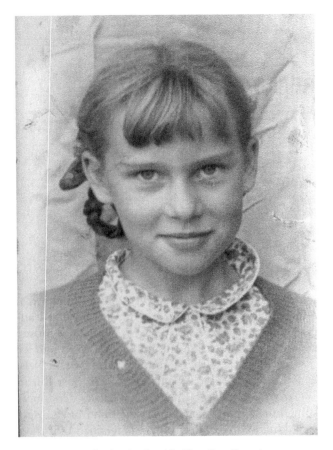

FIGURE 19.1   Carol's Soviet braids (family album).

and defended Russia against verbal abuse'.[2] If our childhood contemporaries had had no worries about being different, this might explain why it did not occur to our parents that we were uncomfortable about how their politics might affect us, despite our growing up when the Cold War was at its chilliest and British society so conventional that siblings dared not talk to each other about their parents' divorce. With only 30,000 Party members communism in 1951 was even less conventional than divorce and Doris Lessing noticed that when with strangers, Party members' children had 'the defensive closed-in look of people knowing themselves to be in a minority'.[3] Carol and I were acutely aware that the Party venerated a nation viewed as an enemy by the rest of the British population. I was relieved when my school playground chose Red Indians or Germans as the baddies to be hunted down and brutally dispatched. But increasingly the Russians were made the baddies and I had to pretend I believed to be evil those whom I knew to be good. I became a skilful dissimulator. 'The incredible dread that my sister and I carried around', writes Carol, 'was that Someone Would Find Out'. When I stayed out of school the whole winter of 1950/51 with respiratory problems, my ill health helped me retreat into the safety of home with just 'us' and none of 'them'.

Carol begins her brief memoir with the collapse of the Soviet Union in 1991 when our father disposed of his collection of communist books. ' "This is my pain", he says, as if he alone has suffered. But it is also his daughters' pain and history. It is our childhood. We were the ones born into a secret society'. Because she and I had never discussed our communist childhood, she called the memoir, 'Did I Ever Tell You?' After I read it, we started talking.

I was an anxious child. Even home could be a dangerous place. Once or twice a week my mother took out the hoover from the cupboard under the stairs. Sometimes it refused to start, or worse, made alarming noises while cleaning the carpet in the front room being readied for that evening's Party meeting. Pat would frown at it crossly, switch it on and off, fiddle with its bag, tut-tutting to herself. I scampered into the hall to sit on the staircase, far enough away to be safe should the hoover blow up. On a Saturday when there was no EC meeting in King Street, no Fire Brigades Union school in Yorkshire, nor a weekend peace congress in Conway Hall, not even a man my father had to see about a dog (a favourite phrase), on such a Saturday morning the hoover would meet its match. It was on good behaviour with my father; no fear of it exploding when he was in charge. A memory: my mother comes out from the kitchen where she has been making our weekend suet pudding, her nose and hands all floury. As he guides the docile machine around the living room, my father puts his other arm around her waist, and kisses her firmly on the lips; the hoover purrs with satisfaction.

I was eight years old when the *Daily Worker* published accounts of the Rosenbergs' trial as Soviet spies followed by news of the worldwide campaign to stop their execution. Even the Pope asked for clemency. The Rosenbergs had two children, aged ten and six. Michael, the older one, wrote a letter to President Eisenhower vainly begging him 'not to let anything happen to my mummy and daddy'. The *Worker* published a picture of the two children taken with their grandmother outside the White House. And another of Michael, his arm around his younger brother. It required little imagination to transpose this to Carol and me. The day after the execution, the *Worker* explained how someone dies in the electric chair. I was a precocious reader.

The healthy heart and a normal constitution can resist for a time even higher voltages, and far from succumbing instantly, the victim may suffer a slow and cruel agony .... A damp sponge has been placed under the main electrode on the bead, and the dimensions of the foot electrodes have been increased so as to give a greater area of contact. But healthy victims literally boil in their own blood. In the veins and arteries the temperature of the blood rises, blood vessels burst and in some cases the skull of the victim has been seen to smoke and the hair fall out.[4]

Might my parents endure the same fate? Or if not electrocution, possibly prison? The *Worker* told me that Communists were jailed in America just for thinking.[5] I was taken to a supper party in south London in honour of a trade unionist, an exile who had been imprisoned in America for his communism. If him, why not my father? Because I never told anyone my fears, I could not be reassured. What I wanted to say to my mother was 'Please stop being communist'. But I knew she would tell me why that was impossible. Would repeat to me her dream of a better world, already real and present in the Soviet Union. Carol recalled the song our father sang on long car journeys –

> Soviet land so dear to every toiler
> Peace and progress built their hope on thee
> There's no land the whole world over
> Where man may walk the land so proud and free.

Even then, I preferred 'If I had a hammer' that made no reference to the problematic Soviets. It was a song of peace, freedom, justice 'and the love between all our brothers all over this world'.

British communists enjoyed singing together. 'There were regular parties, although they weren't called parties'. Carol writes,

> They were Socials. Perhaps the Party couldn't have a party. All the female comrades made savoury what-nots; my mother's set piece were cheesy pastry turnovers. I remember them as very good. Our kitchen table was covered in dozen or so bottles of beer, a green bottle of gin and a bottle of Rose's Lime Juice … My mother used to invent paper and pencil games which involved a chase from room to room following the clues stuck on the wall. Sometimes nobody managed to solve them; she was often too literary for the comrades.

After we moved from Chingford to New Malden, the social's highpoint was local Party member Elin Williams on the guitar. Married to the solicitor, John Williams, Elin was best-known for her song about Harry Pollitt who when he gets to heaven, chalks slogans on the pearly gates and brings the angels out on strike.[6] Elin also sang Woody Guthrie favourites from the years of the Great Depression but the one I most liked was about the very fat man who watered the workers' beer.[7] Our father would round off the evening with his pleasant baritone rendition of Joe Hill. Carol remembered when as a small child at a Party summer fete, I heard over the PA system a recording of Paul Robeson singing Joe Hill. 'Daddy sings it better than that man', I said. She also recalled the folksinger Ewan MacColl coming to our house, 'Turned round a kitchen chair, straddled it, put his hand to his ear and wailed. I preferred the local talent'.

Carol had joined the Young Communist League in 1953 – the same year we moved to New Malden, the year Stalin died and the Rosenbergs were executed. She writes,

> I didn't think about it. I didn't question what I was doing, I didn't even expect that was what my parents wanted. It just seemed inevitable, like cleaning my teeth and going to school. For a few years, life was very grey. Now I was expected to collect 'dues' and do a *Challenge* round every Sunday morning. On some awful occasion we went 'over to Dickerage', the local Council estate to do cold calling for *Challenge*. It was very similar to the Jehovah's witnesses that come to my door these days.

I confessed to her after my second glass of wine: I had regularly stolen money from the *Daily Worker*. Carol laughed. Topped up my glass. 'So did I!' She includes our thieving in the final version of her memoir that describes how our home was used for Party meetings.

> Other children didn't have Meetings in their houses. Other people only had their friends to their houses. They didn't meet strangers outside the lavatory. Greasy, unhappy, thin men from the aircraft factory, the lecherous carpenter and the fat, emergency-trained teacher with the cowl-neck dress that didn't fit and the wobbly arms and the endless cigarettes. There was sometimes a white-haired pair of 'intellectuals' with a smelly dog. My mother was beautiful and gracious. She welcomed them to her home. She smiled and gave them tea from the large aluminium pot and took the minutes. Contributions for the tea went into the collection box for the '*Daily Worker* Fighting Fund' (My sister and I used it regularly to supplement our pocket money).

Some of the meetings were about organizing the annual *Daily Worker* bazaar, an annual event where comrades sold to each other stuff made for that purpose.

> A local hall was taken for a few weeks before Christmas and every woman comrade cooked, sewed and knitted. Maybe the men did something but I can't remember what. My mother cooked. Usually very good fruity mincemeat and so many jars of green tomato chutney. There were baby clothes made from re-cycled jerseys and carpets made from old slippers [sic]......

Pat was devoted to the *Worker*. When driving home from a rally in Hyde Park or Trafalgar Square, John, at her request, would take us along Farringdon Road where, as we drove past the *Daily Worker* building, she led us in a rousing cheer. The building has long since been knocked down, but when I have occasion to be in that part of Farringdon Road I give a silent cheer, perhaps in fond memory of our mother's attachment or possibly at the recollection of how I got my own back against the *Worker*.

It was forever running out of money, dependent for survival on its loyal readers. I felt sorry for Barbara Niven who was in charge of the Fighting Fund. Every day, the valiant Barbara urged the comrades onto greater efforts. There would be frightful consequences should we fail to meet the monthly target. For example, on the tenth of March 1954, the Fighting Fund missed its target by £546.

> There were record collections from the workshops, new collections from workmates and friends, special sacrifices from families – all of them for 'No Arms for the Germans'. A crowning gift of £1 came from an old age pensioner of 89 who had been waiting impatiently for an insurance bonus. His concern was lest it didn't arrive in time for us. But this finish is a hard blow to us. ... Lift us from this position of deadly danger ... with a really substantial rise.

Comrades who came to our house played their part. Pennies were dropped into a cardboard shoebox that had held our sensible Start-rite sandals. Because our mother was hopeless at any handicraft, our father or another comrade must have cut the coin slot into its lid, pasting on the side of the box 'The Daily Worker Fighting Fund'. This neatly hid Start-rite's iconic siblings, arm-in-arm at the start of their long journey on the lonely road ahead. The box was on the hall table, next to the phone with a contribution to the Fighting Fund obligatory should a comrade make a call (the FBU paid our phone bill). Even if not making a phone call, it was difficult to reach the front door without Pat pressing the visitor to drop some pennies into the Start-rite box. When the box felt sufficiently heavy, it was emptied and the cash used for a postal order to send to Barbara Niven.

With no regular checking of the contents, we would have to been caught red-handed for our thieving to be discovered. It was easy enough to help myself. Take off the lid, remove a penny or two and replace the lid. I did it when on the point of leaving the house to go to school. In Chingford, the primary school had been close by, at the top of our quiet street but in New Malden it was a twenty-five-minute walk mostly along a dreary, main road. When it rained, I stole the money for a bus fare. Travelling to school in the comfort of the bus was a small recompense for the work I put in to keep my communist identity a secret. In any case, our family had complicated views on money. A large book on my parents' shelves, *The Robber Barons*, was not as I had long imagined, about the Sherriff of Nottingham as portrayed in radical children's author, Geoffrey Trease's *Bows against the Barons*, but rather an account of the bloated American capitalists who oppressed the poor workers. My mother was pleased when the news on the wireless mentioned falls in the values of shares. 'After all', she told me, 'we don't have any'. The more troubled the stock exchange, the better. Property was theft. When capitalism collapsed from its own contradictions, the workers would be liberated. 'Then, there will be no money', said Pat cheerfully as she counted out on the kitchen table how much was left in her purse prior to writing her shopping list on the back of an old envelope.

Yet I knew it was wrong to take and spend what was not mine. My cousin Evie had been caught stealing from her mother's purse and was taken to see a child psychologist who attributed Evie's thieving habits to her feelings of not being loved because she had been adopted. Evie's thieving was a cry for attention, my mother told me, with an affirmative hug to show how much she and Daddy loved me. I knew they did. If only they hadn't also loved the Party.

Notes

1 Carol Horner's unpublished memoir, 1997.
2 Phil Cohen, *Children of the Revolution, Communist Childhood in Cold War Britain*, London, 1997.
3 For the conventional 1950s, see David Kynaston *Family Britain*, London, 2010; Lessing, 162.
4 *Daily Worker*, 22 June 1953.
5 *Daily Worker*, 29 June 1953.
6 Sadly, there is no recording available of Elin Williams singing 'Harry Bolshie' but it can heard on YouTube at www.youtube.com/watch?v=mSUO2ilm81I Accessed 20 October 2023.
7 'The Man that Waters the Workers' Beer' by Paddy Ryan can be heard on YouTube at www.youtube.com/watch?v=SybZrbeBQ3I Accessed 20 October 2023.

20

'BOTH BETRAYED AND BETRAYER'

'And the complete deadlock remained unbroken', John Horner told the delegates at the FBU conference in 1955.

> After months of discussion we were back where we started. The situation was hopeless. It was clear from the Home Office circular which was to be distributed to Fire Authorities with a new regulations permitting each of the one and hundred fifty or so local authority fire services would be able to fix their duty hours without being required to consult the Fire Brigades Union. Just like the bad old days before the War. The Union's power broken.[1]

They had delayed the annual conference from June until October so as to devote themselves to campaigning against the new Home Office regulation. 'A thousand firemen crammed into London's Conway Hall. Before our tours had ended, Bro. Grahl and I had spoken to nearly one-third of our total membership'. Still unsuccessful, with just two days before the conference was due to meet, John had at last secured a meeting with the deputy permanent secretary at the Home Office.

> Armed as we were with the solid backing of the energetic, enthusiastic and determined opposition of the rank and file of this Union, we were able on that Thursday night, after months of talk, to say once again, and to say it finally, that firemen were not prepared to accept the draft regulation.

DOI: 10.4324/9781032671352-21

And once Sir Arthur appreciated he was faced with 'immoveable opposition', he reversed the policy. Bro. Horner asked,

> Why this change? Clearly the Home Office saw that the Union was not alone. The Labour Movement had understood that any attempt to weaken the power and ability of any union, to threaten its rights and liberties, was a matter for the Movement as a whole. The government saw a united, determined rank and file. They had had reports of the mood of our members, of the temper of the great meetings. They knew they were facing an impossible task.[2]

John had delivered a victory for the membership. A photograph in the *Firefighter* shows the conference delegates rising to their feet to applaud him. He must have been relieved the conference delegates had agreed to skip a conference for the following year. He was weary not only from the Home Office campaign but also earlier from the rumpus earlier that year when the Communist Party decided which of the Union's two national organizers (both Party members) would lose his job during an FBU cost-cutting exercise.[3] It seemed that the Party's National Industrial Policy Committee [NIPC] was interfering more than it should or John would have wanted them to. As Bob Darke had remarked, trade union leaders like John Horner 'may eat fire in public but the dish is humble pie at NIPC meetings'.[4]

On 5 November, John celebrated his forty-fourth birthday. Pat always used her annual Cooperative dividend to buy John's present and that year she gave him E.P. Thompson's new biography of William Morris after reading the *Daily Worker*'s enthusiastic review that concludes with Morris' stirring lines from *Chants for Socialists* –

> Nay, cry aloud, and have no fear,
> We few against the world;
> Awake, arise! the hope we bear
> Against the curse is hurled.

Five days later, a partly clothed body of a woman was spotted in the Thames above Blackfriars Bridge. By evening she had been identified as thirty-nine-year-old Helen Grahl from Chalk Farm, the wife of Jack Grahl, the FBU's assistant general secretary. On the eleventh, the *Daily Mail* reported the police were satisfied there had been no foul play and that Grahl had told them his wife had recently been depressed.[5] The police told the court there were no suspicious circumstances and the coroner decided she had been 'Found drowned in circumstances not fully disclosed by the evidence' – the customary verdict for suspected suicide.[6]

Jack Grahl was a hard-working, highly competent organizer and a good negotiator. When in Northern Ireland earlier that year 'fighting the case of the Ulster firemen', he was described as ruthlessly single-minded and 'a man who does not mince words'.[7] With a special interest in members' education, Grahl was reputedly an excellent tutor with the 'power to draw people out'.[8] And that November's issue of the *Firefighter* included a letter from a union branch thanking Grahl for his 'fatherly care'. Yet, there had been rumours of Grahl's affairs with women staff and it was alleged that earlier in the year he had charged to the Union the costs of his wife's visit to Czechoslovakia when she had accompanied him there on a Fire Brigades Union trip.[9] Unlike in many of the *Firefighter*'s pictures of Horner, Grahl is rarely shown smiling. Perhaps this is what the FBU's future president, Enoch Humphries, was implying when he told the historian, John Saville, that Grahl was 'a different person in every way', from Horner, volunteering that if he had had to decide between them, he would have given fifty-five to Horner and fifty to Grahl.[10]

It was probably during a tea break in King Street at that weekend's monthly Executive Committee meeting that someone in the Party leadership took John aside and told him to give Grahl an alibi. In the context of stagnating membership and falling *Daily Worker* sales, the meeting was discussing at length the content of a draft 'political resolution' to be presented to the next biennial Party Congress in April 1956. According to the detailed notes, John did not speak and when, exceptionally, a vote was taken he either abstained or, more likely, had left the meeting early.[11] As recounted separately to both daughters, the Party had told John that should the police contact him, he was to say that on the evening of Helen's death, he and Grahl had been together on FBU business. The alibi was needed because on the evening Helen died Grahl had been with her sister with whom he was having an affair. Should this detail be made public, it would place the Party in a bad light – and also, of course, the union.

It may not have been the first time John had been required to lie for the Party; indeed, he hinted as much when telling me about the Grahl affair. Kevin Morgan's sensitive discussion of Harry Pollitt's state of mind at the time of the Nazi-Soviet Pact helps me understand John's compliance: 'Party membership brought with it irrevocable obligations'.[12] For twenty years, John had campaigned and organized for the Communist Party, obediently following its shifts in policy. Like his mentor, Pollitt, he was bound by 'innumerable ties of friendship and loyalty'. And as a good Communist, John had agreed to the principles of democratic centralism that obliged him to accept the orders the Party gave him. If Grahl's affair with his sister-in-law were made public, it would not only damage the Party but also injure his beloved Fire Brigades Union for whom just three weeks earlier John had won a significant victory from a hostile Conservative government.

Although from the newspaper report of the inquest, it appears the police may never have interviewed John and despite the coroner's verdict of suicide, he believed he had given Grahl an alibi for murder. His acute sense of guilt originated from not actually telling a lie but from his having agreed to do so. To have to hide the truth of Grahl's whereabouts on the night of Helen's death gnawed away at John's soul; it seems the lie demanded of him by the Communist Party for a comrade's adultery came to embody the Party's requirement that he deny that Stalin ordered the murders of hundreds of thousands.

There is an entry for 13 November 1955 in Lessing's novel *The Golden Notebook*.

> Ever since Stalin's death, there has been a state of affairs in the CP that old hands say would have been impossible at any time before .... The discussions have slowly developed and there is now a sort of vague plan – to remove the dead bureaucracy at the centre of the Party, so that the CP should be completely changed, a genuinely British Party without the deadly loyalty to Moscow and the obligation to tell lies.[13]

Whether or not John was involved in such discussions, he was sufficiently disaffected by the Grahl affair to decline reappointment to the Party's Executive Committee on expiry of his term the following April. According to one of Segars' informants, Grahl had ignored instructions from King Street to resign from his position as assistant general secretary due to the circumstances of his wife's death.[14] Then, towards the end of February 1956, the new general secretary of the Soviet Communist Party, Nikita Khrushchev, addressed a secret session of the Twentieth Party Congress in Moscow and denounced their former leader, Joseph Stalin, who had ruled over them for twenty-five years until his death in 1953.

Although foreign delegates to the Congress had been excluded from the secret session, some of them had seen the text of Khrushchev's speech and, as they made their way home across Europe, rumours travelled with them. On Sunday 11 March, Pollitt and Dutt formally reported back from Moscow to the monthly meeting of the Communist Party's Executive Committee, the last that John was due to attend. The EC duly approved a statement for publication: the Moscow Congress had discussed the magnificent Soviet achievements in industry and agriculture, as well as the improvements in people's living standards. The only hint that the memory of Stalin the Great Leader was to be downgraded came in an oblique reference to 'ending of the cult of the individual'.[15] Perhaps Pollitt and Dutt were more frank with the EC off the record or possibly the rumours about Khrushchev's denunciation may have circulated during the tea break.[16] But whatever it was John learnt that Sunday in King Street must have triggered next day's crisis.

Our kitchen was moist from Monday's wash brought in from the garden before dark fell. Damp stockings, shirts and socks dangled from the airer suspended over our formica-topped table. Having laid it for our tea, I sat there deep into a book, my reading uninterrupted apart from an occasional drip onto the page, wiped dry with my hankie. Pat stood at the stove, her face enveloped in steam from boiling potatoes. She had taken the lid off the saucepan to check their readiness to be drained and mashed for the shepherd's pie she had made from the remains of our weekend joint. When John opened the kitchen door, she turned and greeted him with a loving smile; I stood up from the table, book in hand, eager to answer the anticipated question, 'What are you reading?'

But his face was grey and grim, his blue eyes, cold and absent. We watched him place his cracked, brown leather briefcase onto the lino floor, just inside the door, as if he were half-minded to pick it up again, turn around and leave us. He hesitated a moment. Then, without speaking, walked to the table, picked up a green dinner plate and hurled it across the room, the silence shattered as the plate broke against the far wall. A second plate followed to splinter into pieces. Then a third. John still mute. Wife at the stove, daughter at the table, frozen momentarily inside the chaos that crashed around us. As he reached for a glass tumbler, Pat was beside him. She stopped the carnage. Put her arms tight around her husband and whispered to him. I watched my big, bold, brave father sobbing like a small child. Saw his chest heave. Pat whispered to me. 'It's alright, dear. Don't worry. Daddy is just tired'. And taking him by the hand, she led him out of the room, upstairs to their bedroom.

Shortly before he died, John recalled an incident during the war when he was by himself in Chingford with the family in Birmingham. He had been carrying a tea-tray upstairs to his solitary bed when he heard a drone above his head. As he reached the landing, the flying bomb's engine cut out. No time to get outside and into the Anderson shelter. So, was this it? After five, long years of war, and victory in sight, was he to be denied the fruits of peace? How could he leave Pat and the girls? He froze, for a second mute and helpless, then hurled the tea-tray down the stairs, the sound of crashing crockery drowned out by the bomb's blast that shook the house. Next morning, he learnt that the bomb had fallen at the top of the street. In telling me this story, John reflected on how the threat of the flying bomb had caused his years of pent-up stress to explode through his smashing of the household crockery. Perhaps he was referring indirectly to that moment in 1956 when he literally cracked up, and about which we never spoke.

As soon as she had put John to bed, Pat telephoned Jessie Charles, his secretary and confidante. By noon next day, Jessie had identified and made an appointment with a 'nerve specialist' paid for by the FBU. Thus, on the Wednesday morning, John missed an urgent meeting of the FBU's general purposes committee concerning a forthcoming visit to the Home Office; Pat had instead taken him to the doctor in Harley Street.[17] That evening she told us our father had been working too hard; he had had a nervous breakdown and the specialist had ordered him to rest. Our job was to help her cheer him up.

On the Friday of that same week, a purported summary version of Khrushchev's secret speech was leaked to Reuters news agency, in time to make Saturday's headlines in newspapers across Europe –

> **MURDERED** Five thousand Russia's best officers were murdered during the blood baths that followed Marshal Tukhachevsky's trial for treason 1937. Under Stalin's purges victims, including children, were tortured. During Khrushchev's speech, Renter's sources say, some delegates shouted 'How did you stand it? Why didn't you kill him?' Khrushchev replied: 'What could we do? There was a reign of terror. If you looked at him wrongly you lost your head the next day.'[18]

Because none of this was published in the *Daily Worker*, it would have been in Sunday's *Observer* that Pat and John first read about the trumped-up treason trials and the purges, the gist of which John had already learnt the previous weekend and that, as he told me years later, part of him had always known. Alison Macleod, a *Daily Worker* staff member, remembered her and her husband's reaction to the news,

> I continued, mechanically to measure my knitting. Jack said: 'You've just heard that the hero of your life is a torturer of little children and all you can think of is your knitting'. In fact, I was thinking what Jack was thinking. First: this is all true. Then, as we turned a blind eye to these crimes, we are guilty too.[19]

John's mother spent Easter weekend at our home in New Malden. Perhaps it was the anxiety about her son's mental health that triggered her heart attack on Good Friday; she died in the ambulance on the way to hospital. The overcast sky and the chill in the air would have matched John's mood when he buried his mother in Walthamstow's Queens Road Cemetery, its trees not yet in leaf. They laid her in the family plot alongside John's father and his brother, Charlie, just fifteen years old when a reckless driver had knocked him off his bike.

FIGURE 20.1   John's mother (family album).

After the funeral he packed into a cardboard box the few photographs of himself when young, along with one of his grandmother and another of his father on his wedding day; also into the box went his father's tobacco jar and shaving mug that had remained on the kitchen mantelpiece in Boston Road after his death in 1944. He took also a postcard from Wasdale Head signed 'Freddie', sent to his mother on his and Pat's first holiday together in 1935; and his Monoux School reports. Emily had been so proud of her youngest, brightest child, had had such high hopes for him. Even Mrs Perks had congratulated her when Freddie had won a rare scholarship to grammar school. And now, his mother was gone leaving Freddie in the abyss. 'You will miss me when I am in Queens Road', she used to half-joke when failing to get her way.

During April, John made sporadic visits to the office, but otherwise stayed at home, his only distraction a weekly visit with his younger daughter to the local Odeon. Westerns were his favourite. You could tell the goodies from the baddies. Except, that is, for 'The Searchers', newly on release and whose depressing complexity matched John's mood. 'That will be the day', says weary, cynical, middle-aged John Wayne travelling through the desert on his long, and eventually futile search. 'That will be the day', repeated John as we drove home from the cinema.

Since his 'nervous breakdown', he had been obliged to delegate much of the Union's business to Jack Grahl. The newspaper reports of Khrushchev's speech published on the weekend of the 17–18 March had coincided with the start of the FBU's yearly National School at Wortley Hall where forty-five firemen were to study the theory of the working-class movement and the Union's national executive met in their annual extended session. For the first time, John was absent and when the two groups came together on the school's penultimate day, it was Jack Grahl who 'very ably' led the three sessions on current problems of firemen and the policies of the union. Then, on the final day, Grahl spoke for two and a half hours on the issue of wages and hours.[20] It was a personal triumph. Grahl also took the opportunity of John's absence from Wortley Hall to improve his personal finances. Having explained to a meeting of the executive's general purposes committee how he was short of money to buy his new house, the committee agreed he could draw his salary in advance up until the end of the year. Grahl then explained that some months earlier after an accident while driving his FBU car, the Union had put in an insurance claim both for the cost of repairing the car and for hiring another while it was out of service. But, because he was able to use another Union car in the interim, there had been no car rental costs. So, would they agree that he rather than the FBU received that element of the insurance pay out? And, amazingly, they did.[21]

Jessie Charles, John's secretary, may have alerted John to what had happened. On the tenth of April he came into the office for a meeting of the general purposes committee to tell them why their decision about the insurance money had to be rescinded.[22] After this, relations between John and Jack Grahl must have broken down entirely, explaining John's reluctance to take the full sick leave that the FBU's president, John Burns, was urging upon him. John eventually agreed to Burns' suggestion that 'the nerve specialist' report to the Union's Executive Council on the state of the general secretary's health. The executive council accepted the specialist's recommendation that four weeks of total absence from the office was advised, with a stay in the country far away from London. John was allocated one hundred pounds to cover the costs of his stay.[23]

In the belief that her presence would aid John's recovery, the specialist recommended their younger daughter accompany her parents and in early May, we drove down to south Devon, the car loaded with school work for me and novels for Pat. John had never been much drawn to fiction but Pat had thrown in a couple of Dickens in the hope he might succumb. We stayed at a small farm guest house in the village of Chillington in Devon's South Hams. Pat must have decided on Devon suitably distant from London and as somewhere never previously visited, hoping the novelty might enthuse John to get out and explore. The guidebook describes South Hams as a marvellous outdoor environment, with rivers, moorland, coasts and sea and the weather befriended us with dry, sunny days. The steep banks in Devon's narrow lanes were replete with wild flowers; the scent of bluebells hung heavy in the woodlands; the lambs gambolled in the fields. Yet, she could not persuade John to leave the premises.

A bored child's poorly composed snapshot catches her parents unaware on the edge of the frame in her photo of the guest house garden. They sit side-by-side, half-shaded by a tree. Pat looks down at the book on her lap. John slouches in his armchair, slack hands loosely clasped on his thighs, book face-down on his knees. Bushy eyebrows drawn close together, he stares ahead into empty space beyond the purview of the camera. In a section of his draft memoir that he removed from his final version, he writes – 'Day after day I sat in the old world garden of our guest house and churned over in my head and openly with my loving patient wife, all that had happened and was happening – and was fearful of what might become'. He felt, he writes, 'both betrayed and betrayer'.[24]

The young woman who ran the guest house had a brother who managed the family farm. It was evident to them both that John required distraction from black thoughts. So when a piglet escaped from its pen, he was summoned from the garden to help catch it. Badly out of shape, John puffed up the lane after a small, squealing animal that managed to wriggle out of his grasp every time he grabbed it. But the episode raised a slight smile, the first we had seen for weeks. Brother and sister then proposed something longer-term to keep John occupied. The young farmer had recently picked up on the cheap from Devonport dockyard, an old, semi-derelict admiral's barge that he had moored in a creek of the Kingsbridge estuary, a few minutes' drive away. If John felt like working with him to make the necessary repairs, he would take us out afterwards on a fishing trip. Pat and I sat in camp chairs by the creek-side, reading books from Boots' circulating library while John scraped and varnished, scrubbed and painted, corked and polished. 'Down at the creek', he remembered 'the dark cloud would lift. [But] Idle and away from the boat, the clouds came down'.

After a week, the *Marilyn* was sufficiently seaworthy for an outing. Having little luck with the fish, on the turn of the tide, the young farmer set course for home. The ebb was running strong in the estuary and when we were within hailing distance of the quay, the boat ran aground on the mud. John stood at the stern and tried to push us off with a boat pole. He called to the farmer for a little forward throttle, 'The diesel roared, I pushed and the boat shot into deep water as I plunged headfirst into the ripe, estuarial mud'. Choosing not to be picked up by the boat, John floundered through the mud to the shore from where he walked around to the quay. There,

> the usual crowd of loafers had been watching with increasing amusement our antics on the mud. Filthy as I was from head to foot, I grinned as I approached the crowd. They in turn began to laugh and so did I. I laughed and laughed.

From the boat, we had watched John's reception on the quayside. It had been months since we had last seen him laugh. I turned to look at how Pat was taking it. She was crying the tears of relief that John never saw. She had wiped them away before we came off the boat. 'We were all still laughing', writes John, 'when we got back to the farm … This time the cloud of depression was really lifting. The years of fruitless political effort, misplaced loyalties and of self-deception were ending'.

The nerve specialist was cautious about John's recovery, concerned that unless he took things easy there might be a relapse. For the time being he was to work very much part-time, leaving Jack Grahl in charge as acting general secretary. It gave Grahl the opportunity to demonstrate his capabilities. Enoch Humphries was to tell Saville that Grahl had had a group of supporters on the Union's Executive Council, and that he 'was making moves to make Horner disappear permanently'.[25] Nor did the rumpus that had broken out in the British Communist Party offer John any comfort. At its scheduled biannual congress in early April, Party members had demanded the leadership tell them the full truth about the Stalinist years. A *Daily Worker* journalist, Malcolm MacEwen, was shocked how Pollitt was 'incapable of abandoning the uncritical solidarity with the Soviet leadership on which he had built his political life and [he] … still preferred secrecy to openness'.[26] In May, Pollitt resigned as General Secretary of the Party on the grounds of ill health, to be replaced by Johnny Gollan, Grahl's Edinburgh contemporary. The leadership agreed to look into strengthening democracy within the Party but otherwise, writes MacEwen, nothing changed with Palme Dutt arguing that ends *did* justify means.

> That there should be spots on the sun would only startle an inveterate Mithras-worshipper … To imagine that a great revolution can develop without a million cross-currents, hardships, injustices and excesses would be a delusion fit only for ivory-tower dwellers in fairyland who have still to learn that the thorny path of human advancement moves not only through unexampled heroism but also with accompanying baseness, with tears and blood.[27]

On Sunday, 10 June, the *Observer* published the full text of Khrushchev's secret speech about Stalin: 26,000 words. Pat and John were discussing it over the kitchen table, still cluttered by dirty plates, marmalade jar and cornflakes packet, when Jimmy, the Party's local literature secretary arrived on the pretext of collecting some monthly subscription. I let him in and sat back down at the table. Pat poured Jimmy a cup of tea, and then made another pot. Jimmy lit his pipe, and John re-lit his. Pat took another cigarette. The child sat quiet, listening to the grown-ups in a room filled with smoke. Jimmy was a good friend; he and his wife had taken me into their home when John was in China and Pat had had to go into hospital.

Jimmy sat with us at the kitchen table until it was time to go home for his Sunday roast. Their conversation was a great relief to all three. British Communists 'had lost the habit of frankness', remembered Alison Macleod. What had they been afraid of? No-one was going to send them to Siberia. They had been silent through fear of losing their illusions.[28] Khrushchev's complete speech revealed his indictment of Stalin to be stronger than the summary versions that had been circulating until then. It confirmed the existence of the Stalinist purges, mock trials and mass slaughter, all of which the British Communist Party had denounced as malicious and hostile slander. 'Men and women with honourable records of service to the working-class movement saw their world turned upside down', wrote John in the last chapter of the final version of his memoir.

Notes

1 *Firefighter*, November–December 1955, 20.
2 *Firefighter*, November–December 1955, 20.
3 See Terry Segars, *The Fire Service: A Social History of a Uniformed Working Class'*, PhD thesis, University of Essex, 1989, 356. For the 'resignation' of the national organizer, Mark Bass, *Firefighter*, February–March 1955, 2.
4 Bob Darke, *The Communist Technique in Britain*, London, 1952, 61.
5 *Daily Mail*, 11 November 1955.
6 *Westminster and Pimlico News*, 25 November 1955.
7 *Belfast Telegraph*, 4 January 1955.
8 *Firefighter*, October 1947.
9 Humphries interview with John Saville, HHC/UDJS/1/28, FBU History; MRC/ MSS 346/ FBU GPC Minutes, 17 May 1956.
10 Humphries interview.
11 LHA/CP/ EC Minutes, 12/13 November 1955.
12 Kevin Morgan, *Harry Pollitt*, Manchester, 1993, 112.
13 Doris Lessing, *The Golden Notebook*, London, 1972, 393.
14 Segars, 356.
15 Addendum to CP/EC Minutes, March 1956.
16 For speculations about what was said at that EC meeting see Macleod, 66.
17 FBU GPC Minutes, 14 March 1956.

18 *Daily Herald*, 17 March 1956.
19 Alison Macleod, *The Death of Uncle Joe*, London, 1997, 64.
20 *Firefighter*, March–April 1956.
21 GPC Minutes, 23 March 1956.
22 GPC Minutes, 10 April 1956.
23 GPC Minutes, 30 April 1956.
24 Draft memoir, FBU records at MRC.
25 Humphries interview.
26 Malcolm MacEwen, *The Greening of a Red*, London, 1991, 183.
27 Cited in Paul Flewers, 'The unexpected denunciation: the reception of Khrushchev's 'Secret Speech' in Britain', *Critique*, 2019, 47, 2, 289–329 (319).
28 Macleod, 47.

21

EXIT

Some resigned from the Communist Party following the publication of Khrushchev's secret speech, but John lingered on. By August he was back at work and in September led the FBU delegation to the Trades Union Congress where he spoke about firemen's long working hours and Grahl took the Party brief on international trade unionism. That same week, the journalist and former Labour MP Woodrow Wyatt published the first in a series of exposés in the weekly *Illustrated* about communism in trade unions which included an inaccurate account of John's election as general secretary in 1939.[1] Unknown to John, a cross-departmental meeting had been convened by the Cabinet Office on 9 May to discuss a memorandum from the Security Service about the Communist Party's efforts to control the trade union movement.[2] With Cabinet Office blessing, the MI5 and the Foreign Office afterwards agreed that relevant intelligence would be shared with the Information Research Department to pass on (unattributed) to friendly journalists.[3] The friendliest of these was Wyatt who had straightaway broadcast a BBC *Panorama* programme that warned members of the Amalgamated Engineering Union of the threat of a communist takeover. Also, with Cabinet Office blessing, and with IRD support, Jack Tanner launched, during TUC week, *IRIS News* to encourage greater participation of rank and file members in their trade unions' decision-making so as to reduce communist influence.[4]

Rather than appear as if swayed by this new anti-communist campaign, John might have wanted to leave the Party in his own good time. Resigning was no simple matter. Could he continue to lead the FBU should Jack Grahl and communists in the FBU Executive choose not to follow him? Perhaps,

DOI: 10.4324/9781032671352-22

above all, like Anna in Lessing's *Golden Notebook*, 'The reasons why we don't leave the Party is that we can't bear to say goodbye to our ideals for a better world', as if only the Communist Party could better the world.[5] The growing Suez crisis served to distract. The Movement for Colonial Freedom was at the forefront in opposing the Conservative government's military response to Egypt's nationalization of the Canal but John was the sole trade union leader to send the TUC's general secretary a telegram calling for a general strike against the invasion of Egypt. Those FBU members who had served in the Royal Navy were especially aggrieved by their union's call for a strike that might put at risk sailors' lives. 'A positive desire to retain imperial power may have eroded substantially by the 1950s', writes historian Stephen Howe, 'but in crisis public reactions would still rally to the defence of a British world role'.[6] Angry letters and telegrams arrived at the FBU head office. That John had acted so impulsively with such little thought to his members' views may have been because he needed to take a public stand on an issue about which he had no doubts as to the rightness of the cause. It contrasted with the confusion he must have felt about contemporaneous events in Poland and Hungary where popular movements were demanding liberation from Soviet control.

When Soviet tanks moved into Budapest to shore up the beleaguered communist government, they encountered fierce armed resistance and after several days of heavy fighting the tanks withdrew from the capital. A new, non-communist government promised free elections and Hungary's departure from the Soviet-dominated Warsaw Pact. On the twenty-eighth of October, the left-wing Labour MP, Tony Benn wrote in his diary,

The Iron Curtain has risen and people are moving freely in and out of Hungary ... the red, white and green have reappeared to replace the hated scarlet banner of the Communist government. Everyone in the world is breathless with hope that this may lead to a rebirth of freedom throughout the whole of Eastern Europe.[7]

But when on the third of November additional Soviet troops were reported to have entered Hungary, it seems that John decided this was the moment to resign.

On Sunday the fourth he and Pat disappeared into the front room after breakfast explaining they were writing a letter and should not be disturbed. After an early lunch, I left with them for the Suez demonstration in Trafalgar Square. A mild afternoon had brought out the crowds, making it the largest demonstration in Britain since John had stood next to Harry Pollitt on the plinth of Nelson's column in 1942 when the crowd had shouted, 'Second Front now!' This time the banners read 'Law not War' and the cardboard placards demanded 'Eden must Go!' and 'Stop the War!' Like me, Michael Rosen, then aged ten, was in the Square with his communist parents.

> Suddenly up comes one of my parents' CP friends and says, 'The tanks have gone in, the tanks have gone in'. I was looking at my parents' ashen faces and they turned to me and said 'Khrushchev has sent tanks into Budapest'.[8]

'The banners were all about Suez', remembered Alison Macleod in *The Strange Death of Uncle Joe*, 'The arguments all about Hungary'.[9]

I stood with my parents on the west side of the square and hunched into his raincoat, John resisted our being pushed inwards by a crowd that flowed up into the street and onto the steps of the National Gallery. Nye Bevan's Welsh lilt boomed around the square and echoed back from the great block of Canada House. 'They are besmirching the name of Britain, have made us ashamed of the things of which were formerly proud'. There was only one course of action: 'Get out!'. A great roar of approval swept around the Square. 'Get out! Get out!' The light was fading with Bevan's final words lost in the rush of starlings coming home to roost.[10] John manoeuvred Pat and me towards our car parked in a side road. Away from the crowds in the Square, central London's streets were quiet and empty on a Sunday afternoon and we shortly arrived in King Street. It was probably the first time John had been there since the Party's Executive Committee meeting in March that had triggered his breakdown. Taking the letter off the dashboard, he crossed the street and pushed it through the Party's letterbox. 'That's done', he said to Pat, 'Let's go home'. Nothing more was said in front of me. Yet while ignorant of the letter's content I knew something significant had happened.

The following Thursday, the Party leadership met in King Street to discuss the Hungary crisis and members' resignations. According to Gollan's scribbled notes, Kerrigan, the Party's national organizer, said something about Horner's resignation as 'a special case' and, next to John's name, Gollan added that of Grahl (at that date still a member): Gollan and Kerrigan had not forgotten the context to this particular resignation.[11] John meanwhile made no public announcement of his departure, most likely preoccupied by his members' continuing fury over the ill-judged Suez telegram. Firefighters organized angry meetings in Liverpool, Birmingham, Manchester, London and elsewhere.[12] On the eleventh of November, John retracted the telegram and the Union's executive apologized to its members for not having consulted them before sending it.[13] Only on the evening of the thirteenth, nine days after our visit to King Street, did he make public his resignation from the Communist Party during a speech to a tumultuous FBU regional meeting in

Newcastle discussing a motion of no confidence in the leadership. John read out to the meeting his resignation letter to Gollan:

> I am not blind to the immense material advances made by the Soviet Union. I remain convinced that Socialism for Britain is the only path. I am no longer convinced however that a party of our type is a necessary condition to achieve Socialism here. You will take the view that I should remain in the Party to seek and set right what is wrong. I can understand that point of view but quite apart from my political doubts and misgivings, my personal feelings on the events of the last six months makes the course I am now following the only one open to me .... In recent years I have visited Hungary twice .... I feel I have been responsible for propagating and advancing policies which have produced this latest tragedy.

By a majority of eighty-five to six, branch delegates then passed a vote of no confidence in the Union's Executive and called on its communist officials to resign from their positions in the Union.[14]

It has been estimated there may have been no more than one hundred communists in a total FBU membership of about 19,000.[15] Most of them immediately followed John out of the party, including the Union's other paid officials and all but two on the Executive Council, plus many others running area and district branches. 'If the senior leaders had left the Party', comments Terry Segars, 'there was no longer any need for those lower down the hierarchy to stay in'.[16] Grahl announced his resignation from the party on the fourteenth, the day after John, issuing a joint statement with Les Cannon, a friend of Grahl's and head of the Electrical Trade Union's education college at Esher.[17] On the fifteenth, the *Daily Mail* published a front-page item with the headline 'Reds "Squander" Union £20,000', alleging that the FBU's travel budget had been spent by the leadership on 'personal luxuries and women friends'. According to Paul Lashmar and James Oliver, the attack on Horner and the FBU union leadership engineered by the IRD may have been provoked by John's Suez telegram.[18] And the IRD congratulated itself for inspiring the *Daily Mail* to spotlight the scandals in the Fire Brigades Union.[19]

The FBU Executive Council issued the *Mail* with a writ for libel.[20] The *Mail* then reported that FBU branches in northwest England agitated for the wholesale departure from office of current or ex-members of the Party.[21] Meanwhile, Jack Tanner warned Wyatt on *Panorama* that the Soviet invasion of Hungary had been seized as an opportunity by some communists to publicly resign from the Party in order to go underground.[22] And the *Economist* reported rumours that some recently announced departures from the Party were bogus, made with the intention to form a communist underground in the FBU until more propitious times. But 'most good judges in the trade union movement ... believe that Mr Horner's own resignation had no such sinister purpose behind it'.[23] These 'rumours' perhaps explain why John always insisted that he had not left the Communist Party because of Hungary.

'In all that time of shock and upheaval', writes John in his memoir's brief reference to these events, 'Pat proved the stronger of the two'. She must have worried he would revert to the depression from which he had so recently recovered. But leaving the Party had re-energized him. For several weeks he toured the regions to re-establish his credibility with the FBU membership, after which he turned his attention to ridding himself of Grahl. As recounted by Enoch Humphries to John Saville, just before Christmas the Executive Council demanded Jack Grahl resign 'for having falsified expenses'.[24] The FBU president, John Burns, sent FBU area officials a confidential letter giving this reason for Grahl's forced resignation.[25]

Pat chose to reveal difficult or embarrassing matters to me when standing behind me to plait my hair. This was how I learnt about female reproduction when Carol started menstruating and it was how she told me that she and John had left the Party. The same stratagem could not be used with Carol, almost eighteen and coming downstairs, late for work. So that she would hear it first from her mother rather than from someone at the office, Pat told her of the resignation in a couple of hurried sentences. Despite the centrality of the Communist Party in the family's life, the parents appear not to have considered the impact on their children of their departure. Carol was to write,

> My sister was sent to the local corner shop to buy a copy of every newspaper. [John's] resignation was in every one, in most on the front page. She tells me that she skipped in the street, because this was the happiest day in her life.

Yet, whereas, I rejoiced for having become an ordinary child, Carol cried non-stop for two days.

> My memories tell me that nobody comforted me or tried to explain. Can that really have happened? I felt spiritually homeless. Everything I had been brought up to believe was untrue, and nobody would talk about it. I suspect my mother must have tried but I was a very sullen and enclosed teenager ... There was an enormous vacuum. It seemed impossible to me that one could exist without a political party.

She arrived in tears at the office of the local Labour Party, where the sympathetic constituency agent, consoled her with a cup of tea and signed her up as a Labour member.

John also intended to join the Labour Party. In a letter to the *Daily Herald*, explaining why he had quit the Communist Party, he wrote,

> After prolonged consideration, I had come to the view that Socialism in Britain must be achieved through the Labour Party as a democratic Party based upon the working class and its organisations. The Labour Party will receive the support of this particular trade unionist.[26]

But did they want him? Labour's National Executive had instructed the constituency parties to seek prior approval from head office before admitting to membership any former communist. Pat had thus been accepted. John was to tell Louise Brodie,

> I said 'To hell with that!' Pat said, 'You're silly'. Tony Greenwood [a Labour MP with a seat on the National Executive] rang me up, 'You're a fool!' But I was buggered if Morgan Phillips was going to look at my application.[27]

Yet, although Phillips, the general secretary of the Labour Party, had a Cold Warrior reputation when Pat eventually persuaded John to apply, he had little difficulty being accepted.

Pat was exhausted. Ashamed and moved by the plight of the Hungarian refugees who had been arriving in England since late November, she had helped organize their settling into new homes. And without being able to afford it, she gave one of them a day's work a week cleaning our house and also found her work with other families until the refugee's English was good enough for office employment. Pat then further raided the savings account to book a ten-day family stay over Christmas at the Devon guest house that had looked after us during John's breakdown.

On a frosty New Year's morning in 1957, we walked to a meeting of the South Hams Hunt. It was not our usual kind of meeting. No serious-faced men and women sitting on hard chairs listening to someone explaining how to change the world. Here were stout and jovial Devon farmers in scarlet jackets swigging sherry from the saddle in preparation for chasing their first fox of the year. My light-hearted parents observed the scene with pleasure. Pat knew all about hunting from reading Trollope while John indulged his inner William Morris's attachment to the customs of rural England. On asking one of the huntsmen what time they were planning to move off, he was told with the greatest brevity that the meet had been cancelled due to the frozen ground. 'Going home, too hard'. 'I know what you mean', replied John, 'It can happen to any of us'. As he was to write in January's *Firefighter*, looking back on 1956, it had been 'a very hard year, a very full year'.[28]

The Grahl affair is at least mentioned in the history and I would argue that my formulation is at least <u>factually correct</u> and the man himself is acknowledged as a brilliant organiser. For me, even having to dissect my thoughts in order to produce no more than three or four dozen words has helped me lay his ghost.

Thus, John's covering letter to Saville about his draft chapter for *Forged in Fire*, 'The Communist Party and the FBU'. Grahl had not gone quietly. John Burns' confidential letter to FBU officials was soon leaked and from the fifteenth of February 1957 until the FBU Conference in late June, the *Daily Telegraph*'s industrial correspondent, Hugo Chevins (urged on by IRD?), relentlessly published fourteen articles reporting how Grahl's resignation 'and other events in which communists and ex-communists have been concerned had created serious dissension among members'.[29] These articles included further accusations about the leadership's financial malpractices and an interview with Grahl who wanted to be reinstated as assistant general secretary, in which case, 'I should oppose Mr John Horner when he next seeks re-election'. Mirroring what must have been John's sentiments, Grahl added,

> While we were both members of the Communist Party, I was prepared to accept party discipline and work with him. But so far as I was concerned the position changed immediately I ceased to be a member of the Communist Party.[30]

Chevins wrongly predicted that the FBU conference would be 'one of the most bitter and acrimonious in the post-war history of the trade union movement'.[31] The conference started with a delegates' private session to debate no confidence in the leadership. Industrial correspondents depended on leaks from the conference floor: 'So convincingly did [Horner] put his case', wrote the *News Chronicle*, 'that the big assault against the leaders melted away into three lone votes'.[32] Even the *Daily Telegraph* conceded, 'It was because of Mr Horner's reasoned case and convincing oratory that [the resolutions] were either withdrawn or found no support'. To ensure there would be no grounds for future allegations of vote-rigging, the conference voted unanimously in favour of the Executive Council's proposal that FBU elections be independently scrutinized by the TUC's auditors. That summer of 1957, the family holidayed in Pembrokeshire, after which John attended the TUC, where he spoke solely in relation to a technical matter. In 1958 he was re-elected general secretary unopposed. He was to stay general secretary until after twenty-five years of leading the Fire Brigades Union; he stepped down in 1964.

Yet Grahl seemed to John to be an evil spirit that could not be exorcised. Possibly influenced by his friend Les Cannon's widely publicized allegations of historic election rigging by the communist leadership in the Electrical

FIGURE 21.1   John Horner with author on holiday, August 1957 (family album).

Trades Union, Grahl wrote to the FBU Executive Council in December 1959 about past 'systematic rigging' of FBU ballots. On receiving no reply, he wrote again and when there was still no response, and unaware that John had already forwarded both letters to Sir Vincent, the general secretary of the TUC, Grahl wrote himself to Tewson, accusing John of having deliberately concealed his letters.

Like everyone else, I have no desire to appear in a court of law. On the other hand fear of it, will no longer keep me from raising my voice against the people who took up the cause of honest men in order to cover up their own dishonesty. In my letter of 28 December last, I have referred to Horner as a Liar and a Coward and I have asked the EC to sue me for libel if they believe I am not telling the truth.[33]

Tewson acknowledged the correspondence, with the observation that it was for the FBU to handle the matter as they saw fit, the same point made to John when acknowledging receipt of Grahl's letters.[34]

Grahl did not give up. At the height of the ETU election-rigging controversy in April 1960, he told the *Daily Mail* how as an FBU official he had fixed a union election in favour of the communist candidate by flushing down the toilet a bundle of ballot papers. When asked to comment, John confirmed that Grahl had been returning officer for FBU elections and explained that since leaving the FBU Grahl had been ill.[35] Grahl then wrote again to Tewson, this time attributing the ballot rigging to another FBU official responsible for counting the votes in John's own re-election as general secretary in 1946. John took no action when this official told him what he had done. 'The above facts', writes Grahl,

> were admitted by Horner in his office in November 1956 in the presence of Burns (at that time President), Bagley (National Officer) and myself. His actual words when challenged by me were, 'Yes, I should have reported the matter to the EC'. To which Burns added, 'Yes, you should have'.[36]

On reading in *IRIS News* about Grahl's letter to Tewson, Bob Darke, the author of *The Communist Technique*, also wrote to Tewson: he had worked closely with Grahl during the war and "I should hope that you treat what he has to say with the utmost reservation ... and I am equally sure that John Horner will handle Jack Grahl quite competently, as he always did in the past'.[37] But what did John know and when had he known it? Had he kept quiet when he should have spoken? There is scarce evidence for any definitive answer. Segars emphasizes that from among the former FBU officials and Party members interviewed for his thesis, only Leo Keely confirmed Grahl's allegations about ballot rigging.[38] When in old age John talked to me about his leaving the Party, he spoke of having been pressurized to interfere with Union elections but left unclear as to whether he had succumbed to the pressure. That John was 'confessing' (his term) leads me to think that even if he had not himself directly interfered, he had been aware of what the Union's other communist officials may have been doing and had chosen to turn a blind eye. Take, for example, the strange affair of Jack Grahl's unopposed election in 1946 as assistant general secretary when John Burns and Harry Short had been nominated as candidates without their knowledge or consent (Chapter 16). By the time their names were withdrawn, it appears it was too late to nominate other candidates.[39]

Rather than on explicit orders from King Street, communist officials in the Union may have decided independently to interfere with FBU elections. Yet, according to Grahl's letter to Tewson (29 February 1960), the Party leadership did otherwise get involved in personnel matters when deciding which of the Union's two national organizers, both Party members, should lose his job during an FBU cost-cutting exercise.

John had believed communists did good things for a good purpose until he had to admit to himself what he had long known: for that same good purpose, communists also did bad things. And, by agreeing to provide Grahl a false alibi for the evening of Helen Grahl's death, John learnt how prioritization of ends over means may spread like a cancer from political to personal morality. John's horror of what Grahl represented was never to leave him, as if Grahl were his alter ego, an evil Hyde to his Dr Jekyll.

Grahl and Horner gave different reasons for resigning from the Communist Party. In *The Communist Technique*, Bob Darke described Grahl 'as so well indoctrinated with Marxism that he used to talk to himself' and Grahl had left the Party because, as he told the *Telegraph* he had become 'absolutely convinced of the fallacy of Communist philosophy [that] in a nutshell ... is rotten'.[40] As for John, reared from his youth on William Morris, his socialism was rooted in his understanding of working-class history and he had little interest in theory: Strachey's introductory explanation of what was wrong with capitalism had been sufficient. John resigned not for what communists believed but for what they had done. He made this point to John Saville after reading Saville's essay, 'The Communist Experience, A Personal Appraisal'. The problem with communism, he wrote to Saville, 'is more than "flawed intellectual structures", as you put it'.[41] The most noble end cannot justify foul means. Fred Parsons had warned John of the dangers inherent in any centrally controlled, top-down organization, however worthy its purpose. If only he had listened.

In 1957, Pat read and passed to me, Edith Bone's account of her seven year's solitary confinement in Hungary. Bone was sixty, when in 1949 she was arrested at Budapest airport, just before boarding a flight back home to London. She was then held for seven years in grim conditions without contact with the outside world. 'After thirty years in the Communist Party', she wrote, '[I] landed in prison for a crime which I had never committed; victimized by my own comrades'.[42] The same communist state that had so welcomed Pat in 1948 had abused and tortured another communist visitor. 'The methods by which they attempted to break down the resistance of their victims was quite simple', writes Bone.

> They deprived them of satisfying the basic natural needs of their bodies and then left it to their own bodies to torture them. If you are deprived of

proper wholesome and sufficient food, of air, of light, of warmth, of sleep, then after a certain time your own body revolts.[43]

Dr Bone was not the first to provide such an account, but Pat would not have read earlier testimonies. She first had to leave the Party to learn why she should never have joined. Then, after John had read Aleksandr Solzhenitsyn's *One Day in the Life of Ivan Denisovich*, based on the author's experience in a Soviet labour camp, he passed it to me to read. It seems Pat and John used these books to communicate to their teenage daughter their shame about their self-deception that they found so difficult to articulate.

John's declining enthusiasm for the USSR proved mutual. Although his friend Boris had retired in 1957, in 1962 John accepted an invitation to lead some half dozen members of the Fire Brigades Union on a visit to the fire services of Moscow, Leningrad and Stalingrad. The visitors were given a pointedly cool reception, lodged, for example, in hotels where at breakfast theirs was the only table served with margarine instead of butter. It was a short visit and the atmosphere sufficiently chilly for him to be glad to be back at Moscow airport, homeward bound. They were already on the plane ready for take-off when it was boarded by three officials who came to John's seat: they told him he was to come with them to answer some questions. He hesitated, knowing that should he get off the plane he would miss his flight – and perhaps much worse might happen. The firemen decided for him. All big burly men, they stood up to form a cordon around his seat. Without reinforcements, it would have been impossible to remove John from the plane and so the officials left. The doors of the plane were closed, the steps wheeled away, the firemen sat down and they were in the air. John concluded the incident had been a piece of theatre, designed to scare him. But the message was clear: Don't try and come back. We don't want you.

The Horners never learnt to love capitalism. They never ceased trying to make a better world, with peace and social justice for everyone, everywhere. Unlike communist contemporaries who went public about their rupture, they chose silence. John never became vocally anti-communist, nor confessed past sins in public. Still a socialist, still a member of the labour movement but now clear in his mind that good, progressive change depends on democratic organizing. In 1957, for the first time since 1944, he represented the FBU as an accredited delegate to the Labour Party Conference. He had chosen to speak to Conference on the non-controversial issue of local government financing.

I had been among the most vitriolic of critics in the Communist Party of Labour's policies, so when I was called upon to speak, I was fearful of the reception I would get in the hall. Hostility, resentment, at least,

I would have accepted and understood, but as I moved down the aisle to the rostrum, a ripple of applause went round the delegates.[44]

Pat became a hard-working member of the Labour Party and within a few years was chairing the local constituency party while also volunteering for the Old People's Welfare Association. The innovation of the Bendix laundrette had freed her from the grind of the weekly wash and its copper boiler and mangle. She came home from the laundrette with tumble-dried clothes in her shopping trolley; damp washing no longer dripped over the kitchen table while the purchase of a refrigerator in 1958 meant less time shopping.

As for John, the energy previously devoted to the Communist Party and its front organizations was now transferred to the new Campaign for Nuclear Disarmament. It was led by Canon John Collins, 'the archetypal Good Cause man', who had been devoted to anti-apartheid and Christian action against Third World famine, before turning his efforts to banning the bomb. The journalist James Cameron remembered the first meeting of the CND's executive committee meeting in January 1958 at Collins' eighteenth-century house in Amen Court, close to St Paul's Cathedral. The committee was composed of more of a 'star-studded gang of worthies' than Cameron was used to, 'Bertrand Russell, Kingsley Martin, Michael Foot, JB Priestley, Ritchie Calder, AJP Taylor, John Horner ....'[45]

On that year's first CND Easter March, Pat and John met up with Violet and Reg, still pacifists, the sisters and their husbands now joined together in the common cause of banning the bomb. And at that year's Labour Party Conference, John moved and lost the vote on a resolution that a future Labour government should unilaterally renounce the manufacture, testing and use of nuclear weapons. He returned to the Trades Union Congress and the Labour Party Conference with the same resolution, year after year, and became known and respected for the moral passion and eloquence of his oratory. In 1959, he said,

The argument against the bomb is unanswerable. Those against the bomb are for life. Can we remain silent when there is a possibility that in 15, 75, or 100 years the truncated distorted remnants of humanity, if they can still think and speak, will curse the generation of the 20th century because they did not get rid of the bomb?[46]

And in 1961, 'What kind of people have we become? We are planning the end of two and a half million years of emergent life and the abortion of all that lies in the womb of time'.[47]

At Labour's conference in 1960, he partnered with Frank Cousins, the leader of the Transport and General Workers Union, to move and win the resolution that committed the Labour Party to unilateral nuclear

FIGURE 21.2   John Horner with Canon Collins and Jacquetta Hawkes at head of CND March from Wethersfield, Easter 1961 (family album).

disarmament. The Labour leadership fought back and the following year, the unilateralists lost the vote and although the Easter Marches of 1961 and 1962 were the biggest ever, the political momentum had been lost. John meanwhile made new friends and re-discovered old ones while Pat was delighted when invited by Priestley and his archaeologist wife Jacquetta Hawkes for dinner at their country cottage. As always, most of her campaigning was at the local level but in March 1962 she travelled to Geneva with Diana, the wife of Canon Collins and Antoinette Pirie, the biochemist, on a self-styled 'women's mission' to lobby delegates at the disarmament conference.[48] The Horners' new social circle influenced their lifestyle. Sometime in the late 1950s, they moved from having tea in the kitchen to dinner in the dining room, with a glass of sherry beforehand. They had become definitively middle class.

After twenty-five years as general secretary, John had become eligible for the equivalent of a fire station officer's pension and retired from the Fire Brigades Union. He had been selected as parliamentary candidate for a Midlands constituency from which its incumbent was retiring at the next General Election. The Horners sold their house in suburban New Malden and bought a country cottage on the edge of the Forest of Dean, just an hour down the new M50 motorway from his future constituency. Once elected, they rented a studio flat close to the House of Commons where Pat worked

FIGURE 21.3   Pat and John in Brighton for Labour Party Conference, 1962 (family album).

as his unpaid assistant, researcher and secretary, handling his constituency correspondence. On Friday mornings, they left London for their cottage where lived with them Pat's widowed father, Geoff Palmer. John served in parliament for six years until losing his seat after having stoutly defended his immigrant constituents from racist attacks fuelled by Enoch Powell, the MP in neighbouring Wolverhampton.

He did not look for another constituency. Carol had broken her back while teaching in Kenya and returned home in December 1968 to spend the rest of her life in a wheelchair. In her first years as a paraplegic, she needed all the help and care that Pat and John lovingly provided. He built with his own hands an extension to their cottage so she could live with them and meanwhile organized a successful campaign to improve the local community's drinking water supply. He also published a book about industrial democracy; and, until he had to retire at seventy, served on the local employment tribunal.

History continued to fuel his imagination, cheered him in good times and consoled him during the bad. He fitted with William Morris' definition of a romantic with 'the capacity for a true conception of history, a power of making the past part of the present'.[49] No countryside church was spotted without a visit: a discussion of its architectural history; fulminations against its restoration by over-zealous Victorian parish priests; an informed political commentary on the monuments of long-dead local gentry before ascending the church tower to survey the surroundings with observations on the making of the landscape below him. He greatly admired Fernand Braudel and shared with that great historian 'a wide-ranging curiosity, an instant sympathy for new ideas, and an ability to see phenomena from different points of view', all of which had made John such a good negotiator and resulted in friendships with people whose opinions he did not share.[50] Nor did he lose his childhood enthusiasm for the sea. Over the Sunday roast joint, he recounted the ghastly details of how Captain Slocum ate his boots when running out of food while sailing solo around the world. And when, in retirement, John wrote an unpublished historical novel about the last voyage of a certain Captain Thomas Green, hung for piracy in 1705, he reassured Pat that the novel's account of Green's visit to a South American brothel was in no way drawn from his own experience of port life.

In 1981, they moved into a semi-detached house in Ross-on-Wye, much like their first house in Chingford. Some years later, he organized the little box room for writing his memoir: a small table, a chair from the dining room and on the wall above his makeshift desk, portraits of William Morris and Fred Parsons gazed down upon him as he omitted that part of the story for which he could not forgive himself and found so difficult to tell. When the Soviet Union collapsed in 1991, Carol watched as he threw his Communist library into a wheelbarrow, trundled it to the bottom of the garden and made a bonfire. The only book he preserved from the flames was the Webb's *Soviet Communism* – and the newspaper clippings secreted within it.

Notes

1 *Illustrated*, 22 September 1956. The articles were subsequently published in Woodrow Wyatt, *The Peril in our Midst*, London 1956. Following a formal complaint from the FBU, the account of John's election as general secretary was not published in the book.
2 NA/CAB/130/115, 26 May 1956.
3 Paul Lashmar and James Oliver, *Britain's Secret Propaganda War*, Stroud, 1998, Chapter Twelve, 'Internal affairs: IRD's domestic campaigns'.
4 NA/CAB/130/115, *IRIS News*, September 1956.
5 Doris Lessing, *The Golden Notebook*, London, 1972, 156.
6 Stephen Howe, *Anticolonialism in British Politics: The Left and the End of Empire, 1918–64*, Oxford, 2011, 273.
7 Tony Benn and Ruth Winston, *The Benn Diaries*, London, 1995, 38.
8 Michael Rosen, 'Why I became a socialist', Socialist Review, 2004, Jan.1997. http://pubs.socialistreviewindex.org.uk/sr204/why.htm Accessed 4 February 2022.
9 Alison Macleod, *The Death of Uncle Joe*, London, 1997, 144.
10 According to a *Daily Telegraph* report (11 December 1956) John told Woodrow Wyatt for BBC *Panorama* how he learnt of the Soviet tanks in Budapest while in Trafalgar Square where he met a well-known member of the Communist Party to whom he gave his resignation letter. This seems unlikely because the letter

was addressed to Gollan who at that moment was in King Street at the monthly meeting of the party's Executive Committee. More likely, John told this person he had written his letter of resignation.

11 Political Committee meeting, 8 November 1956, LHA/CP/IND/GOLL/02/07.

12 *Lancashire Evening Post*, 8 November 1956; *Birmingham Daily Post*, 9 November 1956.

13 'Fire Brigades Union takes it all back', *Daily Mail*, 12 November 1956; 'A statement by the Executive Council' MRC/MSS 346/4/208.

14 *Hartlepool Northern Daily Mail*, 14 November 1956.

15 Terry Segars, '*The Fire Service: A Social History of a Uniformed Working Class*', PhD thesis, University of Essex, 1989, 277.

16 Segars, 358.

17 *Daily Herald*, 14 November 1956. This contradicts Cannon's claim that he had resigned as early as August 1956 as in Glyn Powell, 'Turning Off the Power: The Electrical Trades Union and the Anti-communist Crusade 1957–61, *Contemporary British History*, 2004, 18, 2, 1–26.

18 Lashmar and Oliver, Chapter 12.

19 'Progress Report on the Work of the English Section of the Information Research Department of the Foreign Office, 1954 — Spring 1957', Memorandum by the Foreign Office, 30th April 1957, TNA, CAB 134/1342 cited in William Styles, 'British Domestic Security Policy and Communist Subversion: 1945–1964', PhD thesis, University of Cambridge, 2016, 124.

20 *Scotsman*, 16 November 1956.

21 *Daily Mail*, 17 November 1956, 10 December 1956.

22 *Daily Telegraph*, 11 December 1956.

23 *Economist*, 'A Question of Free Speech', 15 December 1956.

24 Humphreys interview HHC/ UDJS/1/28.

25 *Daily Telegraph*, 26 April 1957.

26 *Daily Herald*, 26 November 1956.

27 Brodie interview.

28 *FireFighter*, January 1957.

29 *Daily Telegraph*, 25 April 1957. James Oliver has suggested to me that IRD may have been still targeting John Horner via Hugo Chevins (personal communication).

30 *Daily Telegraph*, 23 May 1957.

31 *Daily Telegraph*, 25 June 1957.

32 *News Chronicle*, 26 June 1957.

33 Letter of 29 February 1960, in TUC file on Grahl and the FBU, MRC/MSS 292-91F-109ii.

34 MRC /MSS 292-91F-109ii.

35 *Daily Mail*, 26 April 1960.

36 Letter from Grahl to Tewson 11 May 1960b, MRC/MSS 292-91F-109ii.

37 MRC/MSS 292-91F-109ii.

38 Segars, note 43, 403.

39 Wyatt makes a similar point, referring to *Firefighter* reports of 'the disqualification of potential candidates who "had not accepted nomination" so leaving a clear field to their Communist sponsored candidate'. *The Peril in our Midst*, London, 1956, 57.

40 Darke, 1952, 72; Grahl's interview with the *Daily Telegraph*, 23 May 1957.

41 John misquotes Saville's 'flawed *organisational* [my emphasis] structures' in Saville, 1991. John Horner's correspondence at HHC/ UDJS/1/28.
42 Edith Bone, *Seven Years Solitary*, London, 1957, 98.
43 Bone, 69.
44 Last chapter in final version of John's memoir.
45 *Guardian*, 4 January 1983.
46 *Birmingham Weekly Post*, 25 September 1959.
47 *Daily Mirror*, 8 September 1961.
48 *Guardian*, 17 April 1962.
49 Cited in E.P. Thompson, 'Romanticism, moralism and utopianism: The case of William Morris', *New Left Review*, 1976, 99, 83–111.
50 Peter Burke, 'Braudel's Long Term', *London Review of Books* 1983, 5, www.lrb.co.uk/the-paper/v05/n01/peter-burke/braudel-s-long-term, page 4 of 7. Accessed 11 February 2022.

EPILOGUE

Uncomfortable Encounters with Truth

When visiting my father after Pat had died, he would seek out my views on a matter of current concern to him (women firefighters, the emergence of the world wide web, Scottish devolution ...), or discuss an intellectual or philosophical problem he had been thinking about anew. Relaxed in his old, deep, dark green armchair, his eyes fixed on me when I spoke, he would raise his right hand to his mouth and gently and slowly move the side of the first finger from right to left, then back and forth across lightly closed lips, pondering. On hearing something especially challenging or requiring concentration, he closed his eyes. If not for the finger's regular movement, you might have thought him asleep. When he had heard enough – or I had invited a response – he opened his eyes, bringing his right hand down from his mouth to meet the other hand that had been resting on his thighs. Gently placing the left over the right he held his hands loosely together at a little distance from his body, at about the level of his heart. Then he responded.

I wish we could have thus discussed the Moscow Treason Trials. But I had been discomfited by his unusual manner of broaching the subject. That Friday evening, I had brought down with me from London a steak and kidney pie for us to share with a bottle of wine. Over our meal, I did most of the talking – about my job and to which part of the world I had travelled since last seeing him. Usually on such visits, he quickly did the washing up after dinner while I dried and put away the plates, our chat inconsequential. This time was different. Having placed just one clean plate on the draining board, he came to a halt. Sponge idle in his hand, he stared down at the dirty crockery in the washing-up bowl. He had a confession to make, he said, without lifting his face to me.

DOI: 10.4324/9781032671352-23

How was it, he asked the dishwater, that he both knew, yet did not know the Moscow Trials had been a lie. And not just the trials. The arbitrary dawn arrests. The mass graves. The labour camps. He lifted up his head to stare at me. I had never seen him so miserable. 'What was I thinking of? How did I not know?' I was uncomfortable and forget now how I answered. Once back in the sitting room, I moved the conversation to cheerier topics.

I had let him down. He had wanted my help to enquire into his state of mind from a time before I was born, seeking understanding, if not absolution, for having succumbed to Stalin's Big Lie. At the very least, I could have encouraged him to talk more about it. We now know that two million people were arrested in 1937, around 700,000 murdered ('liquidated') and well over a million sent to labour camps.[1] All this, my father learnt after the collapse of the Soviet Union in 1991. But as he told me that evening while doing the dishes, a secret part of him had always suspected it.

Most victims of Soviet state terrorism disappeared without publicity. The Stalinist regime deflected attention from them through show trials of the leading Bolsheviks who had made the 1917 Revolution. Foreign observers were invited to the trials with detailed accounts of the proceedings widely published, including in the *Daily Worker*, my parents' principal news source. Each trial followed the same template: the prosecution provided no evidence to substantiate its case while the accused freely admitted to murder, economic sabotage and plotting with the fascist powers, all under the direction of Stalin's arch-enemy, the exiled Leon Trotsky. The accused would have had to exercise Satanic powers to have committed everything to which they confessed. The closest analogy is medieval witchcraft trials.

Long after he left the Party, my father acquired two contemporary accounts of the trials. A young British diplomat, Fitzroy Maclean, portrayed the trials as theatre that required good communists to suspend their disbelief, whereas Leon Feuchtwanger, one of Europe's most distinguished authors, concluded the accused had made genuine confessions. Maclean's memoir, *Eastern Approaches*, describes Moscow in 1937/38 during the height of the Great Terror. 'Fear hung over the city like a mist', he writes. 'Everyone lived in terror of everyone else. Everyone denounced everyone else. Agents of the NKVD were everywhere. No one could be trusted. No one was safe'.[2] Maclean and his fellow diplomats talked endlessly about the 1938 trial they had been invited to observe. They puzzled over why the accused had agreed to play their part in a brilliantly executed piece of theatre, despite knowing that whatever they said, they would afterwards be shot.

Feuchtwanger's *Moscow 1937* was first published in Britain as a Left Book Club edition. My parents were members of the Club and must have read it then, but many years later, John picked up and re-read another copy (thirty pence is scribbled on the flysheet). After fleeing Nazi Germany, Feuchtwanger had settled in France from where he visited Moscow shortly after his friend and fellow writer, André Gide, had published a critical account of the Soviet Union's lack of freedom of expression.[3] Feuchtwanger's response to Gide was that the Soviet economy could not be built without 'a temporary modification' to democracy. History, he concluded, 'Cannot be made with gloves on'.[4] And, after observing the second trial in 1937, any doubts that the proceedings were a sham 'melted away as naturally as salt dissolves in water. If that was lying or prearranged, I don't know what truth is'.

John Horner died just a few months after confessing to me his state of denial about Stalin, about his simultaneous knowing and not knowing about the Terror. I wonder now whether we might have the longer conversation I had denied him then? The same old green chair waits for him by my own fireside and when my ghostly father has sat down and is comfortably relaxed, I suggest to him we focus on a meeting of the Hampstead Ethical Society in Finchley Road that he and my mother possibly attended, only ten minutes' walk from their home in West Hampstead Fire Station. It is Sunday evening, the twentieth of February 1938. Hitler has just annexed Austria and already has his eye on Czechoslovakia while Mussolini is sending yet more men and weapons to Spain in support of Franco. The British Cabinet has met that afternoon to discuss the crisis. Everyone expects the foreign secretary, Anthony Eden, to resign because he disagrees with Prime Minister Neville Chamberlain's policy of appeasing Europe's fascist dictators.

I imagine my parents among the one hundred and ten people that show up that evening – four times more than usual for Ethical Society's events.[5] They have come to hear the writer C.L.R. James denounce the Moscow Treason Trials as a 'dirty, bloody mess of lies, deceptions and murder, open and secret', orchestrated by Stalin to explain the frequent industrial accidents, train crashes and food shortages that have plagued the implementation of the Five-Year Plan. There is no transcript from the meeting but James probably spoke much along the same lines as in his article published the previous year in *Fight*, a British Trotskyist publication:

> The Left Book Club, the Friends of the Soviet Union, and all these hangers-on of the Soviet Union who will not face the truth, and who either by their sycophancy or silence protect the Stalinist regime from the consequences of its crimes, these bear a responsibility only less heavy than the criminals themselves.[6]

James is an Afro-Caribbean, Marxist intellectual, currently campaigning for trade union rights for West Indian workers. In 1934, Paul Robeson had performed the title role at Westminster Theatre of James' play about the Haitian revolutionary Toussaint l'Ouverture. Communists should have a high regard for James but despite James' anti-colonialist credentials, the

Party has made him a non-person, an alleged Trotskyist; James' name does not once appear in the *Daily Worker* and, according to publisher Frederic Warburg, the *Worker* refused his advertisement for James' new book, *World Revolution* because it was Trotskyist. 'In view of the emphasis laid by the Communist Party during the last year or two on democracy and freedom of expression', writes Warburg, 'It is depressing to find that they, too, must be numbered among the censors'.[7]

'You were very lucky to have had this chance to hear James', I tell my father. 'And I rather believe your friend John Saville was letting himself off the hook when in 1991 he wrote, "The Trotskyist movement was numerically very small, and intellectually feeble in Britain at that time and appreciation of the nature and character of Stalinism was confined to very few within the broad labour movement".[8] Saville implies that, should the Trotskyists have made a sharper argument, he would have listened to them. 'From what I've read, there was nothing wrong with James' argument', I say. My father looks at me and sighs long and deeply. From his years at Aunt Mill's Baptist Chapel, he had acquired the habit of citing the Bible. 'For those who have ears, let them hear', he says. And again, he sighs.

I suggest to him that until that evening in February 1938, he had never heard of James and that he had not come to the meeting to hear what James had to say. I assume he and my mother are among the many comrades present, primed to support the evening's other speaker, Dudley Collard, a communist fellow-traveller and barrister who toured the country speaking to Left Book Clubs and other groups, asserting the trials were genuine. Then, just when the meeting is due to end, the news comes through of Eden's resignation from the government. What does this mean for British foreign policy? The chairman extends the discussion until 10.30 pm. It seems the audience is less interested in debating the treason trials' veracity than the importance of the Soviet Union's friendship in resisting the fascist powers.[9] I quote to my father the historian Paul Corthorn, 'It was in the interests of the Labour party to see that as little criticism as possible was given to the Soviet Union, which was being prominently portrayed as an essential part of any alliance against Hitler'.[10]

I am sad to see my father so miserable, hunched into his old green chair. If it is any consolation, I say, communists were not alone in colluding in the travesty of the treason trials. I remind him that among Hampstead's leading progressives, only the distinguished journalist H.N. Brailsford exposed the trials as a macabre sham. My parents took the *Reynolds News* on Sundays, did they read what Brailsford wrote about the trials, I wonder. Or did they turn the page, 'for the sake of the anti-fascist cause', as much as for their faith in the goodness of the Stalinist regime? And, you were still only twenty-six, I remind him. And after all, compared with the totally evil regime of Nazi Germany, at least in the Soviet Union they were trying to build a new, more equitable society: in the twenty years since the Revolution, the status of women had improved enormously and health and education services dramatically expanded. I read to him what his friend, Stephen Swingler, whom he had first met in Hampstead, was to write in 1939 – 'To demand the right to free discussion of the issues, as people have done over the Moscow trials, is to demand the right to obstruct and constrain, the right to negate freedom'.[11] 'Is that what you thought then?', I ask him. I lean forward and take his hand.

Perhaps I understand how he and my mother felt. I quote to him what Gide had thought before visiting the Soviet Union (he later changed his mind).

What we have dreamt of, what we have hardly dared to hope, but towards which we were straining all our will and all our strength, was coming into being over there. A land existed where Utopia was in process of becoming reality ... and we entered joyfully and boldly into the sort of engagement this land had contracted in the name of all suffering peoples.[12]

'Are you trying to let me off the hook?' asks my poor father. I shake my head. I wonder how I would have reacted if I had been there that evening in West Hampstead to hear James destroy my dream. Might I also have pushed the truth into a secret part of my mind, so that I could continue believing?

A week after James' talk to Hampstead's Ethical Society, the *Daily Worker* announced a third Moscow trial was imminent. Among the accused was the Party's leading theoretician and intellectual Nikolai Bukharin. He had denied the specific charges against him while admitting he was guilty because, he said, the State required it of him. 'My own fate, he concluded, is of no importance. All that matters is the Soviet Union'. Fitzroy Maclean was to write,

Watching him standing there, frail and defiant, one had the feeling that here, facing destruction, was the last survivor of a vanished race, of the men who had made the Revolution, who had fought and toiled all their lives for an ideal, and who now, rather than betray it, were letting themselves be crushed by their own creation.[13]

Maclean concluded the Soviet Union was a different world from his own. Stalin, the prosecutors, the secret police, the accused, the Soviet public, all had experienced years of Tsarist repression prior to the bloodshed and terror of the civil war and then afterwards were subjected to relentless propaganda. Cut off from contact with the outside world, and 'from all valid standards of comparison. The real and the imaginary, truth and fiction, the actual and the hypothetical 'blurred into each other'.[14] My father knew that he had less excuse than the Soviet public. For him, there were no constraints of history, geographical isolation or state censorship. Yet it was only too easy for him then – as it is for me now – to choose to circumscribe our contacts and sources to those that share our beliefs.

I cannot remember John ever mentioning having read *The Case of Comrade Tulayev*, whose characters are caught up in the preparations for a Moscow treason trial. Victor Serge wrote the novel in 1942 when a refugee in Mexico with a translation first published in Britain in 1951, at the height of the Cold War. If John had heard about it then, he would have viewed it as a piece of anti-Soviet propaganda. Reviewers did not find it as powerful as *Nineteen Eighty-Four* or *Darkness at Noon*. 'It suffers from over-familiarity with the theme', commented one.[15] In her introduction to a recent edition, Susan Sonntag quotes from another book by Serge, *Memoirs of a Revolutionary*: 'French essayist has said "What is terrible when you seek the truth, is that you find it". You find it, and then you are no longer free to follow the biases of your personal circle, or to accept what is fashionable'. We need courage to open our eyes to uncomfortable truths when in pursuit of social justice.[16] In the end, John Horner found that courage.

Notes

1 Karl Schögel, *Moscow 1937*, Cambridge, 2012, 1.
2 Alistair Maclean, *Eastern Approaches*, London, 1967, 16.
3 André Gide, Foreword to *Return from the USSR*, New York, 1937 https://gutenb erg.ca/ebooks/gideabussyd-returnfromtheussr/gideabussyd-returnfromtheu ssr-00-h.html
4 Lion Feuchtwanger, *Moscow 1937*, London, 1937, 168.
5 Archives of the Hampstead Humanist Society, Bishopsgate Institute.
6 C.L.R. James, *Fight*, 2, 5, April, 1937, 6–9.
7 Letter to the *News Chronicle*, 8 May 1937.
8 J. Saville, 'The Communist Experience', 4.
9 *Hampstead and Highgate Express*, 26 February, 1938.
10 Paul Corthorn, 'Labour, the Left, and the Stalinist Purges of the Late 1930s', *The Historical Journal*, 2005, 48,179–207 (204).
11 Darren Lilliker, *Against the Cold War. The History and Political Traditions of Pro-Sovietism in the British Labour Party 1945–1989*, London, 2004.
12 Gide (no page numeration).
13 Maclean, 86.
14 Maclean, 16.
15 *Times Literary Supplement*, 16 March 1951.
16 Susan Sonntag 'Introduction' to Victor Serge, *The Case of Comrade Tulayev*, New York, 2004, xxi.

BIBLIOGRAPHY AND SOURCES

Bibliography

Adonis, Andrew, *Ernest Bevin, Labour's Churchill*, London, 2020.

Alarcon, Natalia and Oscar Videla, 'Fortaleza local, solidaridad regional, Un ciclo des huelgas de las estabidores portuarios de Villa Constitución (Argentina 1928–1932)', *Historia Regional*, 2022, 4–6, 1–31.

Allen, Steve, *Thompsons, A Personal History of the Firm and its Founder*, Pontypool, 2012.

Bailey, Victor, 'The early history of the Fire Brigades Union', in ed. Victor Bailey, *Forged in Fire*, London, 1992, 3–97.

Beales, Derek, 'David Thomson (1912–1970)' *Oxford Dictionary of National Biography*; published online: 23 September 2004. https://doi.org/10.1093/ref:odnb/38060

Blackstone, G.V., *A History of the British Fire Service*, London, 1957.

Bone, Edith, *Seven Years Solitary*, London, 1957.

Brimble, J.A., *London's Epping Forest*, London, 1950.

Brittain, Vera, *Testament of Youth*, London, 2011.

Brodie, Louise, Interview with John Horner, 1994, *British Library Sounds Collection*.

Burke, Peter, 'Braudel's long term', *London Review of Books*, January 1983, 5. www.lrb.co.uk/the-paper/v05/n01/peter-burke/braudel-s-long-term

Calder, Nigel, *The People's War, Britain 1939–45*, London, 1971.

Callaghan, John, *Rajani Palme Dutt, A Study in British Stalinism*, London, 1993.

Callaghan, John and Ben Harker, *British Communism, A Documentary History*, Manchester, 2011.

Ceadel, Martin, 'The first communist "Peace Society" The British anti-war Movement 1932–1935', *Twentieth Century British History*, 1990, 1, 1, 58–86.

——— *Semi-Detached Idealists: The British Peace Movement and International Relations, 1854–1945*, Oxford, 2000.

Childs, David, 'The Cold War and the "British Road", 1946–53', *Journal of Contemporary History*, 1988, 23, 551–572.

Cohen, Phil, *Children of the Revolution, Communist Childhood in Cold War Britain*, London,1997.

Cole, Margaret, *Growing up into Revolution*, London, 1949.

Colwill, Jeremy, 'Beveridge, women and the welfare state', *Critical Social Policy*, 1994, 14, 41, 53–78.

Cooper, T., 'Politics and Place in suburban Walthamstow', Ph.D thesis, University of Cambridge, 2005.

Copsey, Nigel 'Communists and the Inter-War Anti-Fascist Struggle in the United States and Britain', *Labour History Review*, 2011, 76, 3, 184–206.

Corthorn, Paul, 'Labour, the Left, and the Stalinist purges of the late 1930s', *The Historical Journal*, 2005, 48, 179–207.

Cox, Peter, '"A denial of our boasted civilisation" Cyclists' views on conflicts over road use in Britain, 1926–1935', *Transfers*, 2012, 2, 3, 4–30.

Croall, Jonathan, *Sybil Thorndike: A Star Of Life*, London, 2009.

Croft, Andy, 'The young nen are moving together' in eds. John McIlroy, Kevin Morgan and Alan Campbell, *Party People, Communist Lives: Explorations in Biography*, London, 2001, 169–189.

Darke, Bob, *The Communist Technique in Britain*, London, 1952.

Davis, Tricia, 'Women and Communist Party politics' in eds. Rosalind Brunt and Caroline Rowan, *Feminism, Culture, and Politics*, London, 1982, 85–106.

Davy, Teresa, ' "A cissy job for men; a nice job for girls": Women shorthand typists in London, 1900–39' in eds. Leonore Davidoff and Belinda Westover, *Our Work, Our Lives, Our Words: Women's History and Women's Work*, Basingstoke, 1986, 124–144.

Eade, James and David Renton, *The Communist Party of Great Britain since 1920*, Basingstoke, 2002.

Eyben, Rosalind, *International Aid and the Making of a Better World*, London, 2014.

Feuchtwanger, Lion, *Moscow, 1937*, London, 1937.

Fishman, Nina, 'The phoney Cold War in British trade unions', *Contemporary British History*, 2001, 15, 3, 83–104.

Flewers, Paul, 'The unexpected denunciation: the reception of Khrushchev's "Secret Speech" in Britain', *Critique*, 2019, 47, 2, 289–329.

Freeman, Martin, "An advanced type of democracy"? Governance and politics in Adult Education c.1918–1930', *History of Education*, 2013, 42, 1, 45–69.

Fyrth, Jim, *The Signal was Spain the Aid Spain Movement in Britain 1936–39*, London, 1986.

Gibbons, Stella, *Cold Comfort Farm*, Harmondsworth, 1938.

Gide, André, *Return from the USSR*, New York, 1937.

Hall, Catherine and Daniel Pick, 'Thinking about denial', *History Workshop Journal*, 2017, 84, 1–23.

Harrison, Lucy and Katherine Green, W.E. *The Ex-Warner Estate in Waltham Forest*, 2nd ed., Walthamstow, 2016, 8.

Hassall, Christopher, *Edward Marsh, Patron of the Arts: A Biography*, London, 1959.

Hennessy, Peter, *The Secret State*, London, 2002.

Høgsbjerg, Christian, 'A.L. Morton and the poetics of people's history', *Socialist History*, 2020, 56–77 (58).

Hobsbawm, Eric, *Interesting Times, A Twentieth Century Life*, London, 2002.

Horner, John, 'We must fight together', *Labour Monthly*, November 1942.

———— 'Symposium on affiliation', *Labour Monthly*, June 1943, 172–3.

———— 'Unity, then and now', *Labour Monthly*, March 1946, 75–77.

———— 'The Southport TUC', *Labour Monthly*, October 1947, 299–302.

———— 'My six hundred million friends', *Labour Monthly*, January 1955, 29–33.

———— *Studies in Industrial Democracy*, London, 1974.

———— 'Recollections of a General Secretary', in ed. Victor Bailey, *Forged in Fire*, London, 1991, 279–359.

Howe, Stephen, *Anticolonialism in British Politics: The Left and the End of Empire, 1918–64*, Oxford, 2011.

Hyde, Douglas, *I Believed, The Autobiography of a Former British Communist*, London, 1952.

Kennerley, Alston, 'Aspirant navigator: Training and education at sea during commercial voyages in British merchant ships c.1850 to 1950, *The Great Circle*, 2008, 30, 2, 41–76.

Kushner, Howard, *On the Other Hand: Left Hand, Right Brain, Mental Disorder, and History*, Baltimore, 2017.

Kynaston, David, *Austerity Britain 1945–51*, London, 2007.

———— *Family Britain, 1951–7*, London, 2010.

Lashmar, Paul and James Oliver, *Britain's Secret Propaganda War*, Stroud, 1998.

Lessing, Doris, *The Golden Notebook*, London, 1972.

Liddiard, Mabel, *The Mothercraft Manual*, 10th ed., London, 1940.

Lilliker, Darren, *Against the Cold War. The History and Political Traditions of Pro-Sovietism in the British Labour Party 1945–1989*, London, 2004.

Linehan, Thomas, *Communism in Britain, 1920–39, From Cradle to Grave*, Manchester, 2007.

MacCarthy, Fiona, *William Morris*, London, 1994.

MacEwen, Malcolm, *The Greening of a Red*, London, 1991.

Maclean, Alistair, *Eastern Approaches*, London, 1967.

Macleod, Alison, *The Death of Uncle Joe*, London, 1997.

Maguire, Thomas, 'Counter-subversion in early Cold War Britain: The Official Committee on Communism (Home), the Information Research Department, and state-private networks', *Intelligence and National Security*, 2015, 30, 5, 637–66.

Marchildon, G.P., 'War, revolution and the Great Depression in the global wheat trade, 1917–39'. in eds. Lucia Coppolaro and Francine McKenzie, *A Global History of Trade and Conflict Since 1500*, London, 2013, 142–162.

Matera, Marc and Susan, Kingsley Kent, *The Global 1930s, the International Decade*, London, 2017.

Maxwell, F.W., *Nicholl's Seamanship and Viva Voce Guide*, 15th ed., Glasgow, 1927.

McCauley, Martin, *Origins of the Cold War 1941–1949*, London, 1983.

McIlroy, John, 'Restoring Stalinism to communist history, *Critique*, 2013, 41, 4, 599–622.

Morgan, Kevin, *Against Fascism and War: Ruptures and Continuities in British Communist Politics, 1935–41*, Manchester 1989.

———— *Harry Pollitt, Manchester*, 1993.

———— 'True sons of the working class' in eds. Kevin Morgan, Gideon Cohen and Andrew Flinn, *Communists and British Society, 1920–1991*, London, 2007, 143–184.

———— "Colourless, dry and dull". Why British trade unionists lack biographers and what (if anything) should be done dbout it ', *Moving the Social*, 2014, 51, 213–237.

———— 'Communist history, police history and the archives of British state surveillance', *Twentieth Century Communism*, 2019, 17, 67–89.

Morton, A.L., *A People's History of England*, London, 1938.

———— *Collected Poems*, London, 1976.

Murray, Tom, in ed. Ian Macdougall, *Voices from Work and Home*, Edinburgh, 2000, 254–332.

Overy, R.J., *The Origins of the Second World War*, London, 2009.

———— *The Morbid Age*, London, 2010.

Perkins, Anne, and Red Queen, *The Authorized Biography of Barbara Castle*, London, 2003.

Powell, Glyn, 'Turning of the power: the Electrical Trades Union and the anti-communist crusade, 1957–1961', *Contemporary British History*, 18, 2, 1–26.

Powell, W.R., ed. *The Victorian County History of Essex*, V, London, 1966.

Pritchett, V.S., *A Cab at the Door*, Harmondsworth, 1970.

Pugh, Martin, *Hurrah for the Blackshirts!: Fascists and Fascism in Britain between the Wars*, London, 2013.

Reilly, Catherine, ed. *Chaos of the Night: Women's Poetry and Verse of the Second World War*, London, 1984.

Roberts, Geoffrey, 'The Soviet decision for a pact with Nazi Germany', *Soviet Studies*, 1992, 44, 1, 57–78.

Rose, Jonathan, *The Intellectual Life of the British Working Classes*, New Haven, 2001.

Rosen, Michael, 'Why I became a socialist', *Socialist Review*, 2004, January. 1997.

Samuel, Ralph, *The Lost World of British Communism*, London, 2006.

Sansom, William, James Gordon and Stephen Spender, eds. *Jim Braidy, the Story of Britain's Firemen*, London 1943.

Saville, John, 'The Communist experience, a personal appraisal', *Socialist Register*, 1991, 1–27.

———— 'The Communist Party and the FBU', in ed. Victor Bailey, *Forged in Fire*, London, 1992, 225–228.

Schögel, Karl, *Moscow 1937*, Cambridge, 2012.

Segars, Terry, Interview with John Horner, 8 July 1975, *British Library Sounds Collection*.

———— *The Fire Service: A Social History of a Uniformed Working Class*', Ph.D thesis, University of Essex, 1989.

———— 'War, women and the FBU', in ed. Victor Bailey, *Forged in Fire*, London, 1992, 139–157.

Sibley, Tom, '*Anti- Communism: Studies of its Impact on the UK Labour Movement in the Early Years of the Cold War*', Ph.D thesis, University of Keele, 2008.

Smith, Paul, P. Fosh, R. Martin, H. Morris, and R. Undy, 'Ballots and union government in the 1980s'. *British Journal of Industrial Relations*, 1993, 31, 3, 365–382.

Sommerfield, Penny, *Women Workers in the Second World War*, London, 2012.

Sontag, Susan, 'Introduction' to Victor Serge, *The Case of Comrade Tulayev*, New York, 2004.

Stapleton, Susannah, *The Adventures of Maud West*, Lady Detective, London, 2019.

Stewart, John, 'Hyman Levy', *Oxford Dictionary of National Biography*, Oxford, 2004.

Stirling, Martine, 'Women's parliaments in the second world war', *Women's History Magazine*, 2013, 72, 19–29.

Strachey, John, *The Coming Struggle for Power*, New York, 1935.

——— 'Totalitarianism' in ed. Victor Gollancz, *The Betrayal of the Left*, London, 1941, 202–203.

Stueck, William, *Rethinking the Korean War*, Princeton, 2013.

Styles, William, *'British Domestic Security Policy and Communist Subversion: 1945–1964'*, Ph.D thesis, University of Cambridge, 2016.

Tames, R., *William Morris. An Illustrated Life*, 1834–1896, Aylesbury, 1983.

Taylor, A.J.P., *Origins of the Second World War*, Harmondsworth, 1964.

Thompson, E.P., 'Romanticism, moralism and utopianism: The case of William Morris', *New Left Review*, 1976, 83–111.

Thompson, Willie, *The Good Old Cause*, London, 1992.

——— 'British communists in the Cold War, 1947–1952', *Contemporary British History*, 2001, 15, 3, 105–32.

Thorpe, Andrew, 'Locking out the communists. The Labour Party and the Communist Party, 1939–46', *Twentieth Century History*, 2014, 25, 2, 221–50.

Todd, Selina, *Young Women, Work, and Family in England 1918–1950*, Oxford, 2005.

Trammer, Jeremy, 'Odd bed-fellows: British Christians and communists in the struggle for Peace', *Revue LISA/LISA e-journal [En ligne]*, 2011, IX, 1.

Walker, Harold, *Mainly Memories 1906–1930*, Waltham Abbey, 1986.

Webb, Sidney and Beatrice, Webb, *Soviet Communism, A New Civilisation*, Vol. 1, 2nd ed., London, 1937.

Wheatcroft, 'Towards explaining Soviet Famine of 1931–3: Political and natural factors in perspective', *Food and Foodways*, 2004, 12, 2-3, 107–136.

Wilford, Hugh, 'The Information Research Department: Britain's secret Cold War weapon revealed', *Review of International Studies*, 1998, 24, 1998, 353–369.

Wyatt, Woodrow, *The Peril in our Midst*, London, 1956.

Primary Sources

Bishopsgate Institute
Friends House Library
Hull History Centre
Labour History Archives, Peoples History Museum
London Metropolitan Archives
Marx Memorial Library
Modern Records Centre, University of Warwick
National Archives at Kew
Waltham Forest Local Records Office
Wellcome Digital Collection

Newspapers and Periodicals

Ballymena Weekly Telegraph British Newspaper Archives (BNA)
Belfast Newsletter BNA
Belfast Telegraph BNA
Birmingham Daily Post BNA

Birmingham Weekly Post BNA
Chelmsford Chronicle BNA
Daily Herald BNA
Daily Mail Gale Primary Sources
Daily Mirror BNA
Daily News BNA
Daily Telegraph BNA
Daily Worker UK Press on Line
Derby Daily Telegraph BNA
Dundee Evening Telegraph BNA
Economist Gale Primary Sources
Firefighter Fire Brigades Union, Warwick Digital Collections
Friendship Friends Hall, WFLRO
Hampstead and Highgate Express Camden Local Records Office
Hartlepool Northern Daily Mail BNA
Illustrated British Library
Illustrated London News BNA
IRIS News British Library
Irish Democrat https://archive.irishdemocrat.co.uk
Labour Monthly Google Books
Lancashire Evening Post BNA
Leicester Chronicle BNA
Liverpool Journal of Commerce BNA
Manchester Guardian Proquest Historical Newspapers
Middlesex County Times BNA
Monrovian   https://oldmonovians.com/history/the-modern-school/sir-george-monoux-college.html
Observer Proquest Historical Newspapers
Penrith Observer BNA
Reynolds News BNA
Scotsman BNA
Sheffield Daily Telegraph BNA
Sunday Mirror BNA
Surrey Mirror BNA
Times Gale Primary Sources
Walthamstow Guardian British Library
Walthamstow Observer British Library
Wayfarer Friends House Library
West London Observer BNA
Westminster and Pimlico News BNA

INDEX

Note: The letters n and f represent note numbers and figures, respectively.

AFS. *See* Auxiliary Fire Service
Air Raid Protection 115
air raids, England 120, 120–3, 124, 127,
  138, 157 *see also* Second World War
Alley, Rewi 191–2
Attlee, Clement 162, 180, 186, 189
Ambatielos, Betty 180
Anson's Voyage 28
Argentina 31–2, 34, 61
ARP. *See* Air Raid Protection
Ashe, Thomas 40
Aston (Oxon) 123, 124
atomic weapons 165, 182, 183, 225
  see also Campaign for Nuclear
  Disarmament
Auxiliary Fire Service 89, 96–7, 102,
  110, 111–12, 113–15, 116–17, 118,
  121, 125, 126, 129–30, 134, 141,
  159, 162, 164 *see also* Fire Brigades
  Union

Bailey, Victor 5
Barts (St Bartholomew's Hospital) 104,
  106, 109
Baptist Chapel 20, 107, 159, 170,
  234
Battcock, Marjorie 87–8
Bevan, Aneurin 186, 216
Beveridge, William 134, 149, 154
Beveridge Report 149–50, 175

Bevin, Ernie 116, 133, 142, 143, 144,
  162, 180, 187
Birch, Reg 172
Birmingham 48, 130, 146, 157–8, 165,
  168, 206
Black Circular 73, 102, 163
Blitz, the. *See* air raids, England
Bone, Edith 223–4
Booty, Herbert 47, 48
Boston Road (Walthamstow) 8, 10,
  15–16, 28, 35, 37, 40–1, 77, 106,
  120, 208
Bradley, Ben 67–8, 73, 93, 115
Bradley, Jim 92, 94, 97, 102
Bradley, Len 73, 93, 101, 102
Bramley, Ted 93
British Peace Committee 183–4, 187–8
British Union of Fascists 71
Brittain, Vera 57
Brockway, Fenner 181
Brodie, Louise 5–6
Buenos Aires 27–8, 34, 56, 61, 68, 176
Burns, Emile 71
Burns, John 128, 160, 160f, 170, 174f,
  187, 209, 218, 220, 222–3

Cab at the Door, A (Pritchett) 46
Campaign for Nuclear Disarmament
  139, 225, 226f
Campbell, Johnny 182f, 183

Cannon, Les 217, 220–1
Cassini, Leonard 131
Castle, Barbara 181, 190
Central School (Walthamstow) 17
Chancery Lane Safe Deposit Building 117
Chevins, Hugo 220
Chingford 37, 39, 70, 74, 77, 81, 104–5, 120, 121–2, 138, 146, 148, 153, 158, 165, 180f, 198, 200, 206, 228
Chou En Lai 191
Churchill, Winston 127, 138, 148–9, *see also* Second World War
Citrine, Walter 112, 136, 143
CND. *See* Campaign for Nuclear Disarmament
Collard, Dudley 234
Collins, Canon John 225
Collins, Diana 226
Coming Struggle for Power, The (Strachey) 59, 61–2, 63
Communist Party (UK): ban from trade councils 73; classes 85; and the FBU 129, 130, 131–2, 174–5, 186; fear of 168, 170, 172, 175–6, 185–6; 'Fight for Peace' 182; founding 68; and the Labour Party 68, 84, 161–2, 166, 176; membership 68, 132–3, 163, 196, 214, 217; organizations 87–8, 89, 153–4, 181; parties 198–9, 200; 'People's Convention' 137; and the Soviet Union 185, 211, 212; support for a Second Front 138, 143; women's issues 150–1; *see also* Fire Brigades Union, John Horner, Pat Horner, Soviet Union
Cousins, Frank 225–6
Clerkenwell Fire Station 96, 97, 124
Cold Comfort Farm (Gibbon) 123
Corscombe (Dorset) 107–8
Cross of Peace, The (Gibbs) 57
Cubitts 12, 13

Daily Worker 63, 71–2, 74, 148, 149, 199–200 *see also* Communist Party (UK)
Darke, Bob 129, 130, 141, 165, 222, 223
Darling, John (E.W.) 84–5
Dependents and Wounded Aid Committee 89, 90
dialectical materialism 84

Dominion Records 47, 48
Dooley, Pat 84
Dutt, Palme 71, 133, 137, 144, 180–1, 182f, 183, 205–6, 211
DW. *See Daily Worker*

Egyptian National Revolution 42
Electrical Trade Union 217
Elliott, Edith 40, 46, 48
Emergency Powers Act 106
Epping Forest 9, 23, 38f, 40, 53, 54, 74, 75, 79, 120, 155f
Euston Fire Station 93–4, 96, 157
Eyben, Rosalind. *See* Rosalind Horner

Falkland Islands 12–13
Faringdon, Lord 123
FBU. *See* Fire Brigades Union
Feather, Vic 173
Feuchtwanger, Leon 232–3
Fire Brigades Union 1–2, 5, 73, 80, 92–4, 95–6, 97, 99, 101–2, 111–12, 113, 115, 116–17, 119n19, 128, 129–30, 131, 134, 135n19, 138, 141–2, 146, 149–50, 154–5, 158, 159, 161–2, 164–6, 170–1, 172–4, 173f, 176, 180, 181, 185–7, 190, 202, 207, 209, 214–15, 217–18, 220–1, 222–3
Firebrace, Aylmer 56, 66–7, 114
Firefighter 117, 171, 185
Firemen's Charter Campaign 131, 139
First World War 12–13, 41–2
Fleeming Road (Walthamstow) 41
flying bombs 157–8, 206
forest, the. *See* Epping Forest
Forged in Fire (Bailey) 5, 96, 220
Franco, General 86, 89
Franklin, Olive. *See* Olive Parsons
Freeman, Frank 148, 154–5, 171
Freeman, Pam 148, 153–5, 171
Friends Hall 22, 24, 49, 51, 52, 53, 76–7, 85 *see also* Fred Parsons
Friends Hall Peace Group 53, 57
Furness Withy 63

Gallacher, Willie 130, 154
Gamuel Road School 16
Gandhi, Mahatma 53, 69
Garrison, William Lloyd 88
General Strike of 1926 20–1, 22
George the Fifth, Silver Jubilee 74
Gibbs, Harold 92–3, 94, 98, 115

Gide, André 233, 235
Golden Notebook (Lessing)
Gollan, Johnny 164, 211, 216
Gorman, Joseph 58, 69, 72
Grahl, Helen 203, 204, 223
Grahl, Jack 130–1, 162, 164–5, 174f,
    175, 177, 180, 187, 189, 201, 203,
    204, 205, 209, 211, 214, 218, 220–2,
    223
Graves' disease 96
Great War. *See* First World War
Greece 162, 180
Greenwood, Tony 181, 219
Greene, Graham 52

Haldane, Charlotte 89
Hampstead Ethical Society 233
Hawkes, Jacquetta 226, 226f
Hawkwood Crescent (Chingford)
    120–1, 124, 158, 168
Hardwicke Grange, SS, 56, 61
Harrods 27–8
Hobsbawm, Eric 137–8, 149, 189
Hiroshima 165, 185
Home Office 114–15, 116, 126, 128–9,
    131, 138, 142, 159, 164, 202–3, 207
Hooper, Major 83, 94, 105, 159
Horner, Arthur 170–1
Horner, Boy Charlie 9, 17, 19
Horner, Carol 3, 96, 108, 120, 122f,
    123, 138, 150, 151, 151f, 157, 169,
    180f, 195, 196f, 197, 198, 199, 218,
    227, 228
Horner, Charlie 8–9, 11–12, 18, 19,
    20–1
Horner, Emily 9, 12, 19, 41, 207, 208f
Horner, John: birth 8–9; British
    Peace Committee 183–4, 187–8;
    Communist Party 2, 71, 106, 133,
    139, 163, 176, 180–1, 187–8, 190,
    204, 211; death 233; disillusionment
    with the Communist Party 3, 204–5,
    212, 214–15, 216, 223; education
    at Monoux 16–17, 19–20, 25, 26;
    elections 93, 94, 96, 98–9, 101, 129,
    164–5, 226–7; fines 95, 184–5; fire
    service 1–2, 3, 67–8, 83–4, 92–3, 94,
    100, 226; holidays with Pat 75–6,
    107, 192, 209–10, 220; interviews
    5–6, 102, 112; Labour Party 219,
    224–5; letters 65, 77, 108, 158, 163,
    184, 219; London Branch Committee
    93–4; marriage to Pat 79–80; meeting

Pat 1, 37, 38–9; nervous condition
    206–7, 209, 210, 211; obituary 2;
    photographs of 25f, 30f, 38f, 60f,
    109f, 140f, 152f, 155f, 160f, 174f,
    180f, 188f, 221f, 226f, 227f; reading
    and writing 2–3, 19–20, 28, 71–2,
    110, 117, 171, 176, 185, 190–1,
    228; religion 20, 22, 23, 69, 74, 77;
    reputation with the Fire Brigades
    Union 95–6, 101, 113, 126, 129,
    159, 203, 218; seafaring 13, 28,
    29–30, 32, 34, 35, 56, 59; speeches
    92–3, 117–18, 119n19, 139–40, 141,
    171, 180, 181–2, 202, 217; trip to
    China 190–1; trip to Hungary 172,
    176–7; trip to Moscow 187–8, 224;
    unemployment 55–6, 59; views on
    capitalism 61; William Morris 19–20;
    work at Harrods 27–8
Horner, Pat: childhood 40–1, 42;
    Communist Party 83, 169, 224; death
    3, 231; Dependents and Wounded
    Aid Committee 89; education 42–3,
    44–5; employment 46–7; family
    40–1, 42; Graves' disease 96, 104,
    109, 152; holidays with John 75–6,
    107, 192, 209–10, 220; housewives'
    associations 149–50, 152; interest
    in Spain 86; Labour Party 225;
    marriage to John 79–80; Medical Aid
    for Spain 88–9; meeting John 1, 37,
    38–9; peace movements 56–7, 58,
    183; photographs of 39f, 43f, 76f,
    109f, 123f, 152f, 155f, 174f, 180f,
    227f; reading 43, 169, 171; settling
    Hungarian refugees 219; trip to
    Hungary 172; work at the NIIP 152
Horner, Rosalind: anxieties about her
    parents 198; birth 157–8; childhood
    years 197–8, 206; photograph of
    221f; thieving 200–1; trip to South
    Hams 209–10; visiting John 231–2
Horner, Winnie 28
Houlders Brothers 29, 54, 56, 62
Housewives' Clubs 150–1, 152–3
Humphries, Enoch 204, 211, 218
Hungary 172, 215, 223–4
Hunger Marchers 65, 66
Hyde, Douglas 66, 137, 139

imperialism 61–2
intelligence services. *See* Security
    Services

India 12, 42, 53, 68, 74, 180, 181
International Research Department
    188–9, 217, 220
IRD. *See* International Research
    Department
IRIS News 214, 222

Jackson, Major 114–15, 126
James, C.L.R 233–4

Kerrigan, Peter 172, 175, 183, 196f,
    216
Keynes, Geoffrey 109
Khrushchev, Nikita 205, 207, 209, 212,
    214, 216
King, Truby 150
Kingdom, Percy 73, 93, 94, 95, 96,
    97–8
Korean War 185–6, 189
Kuropaty 3–4

Labour Party, conferences: 1943 133,
    161–2; 1946 166; 1957 224–5; 1960
    225–6
'Labour's Struggles in Latin America'
    32–3
Labourers' Union 11, 73
'Lady of Shalott, The' (Tennyson), 45
Lake District 75, 76f, 121
Latham, Reg 70, 72, 105, 120, 146,
    147f, 225
Lawrence and Wishart 5
Lawther, William 175
le Mare, Arthur 51, 53, 56, 72, 85, 121,
    146
Leadenhall Street 19
Left Book Club 4, 85, 86, 89, 148, 234
left-handedness 42
lend-lease agreement 168
Leslie, Henrietta 51
Lessing, Doris 187–8, 196, 205, 215
Levy, Hyman 71
Lewis, Frederick 63
LFB. *See* London Fire Brigade
London Branch Committee, Fire
    Brigades Union 93–4
London Fire Brigade 56, 66–7, 73,
    97–8, 99, 103n10
Low, David 189

MacColl, Ewan 199
Maclean, Fitzroy 232, 235
MacMurray, John 76–7

Maisky, Mr. (Soviet Ambassador) 138
Mass Observation 144, 148
Massey Shaw 142
Maud West's Detective Agency 46–7
MCF. *See* Movement for Colonial
    Freedom
Medical Aid for Spain 88–9
Meerut Trial 68, 115, 139
Merrells, Chick 95, 113, 164
MI5 172, 214
Michaelson, David 84, 188
Monoux School 16–17, 19–20, 25, 26
Morris, William 1, 9, 13, 19–20, 52,
    203
Morrison, Herbert 1, 95, 124, 128–9,
    131, 133, 164
Morton, A.L. 85–6
Moscow News 3
Movement for Colonial Freedom 181,
    190, 215
Murray, Tom 114, 130

Nagasaki 165
National Fire Service 128, 131
National Union of Miners 170–1, 175
Nazi-Soviet Pact 112, 136, 137–8, 204
New Malden 198, 199, 200–1, 207, 226
Nineteen Eighty-Four (Orwell) 185
Niven, Barbara 200
No More War Movement 1, 56–7, 58,
    69, 70–1, 72

Odlin, Gus 99, 112, 120
Orange River, SS. 29, 30, 31, 33
Orwell, George 185

Pain, Peter 114, 125, 165
Palmer, Alice 40–1, 46, 47, 48, 105,
    106, 107, 108, 121, 146
Palmer, Geoff 40–1, 42, 44, 48, 106,
    113–14, 130, 146, 168, 227
Palmer, Mavis 44, 48, 104–5, 108, 121,
    146, 158, 165
Palmer, Violet 41, 42, 51, 52f, 53, 69,
    70, 72, 77, 80, 104–5, 108, 121, 146,
    147f, 180, 225
Parsons, Douglas ('Harry') 53, 58n7, 83
Parsons, Fred 22, 23f, 25, 52, 53, 75,
    146–7, 223
Parsons, Iris 22
Parsons, Olive 83, 85
Parsons, Owen 65, 83, 115
Peace Pledge Union 71, 73, 80, 106, 114

People's History of England, A
   (Morton) 85–6
Perks, Doughy 15, 16
Phillips, Morgan 171, 219
Pirie, Antoinette 226
Pischikevich, Boris 174, 188, 224
Pollitt, Harry 5, 83, 106, 115, 133–4,
   137, 138–9, 140, 142, 143, 144, 162,
   163, 165–6, 176, 182f, 183, 190,
   198, 204, 211, 215
Poznyak, Zenon 3, 4
Princesa, SS, 35
Pritchett, V.S. 46
Priestley, J.B. 89, 226
Pritt, D.N. 139
Pulleybank, Professor 190

Quakers 1, 22–3, 53, 56, 69, 73, 75,
   108, 146–7
Queens Road Cemetery, Walthamstow
   18, 68, 207

Randall, Sam 73, 75, 93, 98, 99, 101–2
Requirements for Second Mate,
   Steamships (Nicholl) 35
Reynolds, Reginald 69
Robeson, Paul 183, 199, 233
Rogers, Jack 170, 173
Rosenbergs' execution 197, 199
Rust, Bill 139, 144
Rust, Tamara 140f, 153

Saville, John 5, 174, 180, 184, 189, 204,
   211, 218, 223, 234
'Say Not the Struggle Naught Availeth'
   169
Sea, The (Whymper) 28
Second World War 92, 105–6, 107,
   108–9, 116, 120, 138, 143, 157,
   158–9, 165
Security Services 6, 162, 180
Segars, Terry 102, 111, 112, 130, 176,
   217, 222
Serge, Victor 236
Short, Harry 94–5, 97, 99, 101–2, 105,
   113, 124–5, 164, 222
'Sigurd the Volsung' (Morris) 19–20,
   132
Silverman, Julius 181
Solzhenitsyn, Aleksandr 224
Sorensen, Reg 11, 242
Southwark Fire Station 9, 67, 71, 73,
   80–1, 114–15

Soviet Communism, a New Civilisation
   (Beatrice and Sidney Webb) 4
Soviet Union: as an 'Evil Empire' 181,
   185; as a communist country 62;
   famine 62, 63; foreign sympathy
   for 181, 185, 196, 205; invasion
   by Germany 138, 139, 143, 148–9;
   invasion of Poland 137; Kuropaty
   shooting 3–4; negotiations with Great
   Britain 105; non-aggression pact with
   Germany 105–6, 136; in the Spanish
   Civil War 86–7; treason trials 207,
   231–2, 234; women in 150
   see also Communist Party (UK),
   Nikita Khrushchev, Joseph Stalin
Spanish Civil War 86–7, 89–90
Special Branch 163
Spradberry, Walter 52
Squire, J.C. 49, 56
St Bartholomew's Hospital. *See* Barts
St Clair, Charles Nugent 35
St Dunstans 16
Stalin, Joseph 3, 62, 105, 133, 143, 170,
   187, 189, 195, 199, 205, 207, 211,
   212, 232, 233, 234, 235
Stalingrad 132–3, 139, 148, 171
stoicism 69
Strachey, John 59, 61, 62, 63, 72, 163
strikes: at the Falkland Islands 13;
   General Strike (1926) 20–1, 22; in
   London 11–12; on the SS *Orange*
   River 32, 33
Suez 215–16, 217
Swingler, Stephen 181, 235

Tanner, Jack 139–40, 189, 214, 217
Tasmanian Transport, SS 35
Tewson, Vincent 175, 189, 222
Testament of Youth (Brittain) 57
Third Afghan War 42
Thompson, E.P. 203
Thompson, W.H. 115, 117
Thomson, David 25, 26
Thorndike, Sybil 45, 88
Tiptree 16
Trades Union Congress 102, 112, 136,
   140, 143, 148, 150, 154, 159, 163,
   170, 171, 173, 175–6, 187, 189, 190,
   203, 215, 220, 221, 229, 235
Transport and General Workers Union
   116, 175–6, 186, 225
TUC. *See* Trades Union Congress
Tudor-Hart, Alexander 88

Uncle Arthur 16, 28, 55, 80
Unity Theatre 183, 184f
Universal History 2
USSR. *See* Soviet Union
Utting, Hilda 85

Villa Constitución 31, 34, 73

Walthamstow 9–10, 11, 13, 15, 20, 21,
   25, 37, 41–2, 43, 47, 53, 56, 68,
   70–1, 72, 73, 96, 97, 104, 121
Walthamstow Guardian 17–18
Walthamstow High School for Girls
   44–5
'Waste Land, The' (Eliot) 53
Webb, Harry 95
Webb, Beatrice and Sidney 4
West Hampstead Fire Station 80–1, 81f,
   89–90

West, Maud 46–7, 48
Whitt, Percy Bysshe 19–20, 26
Wilbur, Jay 47
William Morris Hall 11, 71
Williams, Elin 198
Williams, Jack 68
Williams, John 188, 198
Willis, Bob 99, 108
Winns Avenue school 42–3
Women's Parliament 153
World Disarmament Conference (1932)
   53–4
World Federation of Trade Unions 32,
   175, 189
World Peace Council 182
World War I. *See* First World War
World War II. *See* Second World War
Wortley Hall 209
Wyatt, Woodrow 214, 217

For Product Safety Concerns and Information please contact our EU
representative GPSR@taylorandfrancis.com Taylor & Francis Verlag GmbH,
Kaufingerstraße 24, 80331 München, Germany

Printed and bound by CPI Group (UK) Ltd, Croydon, CR0 4YY
08/06/2025
01897005-0014